ENTITLED TO SLAVERY

ENTITLED TO SLAVERY

*A Blueprint for Breaking the Chains
that Threaten American Exceptionalism*

MICHAEL P. ABBOTT, JR.

ENTITLED TO SLAVERY

Copyright © 2017 by Michael P. Abbott, Jr.

World Ahead Press is a division of WND Books. The views and opinions expressed in this book are those of the author and do not necessarily reflect the official policy or position or WND Books.

Paperback ISBN: 978-1-944212-80-3
eBook ISBN: 978-1-944212-81-0

Printed in the United States of America
16 17 18 19 20 21 LSI 9 8 7 6 5 4 3 2 1

To Rearden
You are my true life's work.

Endorsements

To look at this book means that you know there are critical issues our nation and other countries are facing. In fact, the swimming pool of solid and creative thought has become a cesspool with poison as the mental, emotional, spiritual, and physical chlorine.

Why? That's an eternal question that Michael Abbott, Jr. answers from the Word of God, through the God of the Word. Michael is my wise friend. He is an executive who speaks straight and clear. He writes in the age of the executive and businessman/woman. The Lord has His hand on this young man . . . please do not just look at this book; you have to listen to his words.

Michael does not just deconstruct but he constructs . . . he strips our blinders and shows us the false deities within Secular Humanism. He lets us see the false gods and failures of Fascism. He brings us face to face with the false gods of Tolerance and its intolerant worldview toward followers of Jesus Christ. Michael builds ways that you can think and act now to bring real change. Now! Not a decade later, but NOW.

Our country and many other nations are upside down. We have relativized the absolutes and absolutized the relatives. This inception is actually a deception.

"This book needs to be a standard textbook in home schools, in private schools, in public schools, in Christian schools . . . and most importantly in your thinking and living personally and with your family. Look, purchase, read, study, listen and act. I am locking arms with Michael. How about you?"

- DR. GREG KAPPAS, DOCTOR OF MINISTRY, MASTER OF THEOLOGY, MASTER OF DIVINITY. FOUNDER AND PRESIDENT, GRACE GLOBAL NETWORK, AN ORGANIZATION THAT HAS PARTNERED IN PLANTING OVER 48,000 CHURCHES ACROSS THE GLOBE; ADJUNCT FACULTY, GRAND CANYON UNIVERSITY AND GATEWAY SEMINARY -PHOENIX

"Michael has done an excellent job of researching and writing this book. He is an extremely passionate and gifted writer."

- DR. DON WILSON, FOUNDER AND SENIOR PASTOR, CHRIST'S CHURCH OF THE VALLEY, ONE OF THE TWENTY LARGEST CHURCHES IN THE UNITED STATES OF AMERICA

Contents

Acknowledgments

Outside of family, writing this book was the most fulfilling experience of my life. It was also the most challenging! I am thankful, first and foremost, to the Lord for blessing me with a message to share with my fellow countrymen. To your holy name be all the glory.

To my wife, thank you for carrying our most precious gifts. Thank you for sacrificing so many nights not only to allow me to complete this work, but also to tend to the inopportune appetites of our young children! Thank you for your dedication to educate our children inside of our home and your willingness to fumigate our home from the destructive influence of the television. Most importantly, thank you for building a family with me.

Rearden, it will take you a long time to understand how you served as the true inspiration for this book. I wrote this for you and Solomon. Never forget that love and civility will always elude a culture that rejects the Gospel of Jesus Christ, so boldly take His message with you everywhere you go.

Jim, I want to thank you for being the perfect embodiment of joy. To my parents, thank you for teaching me right from wrong and disciplining me when I was a child. I could not have written this book had I not learned these difficult lessons. To Brandon, thank you for holding me in such high regard through your words of affirmation. To Joe and Carm, thank you for so actively sharing in our great joy!

To Danny, what an honor to be your friend. Thank you for selflessly donating your time to critique this manuscript. Greg, thank you for promoting my work through your community of influential church leaders. To my new friend Laura, thank you for making the copyedit phase of this process an enjoyable experience.

To Nicoletta, thank you for demonstrating unconditional love for our family. When you interact with Rearden and Solomon, I can see the face of God. To Kerilyn, thank you for your commitment to learning the science of physical therapy. God has blessed me with a life devoid of pain these last few years by working directly through your hands!

Lastly, I want to thank you, the reader, for taking a chance on this young author. This industry features a substantial barrier to entry for new voices, especially those offering contrarian viewpoints. If you gain insight from this book, would you consider promoting it using one of the following three methods?

1. Recommend this book to your church, co-workers, and circle of friends.
2. Write a reader review on Amazon.
3. Engage with me directly at www.AbbottSpeaks.com. Each week, I post anywhere from one to three articles on this personal website. I would be honored to receive your thoughts, comments, and feedback on this book and all of my other writings.

Yes, I do respond!

Preface

The greatest joys in life have as their prerequisite great adversity and tribulation. It is only through this suffering that anticipation and hope can develop within our hearts to produce the jubilation of an unprecedented achievement.

We must remember that the greatest joy in the history of the world never could have been realized without the crucifixion of an innocent man and subsequent martyring of his disciples as they selflessly spread the Gospel throughout a hostile Roman Empire. Though these Roman political elites frantically moved to kill these men to preserve their fleeting aspirations of absolute sovereignty, they were no match for a message that has since converted the hearts and minds of billions of people. In the deep annals of history, Christianity remains the only proven antidote to the suffering induced by the greatest ambitions of the megalomaniacal man.

Two thousand years later, American political elites are frantically scheming to extinguish the Gospel of Jesus Christ in a desperate attempt to resurrect the mindset of the Roman political elites. Astutely observing that Christianity serves as the last remaining impediment to their power, they have clouded their disingenuous intentions behind the seemingly benign veil of "progress" and "enlightenment."

This "progress" has imprisoned a county clerk for refusing to abandon the ways of the Lord in the court system. Her crime? Refusing to render God's ownership of the holy covenant of marriage unto Caesar by issuing marriage licenses to homosexuals.

This "progress" has threatened to strip federal funding from Christian universities refusing to abandon the ways of the Lord in the halls of academia. Their crimes? Requiring a profession of faith from their students and fully integrating this faith into their core curricula.

This "progress" has threatened legal action against churches refusing to abandon the ways of the Lord at the pulpit. Their crimes? Refusing to deviate from orthodox Christian doctrine with respect to human sexuality.

This "progress" has dismantled the viability of upstanding businesses refusing to abandon the ways of the Lord in the marketplace. Their crimes? Failing to use their businesses as political vehicles to undermine their deep-seated religious beliefs.

How could a nation founded on the very principles of Christianity reach the point in which its people so eagerly seek to uproot any last vestiges of the faith?

We never could have reached this point in our culture without first abandoning the central tenets of the faith. The hallmark of modern Christianity has become an unapologetic overemphasis on grace. While grace is indeed a central tenet to the faith, does it carry more weight than the tenet that the Bible is the inspired and infallible word of God? For example, when twenty-first-century churches embrace and perpetuate actions that are in direct contravention to God's law as well as the teachings of Jesus Christ (for example the Presbyterian Church formally sanctioning gay marriage in their church constitution), can we champion grace as the ultimate arbiter supporting our newfound enlightenment? Furthermore, would it be relevant to note that this enlightenment was procured while under the influence of countless hours of secularized media?

God did not bless us with His grace so that we may abuse the gift to meet our perverse desires. Grace does not grant us immunity with respect to the moral decline of our culture. This perspective can only be validated by a steadfast and unbreakable commitment to keeping our Bible at arm's length. The fruits of our faith do not take up residence in our words, but rather our actions. For example, Gallup polls showed America to be a nation that is 77 percent Christian as recently as 2012; however, the Supreme Court mandated marriage as a union between any two individuals just three short years later.[1] If greater than three in four Americans aligned their conduct to the teachings of Jesus Christ, this ruling never could have happened.

The evidence is mounting that we have been misapplying the Christian label to our expressions of faith, and this book explains how our current predicament was only made possible by our resolve to abandon the ways of the Lord in deference to our own understanding. Incredibly, this understanding is wholly grounded on the surreptitious suggestion that one's faith must be compartmentalized on account of the separation of church and state fallacy, a mindset that we shall soon see is only narrowly applied to the Christian believer. This fallacy has given rise to "Comfortable Christianity," the belief that God's grace grants believers an exemption from the responsibilities of the Christian faith while craftily turning these same individuals into agents of their own destruction.

Many Christians lament our current plight, but we are called to confront this time of great adversity and tribulation with the joy of the Holy Spirit. Christians must rise to occasions such as these with the courage, conviction, and boldness of the truth to a culture replete with such spiritual darkness. We have not been called to address the calling of our day with a demeanor of discouraged resignation and fear; this is an opportunity to outwardly reflect the fullness of God's love by being a light to our fellow men! The everlasting love and patience of our Lord has granted us such a providential opportunity to work miracles with our very hands if we would just heed the calling of our faith. At this point, who among us wouldn't consider the restoration of our nation as anything short of a miracle?

If the Kingdom of God is undefeated and the kingdom of man is winless, where is the wisdom in suiting up to support the dominion of the latter? When we up the stakes with the knowledge that our looming slavery will not befall our generation, but that of our children and our children's children, how can we not be compelled to action?

God has so graciously blessed us with this calling of such great purpose. In addition to seeking prayer in earnest, we must first educate ourselves to our culpability in the failure of our various cultural institutions. It is only after we see our fingerprints on these casualties that we can begin to win back the kingdom for Jesus Christ. We know this is the beginning of our journey, while the immortal words of Dr. Martin Luther King Jr. serve as the end:

"And when this happens, when we allow freedom ring, when we let it ring from every village and every hamlet, from every state and every city, we will be able to speed up that day when all of God's children, black men and white men, Jews and Gentiles, Protestants and Catholics, will be able to join hands and sing in the words of the old Negro spiritual:

Free at last! Free at last! Thank God Almighty, we are free at last!"[2]

Do we have the strength to press on toward the goal to win the prize for which God has called us heavenward in Christ Jesus? Unless we commit to unite under this greater purpose, the terms "progress" and "enlightenment" will only continue to elude our haughty culture!

ONE

An Indiscriminately Fertile Field

Do not plant two kinds of seed in your vineyard;
if you do, not only the crops you plant but also the
fruit of the vineyard will be defiled.

~ Deuteronomy 22:9

D espite its ostensibly lofty intentions, secular humanism is paralyzing the greatest civilization in the history of the world. If this trend is left unchecked, America as we know it will necessarily begin a lengthy plunge into obscurity, darkness, misery, and servitude.

This assessment is vehemently rejected by nearly all unbelievers, and a mounting number of modern Christians. These groups of individuals largely consider any suggestion that our nation "hangs in the balance" as little more than irresponsible hyperbole growing from a garden of unguarded cynicism. In fact, an enlightening piece from *The New York Times* succinctly offered an alternative viewpoint. When writing about the appeal of the atypical political candidates running for the office of the presidency, veteran *conservative* columnist David Brooks penned the following excerpt in an editorial titled "I'll Miss Barack Obama" dated February 9, 2016:

> "To hear (Bernie) Sanders or (Donald) Trump, (Ted) Cruz, and Ben Carson campaign is to wallow in the pornography of pessimism, to conclude that this country is on the verge of complete collapse. That's simply not true. We have problems, but they are less serious than those faced by just about any other nation on earth."[1]

Brooks clearly disagrees with my assessment at the beginning of this chapter. Interestingly, just ten months earlier, he confirmed in an interview with *National Public Radio* that he is a "believer" and that there is "something just awesome about seeing somebody stand up and imitate and live the non-negotiable truth of Jesus Christ."[2]

How is it possible that two self-professed followers of Jesus Christ can arrive at such diametrically opposed conclusions when assessing the overall health of our culture? Is either assessment correct? Which conclusion is closer to the truth? Does the disagreement symbolize a rift within the church?

We must begin our journey towards understanding these questions by establishing a foundational knowledge of the fullness of God's love by conducting a survey into the very nature of the human heart. This certainly seems a curious place to start, since a fleeting glance at any "news" outlet would encourage us to direct our concern and attention towards the current national platform embraced by our political party of choice. But alas, this approach would suggest that our ultimate source of understanding springs from the "little g" of government, not the "Big G" of God.

God has abundantly supplied man with countless spiritual blessings, but there are two gifts of monumental significance that must be appreciated when it comes to understanding the essence of man and the evolutions within a society. Each of these gifts is absolute in nature; none of God's children benefit from a greater supply than what has been given to his fellow man. A society will flourish when these gifts are appreciated and respected; whereas, a society will inevitably collapse if they are exploited.

As a testament to His everlasting love, God has blessed all of his children with the first of these two gifts of monumental significance: universal liberty. Commonly referred to as "free will" by Christians, could there possibly be any greater demonstration of love than granting an individual the freedom to act? Liberty introduces the concept of personal responsibility which, when exercised prudently, produces the fulfilling emotion of peace that is so frequently referenced throughout Scripture. Contrary to popular opinion, peace is not a lofty societal aspiration that can only be achieved through the absence of war. Rather, peace is a deep spiritual undertaking that can only be attained individually through a relationship with Jesus Christ. The apostle Paul provides a contextual explanation of peace in Colossians 3:

"Therefore, as God's chosen people, holy and dearly loved, clothe yourselves with compassion, kindness, humility, gentleness and patience. Bear with each other and forgive one another if any of you has a grievance against someone. Forgive as the Lord forgave you. And over all these virtues put on love, which binds them all together in perfect unity. Let the peace of Christ rule in your hearts, since as members of one body you were called to peace. And be thankful."

Liberty is such a fascinating subject because it is simultaneously universal, yet scarce. There is not a single human being on this planet who has not been afforded the blessing of free will from the Creator. Conversely, the history of the world from the earliest collected records to the present verifies that the overwhelming majority of kings, presidents, prime ministers, or other tribal leaders commonly restrict liberty from their fellow man under the justification that there must be an order to society, and only they can be the ultimate supplier of basic human rights. This is the orthodox temperament of the kingdom of man.

Biblically speaking, leaders of a healthy society should strive to function as somewhat of a pass-through entity, extending the blessings of God to the people to the greatest extent possible. From a legal perspective, a society emitting a vibrant spiritual health would thus conclude that people are always innocent until proven guilty. The fruits of such a culture would lead its citizens to determine that "government, even in its best state, is but a necessary evil," as Thomas Paine did in *Common Sense*, published in 1776. The people of this society would likely champion the civilizing pursuit of wisdom, yet another biblical principle. Its leaders might be inspired to state that "if a nation expects to be ignorant and free, in a state of civilization, it expects what never was and never will be," as Thomas Jefferson pontificated in the late eighteenth century.[3]

What if the leaders of a society rejected biblical truths? Rather than passing through the blessings and rights bestowed upon man by his Creator, the ruling class of this kind would gradually advocate government-given rights. After all, if God is either unjust or non-existent, the responsibility falls upon man to organize and control society. These leaders might be tempted to spread distrust among the populace, sensing a growing opportunity for the acquisition of power. The philosophies of such a culture might acclaim entertainment at the expense of wisdom, connections at the expense of character, and intentions at the expense of outcomes. Positions of leadership might be allocated using the principle of political patronage or nepotism as opposed to meritocracy. From a biblical perspective, any governing body seeking to restrict the gifts freely given by the Good Lord from the general public would be reflective of an unhealthy society.

Is liberty an ideal to which we should all aspire through either government or other social organization? Let us partake of the fruits of the tree. Consider the concept of life expectancy before and after the mainstreaming of liberty. Why did the average life expectancy stagnate between twenty and thirty-five years for the span of nearly two millennia between the fall of the Roman Empire and the mid-eighteenth century? Is it merely coincidental that this figure doubled, if not tripled, only *after* granting liberty to the general public? What about basic human needs and the overall quality of life? Is it coincidental that electricity and flush toilets were never commonplace until *after* liberty was extended to the public? Did you realize that the World Bank reports that 100 percent of Americans have access to electricity in 2016?[4] Before the twentieth century, a trip from New York City to Los Angeles would take several weeks. Today, if that trip takes longer than five hours, we grouse at the airline for causing an unnecessary flight delay. This last example gives credence to the suggestion that once liberty is unleashed upon a people, the sky is the limit! It is no wonder that the apostle Paul defines liberty as "the perfect law" in James 1:25. It is a truly remarkable gift.

The fact that we take all of these advances for granted is an absolute indictment on our culture, and frankly, one which should bring us tremendous shame. It is the apex of both hypocrisy and irony that our culture would largely chastise individuals like Paris Hilton for squandering their inheritance while treating our hard-earned liberty with such similar disregard. Do we really not understand that the *only* reason all of these improvements were secured was because our progenitors tirelessly championed the notion of self-determination through government, a value directly aligned with the Scriptures? Without liberty, the odds are strong that I am not even alive to write this book, and you might not even be alive to read it! In this fashion, we directly owe the benefits we enjoy today to our forefathers' conscious application of faith (dare I say their integration of church and state, but we will return to that later). When it is extended to the masses within the framework of a civil society, liberty represents the model standard of governance for all human interaction.

While my love and reverence for liberty is worthy of volumes, I will graciously defer any further esteem in deference to the multitudes of other superb writings on the subject. It is God's second, and far less heralded, gift of monumental significance that I wish to explore over the duration of this chapter. As is the case with liberty, this gift is also largely taken for granted, and it is one that is appreciated less and less as our culture continues to move away from its agrarian heritage. It has become so underappreciated now that it has, in fact, become nearly invisible. This gift of which I speak is God's blessing of a prolific heart of limitless fertility to each of his children.

Deep within every human being rests a heart filled with acres and acres of spiritual soil indiscriminately vulnerable to cultivation. Unlike the soil of the earth, which may be ripe for the harvesting of one crop and unwelcoming towards the harvesting of another, the human heart will produce fruit following the scatter of any type of seed. This is equally true for those scattering the secular seed of the kingdom of man, as well as those scattering the godly seed of the kingdom of light. The heart can never lay barren and does not wither with age. There is no human being alive today who is not producing fruit in accordance with what he has concluded to be truth and purpose.

At every age, the heart is proficient at producing fruit at a rate consistent with the fervency of instruction. As the apostle Paul, the world's most influential Christian evangelist, wrote in 2 Corinthians 9:

> "Remember this: Whoever sows sparingly will also reap sparingly, and whoever sows generously will also reap generously."

The more immersed one is to an idea, the more fruit that person shall bear. Likewise, if one only dabbles occasionally in a various doctrine, his tree shall only bear the fruit of this doctrine in sporadic fashion. This is precisely why a church largely comprised of congregants who only attend service occasionally and read the Bible infrequently produces an insufficient amount of fruit necessary to influence the surrounding culture.

Is spiritual fertility a biblical concept? The answer to this question is a resounding and unequivocal "yes." The biblical significance of fruit is scattered throughout the Old and New Testaments. Fruit is referenced roughly 200 times in the Bible, with five of these references coming in the first chapter of the book of Genesis! Is this merely coincidental, or was God consciously calculating and deliberate in His highlighting of the fertility of the human heart? Is it coincidental that the first recorded teachings of Jesus Christ address good and bad fruit? The following excerpt can be found in Jesus' Sermon on the Mount in Matthew 7:15–20:

> "Watch out for false prophets. They come to you in sheep's clothing, but inwardly they are ferocious wolves. By their fruit you will recognize them. Do people pick grapes from thornbushes, or figs from thistles? Likewise, every good tree bears good fruit, but a bad tree bears bad fruit. A good tree cannot bear bad fruit, and a bad tree cannot bear good fruit. Every tree that does not bear good fruit is cut down and thrown into the fire. Thus, by their fruit you will recognize them."

Even Paul was so bold as to suggest there would be no need for law should there be a ubiquitous pervasiveness of good fruit in a society. In the fifth chapter in his letter to the Galatians, he writes:

"But the fruit of the Spirit is love, joy, peace, forbearance, kindness, goodness, faithfulness, gentleness and self-control. Against such things there is no law."

The Bible contains a multitude of influential seeds through its chronicling of God's law and the liberating teachings of Jesus Christ. By laboriously outlining the painful history of the Israelites when they would abandon the ways of the Lord, the reader begins to develop an appreciation for the fallen and imperfect nature of man, as well as his resultant and desperate need for a Savior. Just as the Bible contains numerous seeds of influence that may be spread throughout a culture, so do the various texts of influence so prevalent in our culture today. From the United States *Constitution* to Karl Marx's *Communist Manifesto*, from Alexis de Tocqueville's *Democracy in America* to Adolf Hitler's *Mein Kampf,* and from Martin Luther's *Ninety-Five Theses* to Charles Darwin's *The Origin of Species*, these texts scatter their own seeds of influence resulting from the life experiences, ambitions, philosophies, and beliefs of man.

These written words contain such immense power because each man is born with a portion of his heart that belongs to the Lord as well as a portion of his heart that belongs to Satan. Regardless of how hardened his heart has become, no man exclusively pursues darkness. Conversely, no matter how righteous a man, his heart will forever be compromised by original sin. These truths prevent any man from pure evil in the same fashion that they prevent man from leading a sinless life. A raw bell curve best demonstrates this principle, with the vast majority of people falling within the normal distribution of the curve. Only a small percentage represent those whose hearts are so hardened that they are dedicated to the pursuit of evil, while a <u>small percentage so earnestly pursue God that they</u> have minimized the control of sin over their lives.

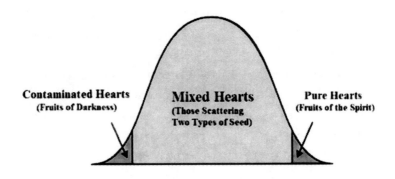

Human Heart Bell Curve Illustration

The hearts of man can never be swayed from this relentless struggle between darkness and the light. As previously mentioned, the portion of the heart belonging to the Lord desperately longs for truth, while the portion belonging to Satan frantically pursues destruction. This is precisely why self-control is essential not only to the believer, but the greater community at large. This facet of humanity led C. S. Lewis, the foremost Christian apologist of the twentieth century, to write:

> "Each day we are becoming a creature of splendid glory or one of unthinkable horror."[5]

Embracing temptations, be it sensual enticements or opportunities for dishonest gain, is the fastest way to destroy a culture since these temptations effectively function as aphids attacking the root structure of good and decent men, preventing their production of nourishing cultural fruit to sustain and improve society. They represent the sprouting weeds that smother a good harvest, moving men to the left on our rough bell curve. If uncontrolled, not only the hearts of individual men but the greater heart of the culture risks full contamination and the near exclusive production of poisonous fruit fatal to consumption.

At the individual level, God has blessed you with a heart that will literally grow any seed and the liberty to pursue which seed you choose to scatter over it. The challenge of guarding your heart is in understanding the emotional soil is just as fertile for harvesting godly thoughts and passions as it is for reaping wickedness and corruption. The emotions that you feed shall flourish, while the emotions that you starve shall wither and decay. Again, this illustrates the two perils facing the Christian exerting the conscious decision not to read the Bible. The obvious consequence is the lost opportunity for the believer to grow spiritually in a relationship with Jesus Christ; however, the true vulnerability is compounded by the understanding that the fertile heart of the believer will constantly yearn for nourishment from a competing source of influence. Much like nature, the human heart abhors a vacuum.

On a larger scale, if an increasing group of Christians were to abandon the teachings of the Bible, the societal fallout could prove catastrophic, depending on how these individuals alternatively chose to pursue enlightenment. If they were to coalesce around a text like *The Communist Manifesto*, for example, this would result in a gradual hardening of their hearts toward Christianity and a gradual softening of their hearts towards the opulence of power. This is not an opinion or personal judgment; the written words of Karl Marx are what best clarify this point:

"The first requisite for the happiness of the people is the abolition of religion."[6]

"For the bureaucrat, the world is a mere object to be manipulated by him."[7]

Thanks to the ever-ripening tree of ungodly customs and practices, we are afforded the luxury of choosing from myriad fully mature fruit with which to solidify our understanding of the true fertility of the human heart. Surprisingly, all we need are two pieces of fruit for our analysis.

The first example comes from a piece of propaganda issued by the Islamic State. In August of 2014, images surfaced of a child dressed as Jihadi John, equipped with a knife and a doll resembling an American "infidel."[8] While it is impossible to determine the age of the child due to the covering around his face, he appears to be between three and six years old. The first image graphically depicts the youngster holding a knife in his left hand and a doll resembling an American baby in an orange jumpsuit in his right. The second image shows the severed head of the doll resting on top of the body with blood sprinkled around the neck. These grotesque images are shown together with the black flag of the Islamic State, a symbol used to encourage, embolden, and ultimately unify the followers of an ideology that is so foreign to our culture.

My focus in this example is on the child. Remember, the more immersed one is to an idea, the fuller and more developed his fruit shall be. The more these seeds are watered, the more quickly they shall grow. Think of the potential of this institutionalized indoctrination of evil into the impressionable minds of an entire culture. Could there be any limit to their destructive power once the tree and its fruit have fully ripened into adulthood? From a biblical perspective, is there no symbolism to the fact that the hated "infidels" to this toxic culture are widely considered to be those societies most likely to embrace a Christian heritage? The spectrum of truth ranges from absolute light to absolute darkness. Is it all that surprising that the further man progresses into darkness, the greater his hostility to the light?

Grant me the license to anticipate the retort that I hardly make a compelling argument by highlighting the easily corruptible mind of a child. Can a reasonable conclusion really be formed using such a fragile example?

I highlight the child to underscore the true fertility of the heart with which we are born. If I may borrow a platitude from the secular manual, allow me to whimsically allege that we were simply born this way. In fact, restoring the unfettered nature of our heart is a paramount desire of Jesus Christ. Read his teachings from Matthew 18:

> "At that time the disciples came to Jesus and asked, 'Who, then, is the greatest in the kingdom of heaven?' He called a little child to him, and placed the child among them. And he said: 'Truly I tell you, unless you change and become like little children, you will never enter the kingdom of heaven. Therefore, whoever takes the lowly position of this child is the greatest in the kingdom of heaven. And whoever welcomes one

such child in my name welcomes me. If anyone causes one of these little ones—those who believe in me—to stumble, it would be better for them to have a large millstone hung around their neck and to be drowned in the depths of the sea. Woe to the world because of the things that cause people to stumble! Such things must come, but woe to the person through whom they come!'"

Although the topsoil of our hearts is virtually untainted at birth, our subsequent sinful indulgences symbolize the "piousticides" (killers of piety) we choose to spray over our respective gardens. Lamentably, many of us occasionally choose to spray these piousticides on the gardens of others, which is so clearly demonstrated by the case of this indoctrinated Muslim child. Unfortunately, the child's spiritual leader is spellbound by the father of sin. A man's decision to mislead himself is tragic, but his premeditated commitment to misleading others is the very definition of evil.

Should the reader remain unconvinced, simply focus your attention upon the Muslim adult in this image. Has his heart not become hardened from years of unadulterated immersion into a militant theology? Was he not merely an unblemished little boy, perhaps as recent as twenty to thirty years ago? Was he not the joy of his mother when he took those first steps as he reached the enchanting age of one? Here again, the words of Jesus Christ are so revealing in his Sermon on the Mount in the book of Matthew 5:

"You have heard that it was said, 'Love your neighbor and hate your enemy.' But I tell you, love your enemies and pray for those who persecute you, that you may be *children* of your Father in heaven. He causes his sun to rise on the evil and the good, and sends rain on the righteous and the unrighteous." (emphasis mine)

It would be challenging to find a more poisonous piece of fruit than the widespread cultivation of terrorism amid a culture clouded in darkness; however, our own culture of egocentric narcissism presents a fairly compelling candidate.

Our second piece of ripened fruit comes from a blogger named Kristen Brown. On March 1, 2016, Ms. Brown composed a blog entitled "I Had an Abortion and It Was a Totally Joyful Experience."[9] Sensing that her scandalous title was insufficient to convey her jubilation, she created a backdrop of smiley faces, champagne bottles, and party hats to function as the red carpet leading into the sacred, innermost thoughts and emotions of her sullied heart.

The article abounds with illustrations that help us understand how the poisoning of an individual heart leads to the perversion of justice. Before we begin unpacking her article, try and develop an appreciation for the association between understanding the fertility of the human heart, identifying secular trade winds, and the spiritual gift of prophecy. For example, juxtapose the following writings of the prophet Isaiah with the perspicacious observations of George Orwell in his landmark dystopian novel, *1984:*

Isaiah 5:20-21	George Orwell, 1984
Woe to those who call evil good and good evil, who put darkness for light and light for darkness, who put bitter for sweet and sweet for bitter. Woe to those who are wise in their own eyes and clever in their own sight.	The three slogans on the white face of the Ministry of Truth came back at him: WAR IS PEACE FREEDOM IS SLAVERY IGNORANCE IS STRENGTH

What type of seed scatter would produce such a vindicating celebration of "independence" at the expense of the most innocent of life? How did we *progress* to the point of rejoicing in the Great American Holocaust, an abortion movement that has terminated the lives of nearly 60 million babies since the 1973 Supreme Court decision of *Roe v. Wade?*

I want to be clear at the outset of our discussion that I am handling the case of one individual, and the following comments are not intended to be taken as representative of every woman who has had an abortion. Ms. Brown certainly demonstrates disturbingly radical viewpoints throughout the article, which is best demonstrated by the title of her blog. I struggle to believe that any more than a mere fraction of women who have had an abortion exhibit such a fanatical degree of euphoric liberation. In the interest of understanding our potential fertility, however, we cannot forego the opportunity to explore the concepts of faith, relationships, and gratitude from her perspective.

Faith undergirds the human spirit. It is not merely an emotion constrained to those identifying as religious or spiritual. Individuals ascribing to Judaism, Christianity, Islam, and myriad other religions have the same inherent faith as those professing atheism. Faith provides everyone with a sense of purpose and comfort. On her personal web page, Ms. Brown takes pride in her work of writing "about how technology is impacting the future of our bodies, our brains and our culture." Perhaps the threat of losing this purpose helps explain why her decision to pursue abortion was relatively easy: *"I never wavered in my decision and I have not once regretted it since."*[10]

Ms. Brown unintentionally outlines her faith structure in the first two sentences of her article. In writing *"I shouldn't have been pregnant. I was on the pill,"* she professes her allegiance to the false god of scientific development. Why would this god forsake her in her pursuit of cultural understanding? For Ms. Brown, the crisis of an impending pregnancy lies not within the decision to terminate life; it is the threat that emerges at the intersection of convenience and responsibility. This threat jeopardizes her apparent core value of power, a theme that is referenced nine times in her brief editorial.

Control is of paramount importance to her. In fact, the article begins with her terrifying fear of losing control over her life: *"I knew that I was (pregnant) because I could feel my entire body rebelling against me – I was no longer in control . . . Getting pregnant was one of the darkest points in my life. I was broke from quitting my job, going back to school, and then accepting a low-paying fellowship . . . I will never forget the feeling of panic and terror that comes with the sensation that you are losing control of your body."* These latter references to financial hardship reinforce her value of control (power), in addition to displaying a terrifying fear of accountability to anything outside of herself.

Compounding this personal constitution is her desperate human need of companionship, a void equally circulated throughout the human race. Ms. Brown is not shy about acknowledging her absence of friends or vocalizing her sorrow over spending *"yet another friendless Friday night."* On one of these friendless nights, she reached out to a *"nice enough guy"* through a dating site to attempt to fill this void. Her description of the events leading up to their passionate encounter is brusque. It takes her only five short sentences to move from her initial dinner date solicitation to what appears to be an utter disgust with her actions. Why else would she express the following sentiments? *"The next day, I . . . blocked his number, unfriended him on Facebook, and sincerely hoped to never see him again."* Why the desire never to see him again but to save the mortification of the entire episode?

Lastly, perhaps as a validation to her faith construct, she expresses a near-reverent sense of gratitude after the deed has been done. *"I felt powerful, as if there were no obstacle I couldn't surmount. I felt a deep sense of freedom, knowing that my only responsibility was to myself. I was overcome with gratitude and optimism and a new-found sense of control."* This gratitude is a validation of her faith in the god of scientific development, who ultimately delivered her from the throes of raising a child through a pill prescribed by Planned Parenthood. The success with which the medication "solved the problem" confirmed the infallibility of her faith by restoring the power she so desperately wanted over her life.

Only a culture so absorbed with political correctness would find the following statement offensive: the ultimate fulfillment of womanhood is the rearing of children. Conversely, the barren womb represents the ultimate adversity facing a woman. This biblical truth is witnessed throughout the Old Testament. Sarai, the wife of Abram in Genesis, is so desperate for children that she pushes her husband into the arms of another woman to conceive. The book of 1 Samuel 1 uses the terms "deep anguish" and "misery" to describe the emotions on the heart of the barren Hannah before she was blessed with a child after impassioned prayer and pleading before the Lord. Lastly, consider the story of Michal upon witnessing her husband David's jubilance upon bringing the Ark of the Covenant to Jerusalem.

> "As the ark of the LORD was entering the City of David, Michal daughter of Saul watched from a window. *And when she saw King David leaping and dancing before the Lord, she despised him in her heart* . . . . When David returned home to bless his household, Michal daughter of Saul came out to meet him and said, 'How the king of Israel has distinguished himself today, going around half-naked in full view of the slave girls of his servants as any vulgar fellow would!' David said to Michal, 'It was before the Lord, who chose me rather than your father or anyone from his house when he appointed me ruler over the Lord's people Israel—I will celebrate before the Lord. I will become even more undignified than this, and I will be humiliated in my own eyes. But by these slave girls you spoke of, I will be held in honor.' *And Michal daughter of Saul had no children to the day of her death.*" (2 Samuel 6:16, 20–23, emphasis mine)

How can the reader *not* infer a certain degree of punishment upon Michal for her hostility toward her husband? Contrary to the women of the Old Testament, our secular "enlightened" culture now considers the rearing of children to be the ultimate punishment facing the career woman.

How do we use these two cases to identify the secular trade winds of our culture? What shall we make of environments that condition children to kill and women to scorn motherhood? The prophet Isaiah foretold that anguish and despair would befall those professing a secular wisdom, while George Orwell anticipated a time in which society would equate ignorance with strength. Woe to the church that refuses to scatter the seeds of righteousness, indeed!

There is an old adage in any field of investigation that encourages the individual to, in effect, peel back the layers of the onion. This is a metaphor that encourages an individual to methodically sift through the various consequences of an issue until he can objectively identify its underlying cause. If we were to peel back the layers of the onion to attempt to understand today's culture, we would start by removing all of the fruit of the earth, both pleasant and foul. After this laborious process, we would surprisingly discover root structures leading to only two trees. The first tree is the tree of the kingdom of light, the Kingdom of God, which produces all of the good fruit that is spread throughout the earth. When man witnesses love, joy, peace, forbearance, kindness, goodness, faithfulness, gentleness, and self-control, he is partaking of fruit from the tree of the Kingdom of God. In today's culture, however, this tree is greatly overshadowed by the other, larger tree that now intercepts much of its light and water supply. That tree is the tree of the kingdom of darkness, or the kingdom of fallen man. This tree produces the deceptively tempting fruit leading a man to develop haughty eyes, a lying tongue, hands that shed innocent blood, a heart that devises wicked schemes, and feet that are quick to rush into evil. Such men are prone to become false witnesses who pour out lies and stir up conflict within the community.

Moses' warning to the Israelites at the beginning of the chapter was not solely agricultural in nature. He was concurrently warning against the scattering of two incompatible worldviews over the fertile field that is the human heart. When scores of Christians choose to dilute the living waters of a biblical worldview with the emptiness of secular humanism, the public vineyard slowly becomes defiled. This leads to the perversion of the two gifts of monumental significance and gradual collapse of the cultural institutions that were initially constructed to promote a healthy society!

For example, the Christian reveres liberty as a cherished gift from his Creator; however, the secular humanist views it as a tremendous liability. The Christian guards against the open fertility of his heart; however, the secular humanist actively exploits the gift at every turn. While Jesus was indeed referring to money in the following teaching, might there have been a connection between the concept of "serving two masters" and "planting two kinds of seed?" Again, read his sentiments from the Sermon on the Mount in Matthew 6:

> "But if your eyes are unhealthy, your whole body will be full of darkness. If then the light within you is darkness, how great is that darkness! No one can serve two masters. Either you will hate the one and love the other, or you will be devoted to the one and despise the other. You cannot serve both God and money."

The world is filled with good and bad seed as numerous as the sand on the shore or the stars in the sky. The Lord has abundantly blessed you, as one of His children, with the liberty of choosing which seed you shall sow upon your own heart and also the vineyard that is your community. While you retain the free will to sow what you please, be mindful that Moses had issued a law forbidding the Israelites from planting two separate kinds of seed over their vineyard. This is more of a protective than a restrictive law, and it includes intellectual as well as physical seed. The Bible chronicles cyclical tales of prophets failing to convict the hearts of Israelite societies who ignored this directive at their own peril. If man is not actively pursuing the Lord and all of His ways, then by definition he is only *progressing* to a higher state of idolatry.

With this grounded foundation of knowledge on the topics of liberty and fertility, the time has come to turn our attention to the wisdom of the world. The kingdom of darkness is spreading at an unheralded pace as we are now witnessing continuous ideological victories of progressivism and secular humanism in our culture. These victories have only been possible, however, because of the wide-scale Christian acceptance of the surreptitious claim that any religion must be compartmentalized on account of the separation of church and state. But just what does constitute religion? Could it be possible that the progressive has in fact fully integrated church and state while deceptively forbidding the same luxury from his Bible-believing counterparts with a duplicitous zeal? The subject of our next chapter will be to search for any traces of hypocrisy within this widely accepted mandate.

TWO

Erecting the Golden Calf

*"It doesn't matter what the friggin' legal and ethics
people say, we need to win this m----f---er."*
~ Scott Foval, Wisconsin State Director,
Americans United for Change

The fifteenth-century artist Leonardo da Vinci
sagaciously pronounced that simplicity is the
ultimate sophistication. In keeping with this profundity,
the simplest means of understanding human governance begins
with an appreciation of the following assertion: the pendulum
of earthly authority ranges from the absolute, *voluntary*
submission before the Lord in humble reverence on the right,
to the temporary, *involuntary* capitulation before men whose
hearts have yielded to power on the left. While we fancy
deceiving ourselves that we have evolved beyond such a basic,

even primitive, framework, these are the only two directions in which the pendulum may swing. There are the ways of the Lord, and then there are the ways of man. Though the ways of man vary greatly, they are still the ways of man. As outlined in Isaiah 55, these diverging courses are polar opposites:

> "'For my thoughts are not your thoughts, neither are your ways my ways,' declares the LORD."

The aggregate actions of men provide a constant force driving this pendulum, an object that can never lie motionless in any given culture. In fact, the sixteenth Speaker of the United States House of Representatives, Robert C. Winthrop, initially articulated these thoughts before the Annual Meeting of the Massachusetts Bible Society in Boston back in 1849:

> "All societies of men must be governed in some way or other. The less they have of stringent State Government, the more they must have of individual self-government. The less they rely on public law or physical force, the more they must rely on private moral restraint. Men, in a word, must necessarily be controlled either by a power within them, or a power without them; either by the word of God, or by the strong arm of man; either by the Bible or by the bayonet."[1]

Government is the vehicle most commonly used to move this pendulum. Throughout history, man has devised a multitude of forms of government; however, in nearly every circumstance, the end result has been power being exercised by the strong arm of man. In other words, human governance commonly wields the bayonet as opposed to the Bible, and as a result, the default human condition features poverty, misery, slavery, suffering, and tyranny. While Western civilization has so generously provided a temporary respite to those of us fortunate enough to live in the developed world over the last two centuries, mere societal advancement does not change this default human condition.

Why is this state of despair so common? Why would poverty, misery, slavery, suffering, and tyranny typically result, regardless of whether the central government was monarchical, democratic, parliamentary, republican, communist, or totalitarian? The answer is relatively simple. When governments become instituted among men, the pendulum of earthly authority *always* moves to the left, so long as those in power have not yielded to the ways of the Lord. These various forms of human governance are merely speed gauges controlling the velocity of man's race to absolute power. This point bears repeating. While history proves that a parliamentary style of government is certainly preferable to a totalitarian regime, the reader must understand that both forms advance the interests of the kingdom of man assuming they have not aligned their laws and customs to the ways of the Lord.

If government is the vehicle driving the pendulum of earthly authority, religion is the fuel that powers the car. Contrary to popular opinion, religion does not require a supernatural entity in order to exist. Instead, religion is on prominent display any time an individual grounds his actions in faith and conviction. The reason there will always be an unceasing conflict over the appropriate means of government is because every individual man faces the crisis of balance in life.

As a sinner, his contaminated heart leads to the simultaneous pursuit of both light and darkness by virtue of his daily conduct, yet in the midst of this struggle he desperately yearns to evangelize with others what he believes to constitute truth, meaning, and purpose. In this fashion, every human being engages in his own unique form of evangelism, traditionally spiritual or otherwise. The ensuing evangelism of these millions of separate epiphanies, which almost exclusively contain visions well beyond the capacity of our eyesight, serve as the various religious pursuits of the culture. (If they were either obvious or could easily be seen, there would be no need to evangelize!) The messages that become the most widely accepted ultimately fuel the engine of this vehicle of government.

Just as you have your choice of octane when you need to refuel your vehicle, the culture powers its government by the most widely practiced religion among its people. At some point in time during the twentieth century (the precise point is an endeavor best left to historians), the people of this great nation began to consciously reject the Gospel of Jesus Christ in favor of the gospel of secular humanism. Contrary to the sentiments of Mr. Brooks, this is the reason I conclude our country is on the verge of complete collapse, since the fruits of this doctrine are cancerous.

Before we review and evaluate these fruits, however, we must first develop an understanding of this substitute gospel. After all, this evangelism has established the church of secular humanism as the national church of modern America, converting millions of people and two major political parties into its ranks. These congregants are more commonly known as *progressives*.

Secular humanism is a doctrine whose central tenet is a belief in the ability of man to usher humanity into the utopia of a man-made Garden of Eden. In accordance with this faith, progressives believe there can be no more virtuous act than to champion a cause, political or social, that promises to improve the comfort and security of the masses. This comfort and security is not limited to the physical element, but the intellectual and emotional aspects as well. They believe that life should be a pleasurable experience for people; therefore, any threats to these pleasures, particularly the carnal, must be silenced and eliminated. They reject traditional religion with a militant zeal; however, they make shrewd use of convenient biblical passages to emotionally appeal to those possessing a Judeo-Christian worldview. As we shall soon see in the later chapters of this book, progressives infiltrate the various institutions within the culture (for example, the media, academia, the legal system, and so forth) to evangelize their gospel and win the hearts, minds, and (most importantly) financial resources of those they are fortunate enough to convert to their mission. Progressives have no tolerance for the conscience of their dissenters, since they are perceived as impeding the completion of this utopian construction project. As a result, they provide these nonconformists with the unpleasant option of either boarding the progressive train or tying themselves to the tracks.

Even though secular humanists claim to love people, they hate individual man. This is best expressed by their reverence for and desperate quest to procure power. Who has ever demonstrated their love with the phrase, *I love you so much I want to control you?* Progressives relentlessly promote the virtue of expanding the central government to the size necessary to regulate every aspect of the human experience, while simultaneously disregarding its blatant incompetence when given even a modicum of civic responsibility. They perceive the sea of humanity as a collection of stupid, ignorant people desperately in need of shepherding at the hands of the self-appointed, politically connected few. While this may sound inflammatory, these are merely the words of secular humanist Jonathan Gruber, who explained that Obamacare was ultimately able to pass because "the American people are too stupid to understand the difference."[2]

The notion that progressives deride the general public is also supported by a recent bureaucratic survey conducted by political scientists Jennifer Bachner and Benjamin Ginsberg. Their survey discovered that bureaucrats think they should use their best judgment instead of consulting public opinion on policy pursuits because these bureaucrats believe the American public is ignorant on a wide range of issues.[3] Secular humanists define accomplishments as legal pronouncements that control and restrict the behaviors of man, not those that liberate his potential.

Secular humanists perceive liberty as a threat to their promised deliverance. For this reason, they promote a radical form of egalitarianism that maintains that all people are to be treated equally across their entire lifespan, without regard to the varying degree of effort exerted by each unique individual. Regardless of whether an individual spends his days in the exhaustive pursuit of toil or the exclusive pursuit of leisure, progressives believe unfairness emerges when these two individuals receive conflicting outcomes from their respective pursuits. This radical egalitarianism rejects the theory that the well-being of each member of society is a direct byproduct of the individual decisions made over the course of their respective lives. It rejects the assertion that an individual has the innate capacity to improve his lot in life.

Progressives believe that individuals are merely a product of their environment, helpless to improve their standing in the absence of a centralized administrator dispensing compassion aligned under the ever-mutating framework of a secular cultural ethos. Progressives lament the inequality and wealth disparity that pervades our culture, and they address this problem through solutions that increasingly restrict the liberty of all citizens. Never forget that the paramount cause of inequality in our society today is individual liberty; thus, any desire to restore equality within the culture must necessarily eliminate this liberty.

With respect to this wealth disparity, secular humanist policies promote redistribution as the greatest achievable good in society. Yet while their spoken words and formal policies praise the economic benefits of the redistribution of wealth, their downright hostility to the redistribution of power exposes their intentions as being completely disingenuous. When proposing social solutions, progressives mask their desire for power behind creative emotional appeals designed to convey a message that they are troubled by the current state of society. These appeals generally cast a wide net across society in search of cultivating support to address the negative features of our society that will never change. An example of such a campaign would be the elimination of poverty. Whose heart wouldn't resonate with that? Rejecting Christ's assertion that the poor will always remain among us,[4] the progressive sells the idea that modern civilization can progress beyond the outmoded presence of poverty by bonding together to raise awareness and demand the problem be solved by modifying the purpose of the citizenry, typically through aggressive petitions that shame the conscience. (In reality, the action requested is a simple transfer of faith and sacrifice of personal liberties to a central authority to ensure a level playing field for everyone).

Secular humanism is a false gospel. To put the ideology in terms that an information technology specialist would appreciate, it is completely incompatible and unrecognizable to the Christian operating system of the Bible. Though the progressive ostensibly denies the incompatibility of his pursued actions with biblical affirmations, his actions demonstrate an inconspicuous departure from the ways of the Lord. These inconsistencies can be unrecognizable to the unsuspecting believer, who draws inspiration from the prospect of contributing to what he perceives to be a series of outwardly noble missions. Make no mistake, however, as a careful study reveals no less than five irreconcilable differences between the core beliefs of the progressive and the teachings of Jesus Christ.

Most notably, the social crusader ardently rejects the concept of original sin by holding the belief that human nature can be perfected if only everyone were to ascribe and commit to achieving social justice collectively. If this were true, why was Christ's sacrifice necessary? Second, progressives require that faith and belief be redirected away from their traditional sources in favor of allegiance to an unprecedented pursuit of utopia. If utopia were indeed achievable, man could simply create heaven on earth, resulting in the elimination of all human suffering. This violates the scriptural affirmation that we are to affix our mind on the heavenly realm. If heaven were attainable of our own creation, then by implication we are fixing our mind on earthly things. Paul provided advance warning of this enticement in Philippians 3:

"For, as I have often told you before and now tell you again even with tears, many live as enemies of the cross of Christ. Their destiny is destruction, their god is their stomach, and their glory is in their shame. Their mind is set on earthly things. But our citizenship is in heaven. And we eagerly await a Savior from there, the Lord Jesus Christ."

Third, secular humanists possess a rigid faith in their ability to control the outside environment. From the climate-related concerns of rising sea levels and polluting carbon emissions, to the unwavering convictions that guns create violence and entrepreneurs exploit workers, these secular mercenaries believe it is well within their power to control the climate, eliminate poverty, eradicate crime, and prevent the general human tendency for people to take advantage of one another. How can we Christians be so gullible? Can man control the wind? Could a bureaucrat have prevented Cain from slaying Abel? Would life be better without power plants, electricity, automobiles, defense weapons, and employment opportunities? The only reason these seductions gain traction is because there is an epidemic of biblical illiteracy in our society. If the Bible is indeed absolute truth, the story of the great flood in the book of Genesis invalidates the doomsday environmental concern of the progressive.

"As long as the earth endures, seedtime and harvest, cold and heat, summer and winter, day and night will never cease" (Genesis 8:22).

The believer also wouldn't be swayed by the empty, idealistic promises appealing to the social issues if he were to simply meditate on the teachings of Jesus Christ:

"Nothing outside a man can make him 'unclean' by going into him. Rather, it is what comes out of a man that makes him 'unclean'" (Mark 7:15).

If everything that defiles a man literally comes from within, why do secular solutions archetypically address the *outside* environment? Can molding the environment fix the brokenness of individual man?

Fourth, secular humanists seek to suppress and uproot the influence of institutions supporting a biblical worldview by employing a joint strategy of ridicule and infiltration. In April of 2011, two individuals who would later become senior officials of the Hillary Clinton presidential campaign exchanged emails in which they asserted that Catholic teachings represented an "amazing bastardization of the faith."[5] These officials also used the phrases "severely backwards" and "totally unaware of Christian democracy" when referencing Catholicism. The following year, Sandy Newman, president of the progressive organization Voices of Progress, emailed senior staffer John Podesta to begin contemplating how they could "plant the seeds of revolution" in the Catholic church. The stated goal was to foment a "Catholic Spring, in which Catholics themselves demand the end of a middle ages dictatorship."[6] Despite being a self-professed Roman Catholic, leaked emails reveal Podesta was on board with the proposal, helping to create a fictitious front group named Catholics in Alliance for the Common Good as part of a "bottom up" strategy to incite a mutiny within the Catholic church.[7]

Even worse, during Clinton's delivery of the keynote address before the sixth annual Women in the World Summit in April of 2015, she explained that our "deep-seated cultural codes, religious beliefs and structural biases have to be changed" to acquiesce to the demands of the powerful abortion lobby.[8]

Despite living a life lacking any evidence of spiritual conversion, Clinton apparently has no qualms misrepresenting her faith for personal gain. When marketing her autobiographical book in an interview with *The New York Times* in 2014, she shamelessly provided the following response to the question of which book made her into the woman she had become:

> "[T]he Bible was and remains the biggest influence on my thinking. I was raised reading it, memorizing passages from it and being guided by it. I still find it a source of wisdom, comfort and encouragement."[9]

Clinton is the poster child of secular humanist duplicity. Five years after the aforementioned email exchanges, she continued her relationship with at least two of the senior level staffers involved in collusive brainstorming efforts to dismantle the Catholic church. For someone claiming to be so heavily influenced by the Bible, why would she continue to employ staffers plotting a revolution to overthrow institutions built upon its teachings? Why would she fight so aggressively to preserve American genocide? Why would she want to change our deep-seated religious beliefs? This duplicity suggests that this faith construct can produce a completely bankrupt conscience that only hardens following a decades-long pursuit of absolute power.

These examples also show that there are no ethical limitations to the methods employed by progressives. Even the sanctity of unborn human life is not off limits so long as every knee shall bow before the idol.

Finally, progressives reject the philosophy that people are an end in themselves. Instead, they will not hesitate to malevolently abuse people as the means to the ultimate end of erecting their golden calf of utopia. A video investigation released by *Project Veritas* in October of 2016 flawlessly highlighted this attribute by capturing the raw emotion of Scott Foval, the secular humanist field director of the progressive front group Americans United for Change. In the video, Foval confesses to the role he plays in deploying paid operatives to incite violence at Republican campaign events. His reprehensible comments reveal how this philosophical worldview can utterly contaminate the human heart:

> I'm saying that we have mentally ill people, that we pay to do s—t, make no mistake. Over the last twenty years, I've paid off a few homeless guys to do some crazy stuff, and I've also taken them for dinner, and I've also made sure they had a hotel, and a shower. And I put them in a program. Like I've done that. But the reality is, a lot of people especially our union guys. A lot of our union guys . . . they'll do whatever you want. They're rock and roll. When I need to get something done in Arkansas, the first guy I call is the head of the AFL-CIO down there, because he will say, "What do you need?" And I will say, I need a guy who will do this, this, and this. And they find that guy. And that guy will be like "Hell yeah, let's do it!" . . . It doesn't matter what the friggin' legal and ethics people say, we need to win this m-----f---er.[10]

As evidenced by this example, nothing is off limits to a person who embraces the "means to an end" mindset. This episode explains how the seeds of progressivism can produce a harvest in which human beings disgracefully brag about manipulating the very destitute whose interests they claim to defend. The investigation also uncovered Foval's confession that he and various other likeminded organizations coordinate to "stage very authentic grassroots protests" at events that do not march in complete lockstep with their worldview. Though Foval was subsequently fired once the undercover investigation gained publicity, the damage had already been done. The goal of his organization's actions, of course, was to manipulate public opinion by using the media to distort the democratic process through the widespread dissemination of a false narrative. We will further explore this progressive strategy in chapter five. For now, however, I ask you: is this not the exact same method employed by the very father of lies in the garden?

Despite all of the collateral damage produced by their methods, progressives continue to dedicate their lives to evangelizing the social gospel of secular humanism throughout the primary institutions of society. The pursuit of utopia is a vision that gives them meaning and purpose. Thus, the entire array of solutions proposed once this philosophy is embraced fully integrates a utopian faith when communicating with the governing authority. In other words, the progressive has firmly enjoined church and state in his pursuit of utopia. After all, what could be more virtuous than achieving Eden of your own volition?

Let us now partake of the first fruits of the tree of secular humanism. It has been just over 50 years since two landmark Supreme Court cases have launched daggers into the heart of the influence of Christianity upon America. In *Engel v. Vitale* in June of 1962, the Court effectively removed prayer from public schools, citing prohibitions of the First and Fourteenth Amendments to the Constitution. One year later, the Court mandated that no state law or school board may require that passages from the Bible be read in the *Abington School District v. Schempp* case. The case further prohibited the reciting of the Lord's Prayer in the public schools of a state at the beginning of each school day.

These first fruits have led to fifty years of cultural experience living in a world that does not welcome the Gospel of Jesus Christ. What do we now have to show for this "progress?" Christians are instructed to be the light of the world, so with boldness, allow me to humbly shine the light on the benefits of this movement that we so mindlessly champion:

- By and large, we walk with our faces down in desperate fear of making eye contact with a stranger;

- any man desiring to mentor or befriend a child is assumed to be a pedophile;

- it is now unsafe for a woman to walk alone in nearly all major metropolitan cities, in many instances even in broad daylight;

- allowing your child to play unsupervised at a park constitutes criminally negligent child abuse; and

- domesticated animals are referred to as "children" by a rising percentage of their owners, while actual children were referred to as "punishment" by then Illinois Senator Barack Obama while campaigning for the presidency in Johnstown, Pennsylvania, in September of 2008.[11]

This bullet-pointed list of outcomes inescapably ensues pursuant to the theory of triangular congruence. Picture an equilateral triangle with God, individual man, and the society at large serving as its three corners. Man's horizontal relationship with his counterpart is always a reflective byproduct of his vertical relationship to his Creator. The closer man is to God, the closer he must also be to his fellow man, resulting in a smaller triangle. Conversely, the further man is from God, the further he must be from his fellow man. Alternatively stated, when we *consciously* detach and dissociate from God, we *unconsciously* detach and dissociate from our fellow man.

In keeping with this theory, the deeply rooted distrust that permeates through our modern culture is merely symptomatic of our broader distrust in God. This distrust has given rise to the burgeoning narcissism in our culture, which is commonplace to societies that resist accountability for their actions. Put simply, since we have elected to scatter two dissenting worldviews over our culture, the secular fruits of distrust and narcissism have defiled the biblical fruits of trust and humility.

Think critically: would Jesus Christ really sanction the overthrow of the Bible and eradication of prayer from the minds of the same demographic whom he distinctly referred to as those who are greatest in the kingdom of heaven? The Bible is the divinely inspired and infallible Word of God, while prayer is the most powerful act of communication uniting us with our Creator. Would Jesus Christ abate his teaching to acquiesce to the removal of these two foundational elements of the Christian faith simply on account of a worldly suggestion to separate Christian values and principles from state governance?

Abandoning the Bible, prayer, and any references to Christianity in the public education of three full generations of Americans (Baby Boomer, Generation X, and Millennial) serves as irrefutable evidence that the people of this great nation have indeed changed their religion. This faith exchange explains why our centralized form of government is migrating away from a representative democracy in favor of an authoritarian dictatorship, since our heightened preference for the ways of man has increased the degree of pressure being applied to the accelerator in our governmental vehicle. Since the ways of the man are hostile to the ways of the Lord, the church of Jesus Christ has gradually become subject to the same treatment as 19th century American Indians. Christians are being militantly exiled out of every cultural institution onto the independent reservations of their respective church facilities, forbidden from practicing their customs outside of these confined tracts of land. Without question, we are no longer a Christian nation.

Consequently, it is no accident that our form of government is becoming more authoritarian, with increasing evidence of communist and socialist underpinnings. Social security, healthcare, and unemployment insurance are all socialist-style programs that emerged only after the country formally changed its national religion. These developments are harmonious to secular humanism, since socialism gives the omniscient state an economic system in which it can gradually centralize the ownership of the means of production in order to facilitate the deliverance of utopia. In a progressive society, the state becomes our great provider and deliverer, and it is only by its power that we can attain our salvation and establish the kingdom of heaven on earth. Progressives simply substitute the role of Jesus Christ with the central state authority as the agent that dispenses grace throughout the culture.

In addition to this messianic connection, the unwavering, steadfast commitment of progressives to the moral virtue of socialism provides even more definitive proof that secular humanism is a faith construct. Progressives truly believe that their socialist system of government, if properly perfected, can provide the way, the truth, and the life despite the lack of any discernible evidence existing anywhere along the broad spectrum of human history. Not only does this evidence not exist, but there are countless examples in which this political system has ended with the mass genocide of millions of people. The belief that it can still work because it simply has not been applied correctly is the very definition of faith in the unseen.

The unjust extermination of so much human life requires a more in-depth survey of this political ideology toward which we are so mindlessly gravitating. One of the most ardent advocates of socialism was Vladimir Lenin, the man who helped create the Soviet Union and launch the communist era in Russia in the early twentieth century. Lenin admitted that "the goal of socialism is communism."[12] *The Free Dictionary* defines communism as "a system of government in which the state plans and controls the economy and *a single, often authoritarian* party holds power, *claiming to make progress* toward a higher social order in which all goods are equally shared by the people" (emphasis mine).[13] This definition links the concepts we have explored throughout this chapter, whether it be progressivism, egalitarianism, socialism, or secular humanism.

If communism is the goal of socialism, and socialism is the primary means of achieving utopia, it stands to reason that a survey of the effectiveness of communism as a political system would be prudent. China is one of the most prominent communist regimes in the world today. How effective has communism been in China? In 2005, professor and Nobel Peace Prize finalist R. J. Rummel exhaustively studied this question, and his findings are terrifying. During a period of only thirty-eight years from 1949 to 1987, the communist regime of China under Mao Zedong was responsible for the death of 77 million Chinese people. To add context, this genocide more than doubles the 34.1 million casualties in all wars between 1900 and 1987, which includes World Wars I and II, Vietnam, Korea, and the Mexican and Russian Revolutions.[14] The 77 million figure is greater than the entire populations of the United Kingdom, France, and Italy; in fact, over 90 percent of the countries in the world currently have individual populations that are fewer than 77 million inhabitants.

Perhaps China was an aberration. What became of the communist experiment in the Soviet Union? Under Lenin, Josef Stalin, Nikita Khrushchev, and others, a total of 62 million Soviets fell at the hands of communist rule during the seventy-year period ending in 1987.[15] In other words, Soviet and Chinese communism resulted in the deaths of nearly 140 million people in a time frame that did not even span a full century. This figure would only increase after giving consideration to Romania under the dictatorship of Nicolae Ceausescu, Cambodia under the leadership of Pol Pot, Venezuela under Hugo Chavez, Cuba under Fidel Castro, and North Korea under Kim Jong-Il.

In spite of this history and track record, the progressive seed continues to bloom brightly in America. In fact, Hillary Clinton, perhaps the most prominent contemporary progressive in our culture, enthusiastically voiced this response when asked to expound on her political philosophy while first campaigning for president in 2007:

"I consider myself a proud modern American progressive, and I think that's the kind of philosophy and practice that we need to bring back to American politics."[16]

This response alone should have uncompromisingly repelled any believer in Jesus Christ from affixing their support to her campaign, simply out of fear of what type of poisonous fruit might have blossomed under her leadership. (In reality, the various fruit that has *already* blossomed under her headship as Secretary of State eliminated any need to wonder).

Progressive values completely undermine the well-being of a society because they uproot the influence of the Bible from the people. As a result, trust, liberty, and traditional morality are slowly and painfully extracted out of the culture. When believers engage in the political process, they need to begin a new habit of determining whether their support helps to water the seeds of the kingdom or the weeds of secular humanism.

On November 8, 2016, the broad failure of American Christians led the nation into a situation in which the choice for president featured two secular humanists dedicated to restricting liberty through their mutual endorsement of the supremacy of the state authority. In a series of debates leading up to the election, Hillary Clinton and Donald Trump merely argued over what speed limit was most suitable for travel. Regardless of who won, the notable loser was the American people.

We arrived at this demoralizing presidential choice due to our wide acceptance of what may perhaps be the most successful falsehood ever mainstreamed throughout modern culture: the suggestion that Christians must separate church and state. Incredibly, this whisper has been widely accepted throughout the ranks of believers, despite the fact that it is a suggestion that effectively neuters the Christian faith! The separation of church and state is foundationally opposed to all biblical teachings, and it can only become intellectually enticing once the believer has accepted the relentless message of progressivism being broadcast across virtually all secular channels of society. Once a believer consents to detach his spiritual faith from political affairs, he essentially states that the teachings of Jesus Christ have no place in a modern and enlightened culture. This is the modern equivalent of lighting a lamp and then hiding it under a clay jar. A simple reading of the New Testament Gospels would alert us to the absurdity of this claim. Jesus Christ was constantly at odds with the Pharisees. Who were the Pharisees but the religious *and political* leaders of the Jews in his day? Not even Jesus Christ separated church and state. Did he not clear the temple courts and overturn the tables of the money changers?

The hypocrisy of the church and state mandate is that secular humanists vehemently refuse to separate their faith from state governance, as we have previously explored. Regardless, we should concern ourselves with whether or not this mandate can satisfy a biblical test. Does God's Word endorse a separation of church and state? If the actions of Jesus Christ are unconvincing, consider the words of Paul from Ephesians 6:12:

> "For our struggle is not against flesh and blood, but against the rulers, against the authorities, against the powers of this dark world and against the spiritual forces of evil in the heavenly realms."

Did Paul intend for us to struggle against the rulers and authorities of this world by sacrificing our faith?

If these two arguments remain unconvincing, let us attempt to harden our understanding by making an appeal to the intellect. One fruit from the tree of progressivism has been the notorious *Roe v. Wade* Supreme Court decision in 1973 that legalized abortions across the nation. Since this decision, the lives of nearly 60 million American babies have been extinguished for any number of reasons. If we are honest, we confess the primary motive is selfishness, but that is neither here nor there for purposes of our argument.

Let us open our thought study by using you as our subject! Assume that you are a God-fearing Christian that vehemently objects to abortion, considering it a sinful practice. You believe that life begins at conception, and you hold the opinion that ending the life of the most innocent among us serves as biblical affirmation of governmental corruption as it is stated in Psalm 94, verses 20–21:

> "Can a corrupt throne be allied with you—a throne that brings on misery by its decrees? The wicked band together against the righteous and condemn the innocent to death."

You are open about voicing your displeasure with those in your church, but these lamentations shared with believers inside the church walls represent the entirety of your fight over the course of your life. Upon your death, you kneel before the throne of the Almighty for judgment. Would the Divine Creator, the Lord Almighty, the God of Abraham, Isaac, and Jacob accept your justification for inaction on the worldly premise that church and state remain separate? Or, perhaps, would he remind you of the words of the prophet Zephaniah?

"At that time I will search Jerusalem with lamps and punish those who are complacent, who are like wine left on its dregs, who think, 'The Lord will do nothing, either good or bad'" (Zeph. 1:12).

Your defense would be wholly rejected. Not to speak is to grant a license and authorization to the mass murder of the unborn. It is in this fashion that we share accountability in the decline of our society.

The separation of church and state is merely an ideological transaction that provides fuel to those desirous of a permanent removal of any influence of Jesus Christ upon society. The secular humanist refuses to engage in this transaction because there is no price that can offset his quest for absolute power. Christians, however, willingly engage in this transaction because it provides them with tremendous value as it pertains to the difficulty of taking up their cross.

What benefit does the believer receive in this transaction? What worldly benefit would be worth sacrificing the exclusive societal antidote that is the Gospel of Jesus Christ? From an altruistic perspective, does it promote a greater degree of civility in the community? From a selfish perspective, does it grant power to the believer? Neither suggestion is true.

Christians willingly sacrifice the Gospel because of one essential weakness within human nature. The only force stronger than one man's quest for absolute power is another man's longing to absolve himself of accountability. When the Christian surrenders to this weakness, he indeed procures an informal waiver of accountability to temporarily placate his sinful nature. What he fails to realize, however, is that this metaphorical waiver only provides the short-term benefit of conscience appeasement. With the passage of time, the ultimate cost becomes devastating because, as previously mentioned, it adds fuel to the insatiable and despotic ambitions of the godless dictator.

Being accountable is one of the most challenging aspects of following Jesus Christ, and this difficulty generates an environment conducive to excessively relying upon grace. After all, human nature is fundamentally flawed through original sin to the point of permanent imperfection. Thus, there is an inherent fear in every believer from going "all in" with the knowledge that our next sin will likely precede the evening sunset. Since the believer is so prone to sin, the decision to champion grace and compassion overtakes the instruction to obey the Word of God. This struggle cripples the faith of many a believer, leaving him to cling to grace given an uncertain understanding of how to confront this sinful culture.

This struggle plays right into the hands of the secular humanist. Detecting and broadcasting hypocrisy is of paramount importance to those currently in control of our cultural institutions, whether they be American universities, media conglomerates, or political organizations. Luring Christians to take the bait and champion the notion of a separation of church and state lays the seed for a rampant harvest of hypocrisy, unbeknownst to well-intentioned followers of Christ. For the people who adamantly refuse the integration of church and state are typically the same ones who trumpet how hypocritical Christians are for not living their faith. It is a lose-lose proposition.

The most prominent recent example we have of this dynamic is the wedding cake dispute. Beginning in 2014, progressives had Christians on the ropes attempting to defend their support of bakers, photographers, caterers, and real estate owners who would not offer their services to celebrate the union of two members of the same gender in marriage. This debate challenged the courage and resilience of the believer, placing a premium on his true understanding of the teachings of Christ. If Jesus were alive today, would he bake the cake or facilitate the wedding for these individuals? Would he condemn or condone the union? Either way, progressives were in for a landslide victory merely on account of the rampant division within the church. In fact, the division was so rampant that the Presbyterian sect formally sanctioned gay marriage in their church constitution in March of 2015![17]

It is imperative that the believer process the impact of the removal of Christian influence in American culture. Christianity scatters the seeds of peace, joy, gentleness, self-control, and love through our people, resulting in the cultivation of a godly society. Progressivism scatters the seeds of envy, malice, arrogance, and deceit, advancing the agenda of spiritual darkness. The fallen human tendency to envy now represents the literal foundation of our current economic policy. With this knowledge, how is it righteous to insist upon the separation of Christianity from governance, particularly when the progressive demands allegiance to an unprecedented, collective pursuit of utopia? Remember, the progressive mocks and mercilessly excoriates the Christian believer for displaying a steadfast adherence to what the former perceives to be a complete mystical abstraction. Does not the progressive concurrently demand allegiance to a golden calf that essentially consists of an ideological abstraction?

To best understand this abstraction, simply commit the following phrase to memory:

**Capitalism teaches man how to swim.
Communism teaches man how to drown.
Progressivism teaches man that water doesn't exist.**

Without question, progressivism is the pagan god of our day. This secular philosophy is an idol, a false god, a golden calf. Our culture's enchantment with it is a testament to historical illiteracy, which in part has caused an inability to think critically. The doctrine is a cancer. The inability of so many people to detect it does not mean it is not there; a cancer in a latent stage is still cancer. I implore the reader to apprehend the death toll of those societies who have bowed before the calf, not simply for our own benefit but also to honor the memory of those taken before their time. Should this warning remain unconvincing, please hold the words of Moses close to heart when considering the intentions and rhetoric of socialism and progressivism. As he wrote in Deuteronomy 8:

> "If you ever forget the LORD your God and follow other gods and worship and bow down to them, I testify against you today that you will surely be destroyed. Like the nations the LORD destroyed before you, so you will be destroyed for not obeying the LORD your God" (Deut. 8:19–20).

The demise of the United States of America is merely a foregone conclusion should we refuse to change course, simply through an appreciation of Old Testament prophecy and recent international history.

While progressive leaders as a whole are undoubtedly comprised of hearts that have truly been compromised by the pursuit of power, the overwhelming majority of their disciples truly want the best for their fellow man. These are the same open hearts that would have been ripe *for our harvest* if only we as Christians had observed the Great Commission of Jesus Christ as documented in Matthew 28:

> "Therefore go and make disciples of all nations, baptizing them in the name of the Father and of the Son and of the Holy Spirit, and teaching them to obey everything I have commanded you. And surely I am with you always, to the very end of the age" (Matt. 28:19–20).

The great news is that these same individuals still remain ripe for the harvest; however, if we continue to separate church and state, we had better prepare for a challenging search for grapes among thornbushes. The ripened fruit of a compartmentalized faith structure unpretentiously rebrands the Great Commission into the Great Omission, convincing Christians that their faith must be separated from civic affairs. It represents a masterful public relations victory for the church of progressivism and a feat that never could have been accomplished without a successful infiltration into the most influential institutions of American culture.

While we as Christians largely turned our faith into the Great Omission, progressives have united to construct an elaborate system of evangelism that is nothing short of breathtaking in its effectiveness. Through a successful penetration of academia, popular culture, the media, political parties, trade unions, multinational corporations, financial institutions, and even churches, these secular missionaries have won every single American cultural institution for the church of progressivism. Armed with the financial support of these institutions and the sympathetic stance taken by a rising portion of our younger generations, these legionaries have constructed a new American church. This modern church of secular humanism demands the hearts, minds, and economic resources of all Americans, and it has become powerful enough to threaten the wholesale eviction of Christianity from our culture.

Contrary to the biblical proverb, our new substitute church does not place its trust in the Lord with all of its heart; rather, they lean entirely on their own understanding.[18] They pledge a reverent allegiance to their false god of scientific development, using its breakthroughs to lambaste the irrationality of spiritual faith in what they perceive to be either a non-existent or callous God. To date, they have received little pushback from the faith community. The time has come for that to change.

THREE

The Flat Earth Society

But they did not listen or pay attention; instead, they
followed the stubborn inclinations of their evil hearts.
They went backward and not forward.

~ Jeremiah 7:24

The God v. Science debate is nothing new. It was almost 400 years ago that Pope Urban VIII ordered the astronomer Galileo Galilei, *a devout Christian man*, to stand trial for his conviction that the Earth revolved around the sun, a position deemed heretical by the Catholic Church. Galileo was confined to house arrest for the final eight years of his life as punishment for his heresy, an episode many unbelievers point to as indisputable evidence of an intolerant church. As a matter of secular convenience, this incident is commonly used to conflate the seventeenth-century position of the Catholic Church across all forms of modern Christianity.

Modern believers are presumed to possess a foundational hostility to reason and scientific development. It is long overdue that this preposterous claim be exposed for what it truly is: a defense mechanism used by unbelievers to divert attention away from the uncomfortable inconsistencies of their materialistic worldview. The phenomenon is known as psychological projection, and it was initially abstracted by the neurologist Sigmund Freud. Psychological projection features the projection of unpleasant emotions upon another person or group of people, alleviating the need to admit to or address these unwanted feelings in one's own life. In the case of the scientific community at large, it is far easier to label Christians as "science-deniers" than address positions that can best be considered troublesome, if not outright contradictory.

Start, for instance, with the primary process used to pursue knowledge. Would a true champion of science actively petition for an exemption from the scientific method for certain politically favored positions? Is it in the best interests of a culture to overthrow the scientific method in such circumstances? Could there possibly be a more scientifically ignorant statement than "the science is settled?" Science can never be settled since skepticism is at the very heart of the scientific method.

Take the recent example of sodium consumption. The American Heart Association has a long history of warning civilians about the link between salt intake and heart problems. This "settled science" was viewed as the hard truth, altering the dietary practices of Americans for decades. When exposed to scientific inquiries, however, the thread slowly began to unravel. After studying over 6,000 subjects, seven studies reported in the *American Journal of Hypertension* found no strong evidence that reducing salt intake lowers the risk of heart attacks, strokes, or death in people with normal or high blood pressure.[1] The author of one of these studies, Dr. Niels Graudal of Copenhagen University Hospital, formed this conclusion after interpreting all of the data: "In my opinion, people should generally not worry about their salt intake."[2] When challenged on one of their core beliefs, however, representatives for the American Heart Association remained stoically unfazed. In fact, the association reiterated its stance that the connection is well established and urged Americans to continue lowering salt in their diets.[3]

What about climate change, formerly known as global warming, and previously referred to as global cooling? The whole ordeal would be laughable were it not for the blind and dangerous fidelity of many of its supporters. In addition to being referred to by three contradictory titles within a forty-year period, the movement has simultaneously been blamed for both rising and falling sea levels; flooding and droughts; more and fewer hurricanes; and rising and cooling temperatures. In the mid-1980s, government scientists were warning that the greenhouse effect could cause New York City weather to mirror that of Daytona Beach within a century.[4] Thirty years later in 2015, the city experienced cold weather so severe the local presses referred to it as "Snowmageddon" and the governor of New York shut down the city and declared a state of emergency.[5]

While the entire climate change movement is laced with fear and hyperbole, there is a noticeable lack of scientific integrity when research, facts, data, and studies conflict with the desired narrative. For example, climate change disciples have become so ideological that a pair of scientists who were critical of the apparent consensus on climate change had to use pseudonyms just to get their academic research published![6] Rather than deal with inconsistencies such as these, however, progressives have found it far easier to circumvent their need to testify by calling Christians to the stand on account of their alleged hostility towards science. Instead of having to address broken climate models or climate projections that failed to materialize, progressives subject believers to ridicule by labeling them as "flat-Earthers," changing the narrative just enough to make these uncomfortable conflicts simply evaporate.

This approach could not possibly be any more anti-scientific. When announcing his new climate change policy in 2013, President Barack Obama offered the following lecture to opponents of his scientifically invalidated position:

> "I don't have much patience for anyone who denies that this challenge is real. We don't have time for a meeting of the Flat Earth Society. Sticking your head in the sand might make you feel safer, but it's not going to protect you from the coming storm."[7]

The marriage of these condescending sentiments with an apologetic media was all that was necessary to change the narrative, placing Christians and other skeptics on the defensive while the country drastically and detrimentally changed its energy policy. Remember, a healthy measure of skepticism is at the very core of the scientific method. Wouldn't the party attempting to eliminate any empirical questioning represent the true members of the Flat Earth Society? This allegation, by the President of the United States of all people, is a textbook example of psychological projection, the most regressive scientific position imaginable, and the epitome of hypocrisy!

Legitimate concerns to care for the Earth have, unfortunately, turned into an absentminded worship for many in the field of science. Despite the fact that over 31,000 scientists have signed their name upon a petition denying the validity of climate change and even Nobel Laureate Ivar Giaever has declared President Obama "dead wrong"[8,9] on global warming, supporters have doubled down on the sanctity of their dogma. One of the most vocal members of the sect, former Vice President Al Gore, was so bold as to recommend that climate change deniers be punished for their rejection of "accepted science."[10] An assistant professor at a private university in New York suggested that anyone disagreeing about global warming should be jailed.[11] Without a trace of irony, Massachusetts Senator Elizabeth Warren included the following statement in a speech entitled *The 11 Commandments of Progressivism*:

> "We believe in science, and that means that we have a responsibility to protect this Earth."[12]

Were it not for the man-made creation of *political* science, there would be little evidence to support any degree of truth in this claim. Ms. Warren has, however, found such beliefs effective tools to advance her pursuit of power. Since skeptics of climate change directly threaten this pursuit, the most efficient means of silencing these critics is by providing an exemption to this political creed from the rigors of something as menial as the scientific method. There is nothing scientific about asking a freethinker to sacrifice reason and logic to an unproven hypothesis. Regardless of the legitimacy of climate change, a true rationalist would conclude this tactic from the allegedly "pro-science" community raises a glaring red flag threatening the stated authenticity of their intent.

The problem with moral relativism is that it is very difficult to compartmentalize. It is nearly impossible to maintain an elastic outlook in one field while simultaneously maintaining rigid standards in another. For this reason, it is only logical that ideological discrepancies could surface across other scientific disciplines now that we have identified an irrational flexibility in the approach of the progressive with respect to the scientific method.

The avowed atheist Richard Dawkins once said, "I am very comfortable with the idea that we can override biology with free will."[13] What a remarkable confession. While these remarks were shared in the general context of his allegiance to Darwinian natural selection, a literal interpretation provides an opportunity to scrutinize the secular mindset for potential traces of duplicity. Could it be that those carrying the flag of science also take issue with the seemingly "settled science" of biology?

If you are reading this book, you likely studied biology at some point during high school. Simply put, biology is the science of life. We encourage our children to study this science to understand the mechanics of life, and continued research and dedication to this pursuit of understanding can ultimately lead to advances in many scientific disciplines, including the field of medicine. As a Christian, I am awed by the diversity of animal species, complexity of our DNA, and majesty of a world filled with countless forms of life, all of which I use to reaffirm my conviction in the splendor of our Creator. As a believer, I do not fear biology, and I do not want to curtail efforts to expand our understanding of our genetic composition in any fashion.

Does the secular humanist share this opinion? Let us analyze his approach toward the most basic of biological attributes: the study of gender. At the turn of the twentieth century, American genetic researchers discovered chromosomal differences between the two genders in a number of independent studies. These scientists identified that males possessed the XY chromosome, while females featured the XX chromosome. Although our eyes provide the visual proof necessary to discriminate between the genders by assessing the physical and anatomical features of an individual, this academic development furnished a scientific determination beyond the limitations of our senses. Astronomically few people had any issues with the conclusions drawn by this research. In fact, it has been and continues to be widely circulated throughout the American education system at the secondary and post-secondary level.

From a Christian vantage point, these biological breakthroughs completely validate biblical truths. This scientific understanding ("the settled science") completely reaffirms the binary arrangement of life. There is no contradiction to resolve, as God distinguishes all of life between male and female six times alone in the first seven chapters of the book of Genesis:

"He created them male and female and blessed them" (Gen. 5:2).

While no research has emerged to threaten the validity of the chromosomal understanding of gender, our environment has changed drastically over the past several years. Concepts such as gender fluidity, gender identification, and transgenderism have descended upon the culture with fierce intensity. Instead of addressing these issues head-on, Christians have treated them as they would rain on a Sunday picnic, scattering for cover as they wait to assess the damage. This approach has only emboldened the most confused members of our society.

Desiring to stay ahead of these secular trends and promote an environment of "inclusion," Facebook provided seventy-one different gender options to its users as of June 2014.[14] While the Christian surely identifies this latest trend as a departure from biblical teachings, he has likely given little thought to the underlying significance this action has on the faith construct of the unbeliever. These secular developments can only be construed as nothing other than an utter rejection of biological science, plain and simple. This instance is far from anecdotal, as Google, a number of online dating services and even the University of California have followed suit in migrating away from the binary constraints of gender.[15, 16,17,18] The current application for admission at the University of California features six different options for a candidate's gender. Think of that: a state university formally rejecting biological science . . . on its application for admission into the College of Biological Sciences!

The progressive war on biology is actually being waged on university battlefields on both coasts. In Rhode Island, Brown University student body president Viet Nguyen announced that feminine hygiene products such as tampons and pads would be provided in all men's bathrooms beginning with the 2016–17 academic year.[19] In a letter to all students, Nguyen explained that this action is "long overdue" because "menstruation is experienced by more than just those who identify as women."[20] For being such a highly esteemed Ivy League institution, it sure is unusual that this bold action would precede any scientific account of even one man ever menstruating. Since no such evidence exists, the man of reason can only conclude this to be an act of religious faith. Nguyen even confesses his larger goal is one of pure evangelism. He hopes the action "will motivate other universities and student governments to take similar actions to address this issue of equity." Predictably, Brown's Director of News and Editorial Development praised Nguyen and the Undergraduate Council of Students for showing such "tremendous initiative."[21]

By approving the proposal to place feminine hygiene products in all of its public men's bathrooms, Brown University management unwittingly endorsed the full integration of church and state. Without fully processing the broader meaning of its actions, the university just tailored an administrative policy on an idea wholly grounded in faith and evangelism, as opposed to facts or science. Surely the leaders of an institution of such intellectual prowess can make this most rudimentary connection.

As fully explained in chapter two, secular humanism is every bit as much a religion as Christianity. Since Brown received over $150 million in government grants according to its audited 2015 financial statement, an honest progressive would immediately turn to a campaign of defunding such an overtly inappropriate use of taxpayer funds to advance a religious agenda. [22] Of course, this will never happen, because the church and state restriction is only narrowly applied to those following the Gospel of Jesus Christ. The church of secular humanism, on the other hand, has been granted a conspicuous waiver from the culture. As a result, missionaries at both Cornell University and New York University have already taken steps to infuse this new church doctrine into the men's restrooms of their respective campuses.[23,24]

It would be easy to discount these cultural trends, considering that Facebook facilitates a market of virtual human interaction and online dating services simply connect two consenting adults in their pursuit of intimacy. Regarding the university network, what is the true harm of a checkmark on a formal application or the inclusion of tampons in the men's room? The problem emerges when we develop an appreciation for healthy root structures. Ideologically planted seeds grow rather quickly, particularly in the absence of a competing biblical narrative. When universities nurture an academic community that is openly hostile to science, the resultant seeds of contamination soon reach the desks of those tasked with developing social policy.

Just two years following Facebook's capricious gender expansion, the US Department of Health and Human Services issued rules informing doctors that declining to perform gender reassignment surgery *on children* following a recommendation from a "medical health professional" could be a potentially career-ending decision.[25] In other words, if the contaminated seeds being spread across the university network could reach the ears of just one newly minted doctor, the health and welfare of a toddler could be irreparably harmed. This is symbolic. By ordaining this directive, the national health department is effectively mandating that doctors violate their Hippocratic Oath! This edict, widely circulated through the media in August of 2016, came less than two weeks after two distinguished scientists from Johns Hopkins University published a 144-page report confirming that:

> "The understanding of sexual orientation as an innate, biologically fixed property of human beings—the idea that people are 'born that way'— is not supported by scientific evidence."[26]

Is it the Christian or the unbeliever who is willing to ignore science to the point of openly advocating child abuse?

Of course, gender is just an *attribute* of life. Rather than talking about attributes of life, why not just address the *essence* of life? The believer holds that life begins at conception, a belief most directly supported by the following two Old Testament verses:

"For you created my inmost being; you knit me together in my mother's womb" (Psalm 139:13).

"Before I formed you in the womb I knew you, before you were born I set you apart" (Jer. 1:5).

Although the belief that life begins at conception is a non-negotiable element of the Christian faith, arguments in favor of the (masterfully branded) "pro-choice" movement have slowly infected the minds of many believers. Their chief contention has been so effective since it appeals to liberty, spreading confusion throughout the Christian community: *a woman has the civil right to control her own body.* I must confess, even I agree with this statement on principle! That being said, I do not have the luxury of trusting on my raw emotion without making an appeal to reason. That would sidestep the scientific method.

Never forget that arguments appealing most heavily to the emotions and feelings of an individual typically conceal material scientific weaknesses, since independently tested and validated scientific conclusions eliminate any need to rely upon emotional appeal. To help us firmly root our position in reason, we must explore the scientific evidence behind the following questions: 1) Does life begin at conception? and 2) Does the fertilized egg represent a part of the woman's body during her pregnancy, or does the egg represent its own unique life form?

Biology-online.org, a website branding itself as the world's largest and most comprehensive biology discussion board, presents the following definition of life: "a distinctive characteristic of a living organism from dead organism or non-living thing, as specifically distinguished by the capacity to grow, metabolize, respond (to stimuli), adapt, and reproduce."[27] Contrast this definition with the explanation of how a fertilized egg becomes an embryo, according to the professionally accredited *Web*MD:

> "At the moment of fertilization, the baby's genetic makeup is complete, including whether it's a boy or girl. The fertilized egg starts growing fast, dividing into many cells. After the egg attaches to the uterus, some cells become the placenta while others become the embryo. The heart begins beating during week five. The brain, spinal cord, heart, and other organs are beginning to form."[28]

This scientific position affirms each of the aforementioned, distinguishing characteristics of a unique life. Conception is a process featuring growth, metabolism, responsiveness, adaptability, and reproduction. *Web*MD also recognizes that the genetic makeup of a baby is complete at fertilization. In other words, the baby has his own unique genetic code, otherwise known as DNA, *at the moment of fertilization*. This code is wholly different from that of the mother. This also satisfies the logical test, since the baby is equal parts father and mother. Does a mother possess parts of the father's DNA prior to or after impregnation? Also note the conspicuous use of the term *baby* as opposed to its secular equivalent, *fetus*. This is a striking word choice from such an esteemed institute of the medical community. (As an aside, and as a testament to the magnificence of our Creator, just one unraveled strand of DNA from one tiny cell of this new life contains over three billion bits of information, stretching as long as six-and-a-half feet!)[29]

This is merely one source of information supporting the argument that life begins at conception. It is far from isolated. In April of 1981, a group of internationally known geneticists and biologists shared their professional opinion before a Senate Judiciary Subcommittee tasked with understanding the question of when life technically begins. Excerpts from the testimony overwhelmingly affirm the biblical narrative. Interestingly enough, their judgments were made with a complete absence of opposing testimony. Take a moment to reflect upon the conclusion reached following the two-day address:

> "Physicians, biologists, and other scientists agree that conception marks the beginning of the life of a human being – a being that is alive and is a member of the human species. There is overwhelming agreement on this point in countless medical, biological, and scientific writings."[30]

Isn't it interesting that none of our cultural institutions have taken to mainstreaming this conclusion? With this information, how could a Supreme Court possibly uphold the legality of the *Roe v. Wade* decision that legalized abortion, otherwise known as the murder of the most innocent of life, in the United States over forty years ago? Although he was not directly presented with this question, these sentiments from Dr. Eugene Diamond, former Chairman of the Department of Pediatrics at Loyola University Stritch School of Medicine, seem to explain all we need to know about modern culture's commitment to death:

> ". . . either the justices were fed a backwoods biology or they were pretending ignorance about a scientific certainty."[31]

Lastly, Dr. Gordon Hymie, the late Chairman of Medical Genetics at the Mayo Clinic, offered the following perspective based on his years of research and expertise:

> "By all criteria of modern molecular biology, life is present from the moment of conception . . . . Science has a very simple conception of man; as soon as he has been conceived, a man is a man."[32]

Modern efforts to expand our understanding of biology and life continue to reinforce the biblical position that life begins at conception. In April of 2016, researchers from Northwestern University discovered that human life begins in a bright flash of light.[33] The video is incredible, showing an explosion of tiny sparks at the exact moment a sperm fertilizes an egg. Watching the video causes me to wonder if this explosion might resemble that which happened when God called the universe into being!

Even after digesting all of this information, the hard truth is that no degree of scientific evidence can sway the hardened heart of the abortion supporter. In an interview with Seattle radio station KIRO 97.3 FM, host Jason Rantz asked the National Organization for Women president Terry O'Neill if she would still support abortion rights if science determined that life begins at conception. Demonstrating her completely closed mind to the discoveries of science, Ms. O'Neill tactlessly responded by stating, "I don't care. Of course I would support abortion."[34] Isn't it curious that the same enlightened individuals championing the discovery of life in something as abstract as an amoeba ardently reject the evidence before them supporting an understanding of the beginning of human life?

This inconsistency is worthy of a deeper dive. As previously mentioned, science proves that a baby in process of development has its own unique DNA coding. Science confirms that the heart begins to beat within the first three weeks of pregnancy. Science even reveals a brilliant flash of light at the very moment that a sperm fertilizes an egg!

How can a community that esteems science with such a hyper-religious zeal have no qualms about turning a blind eye to these remarkable scientific discoveries? Why does this community continue to champion child sacrifice in America when the science disproves their supported position?

We cannot understand these questions without developing an appreciation for the duality of science as it is practiced in our culture. Put simply, science represents the existing state of knowledge and the subsequent pursuit of understanding of the material realm. Science represents our current understanding of humanity and the surrounding environment using an anthropocentric predisposition. Since the abstract and the spiritual fall outside of the material realm, these subjects are consequently ignored by the scientific community.

While science represents a state of human understanding, it also doubles as an object of worship in our culture. When campaigning for president, Hillary Clinton openly declared, "I believe in science!"[35] before the thunderous applause of thousands of likeminded supporters. This statement is a symbolic profession. Again, science is the pursuit of human understanding. If an individual believes in (worships) human understanding, then the categorical object of their affinity becomes the human mind. If someone worships their own understanding, then by definition, they worship themselves. In this capacity, the intellectual community is merely using science as a convenient label to conceal the object of their true devotion.

At this juncture, we are presented with the irreparable fissure foundational to a secular humanist worldview: if man is the center of the universe, how can something else be the author and creator of life?

Here is where proponents of this ideology are presented with a terribly difficult decision. On the one hand, they can select the painful option of rejecting the notion that man is the most significant entity in the universe by embracing the discoveries of their most cherished science. On the other, they can harden their view that man is indeed the author and creator of life, a decision that would openly reject the science that they claim to revere.

This is a character-revealing decision. Rejecting a worldview centered on the worship of self would display humility, while rejecting the proven science would duplicitously reveal a stubborn measure of arrogance. Faced with the inconvenient scientific data and a general unwillingness to release control to an authority that lies perpetually beyond their senses, the secular community ultimately chooses to sacrifice science upon the very altar of their own worldview.

This is how abortion becomes the highest sacrament of a secular humanist worldview despite revealing an irreparable fissure within its own methodology. Retaining the right to terminate life at any point, for any reason, bestows the characteristics of an infallible God upon the shoulders of tragically fallible man. To consummate the ideological transaction, the unbelieving community then rebrands the theological issue of life into a political issue, masterfully completing the heartbreakingly creative attempt to abort God from our culture.

People who support abortion reject biological science, the Bible, and the sixth commandment of the Law of Moses. In its place, they concoct surrogate arguments to support their position. Review the following list of arguments in favor of abortion and determine which of them are based on science and which of them excessively rely upon an appeal to human emotion:

- Life doesn't really start until birth. *There is no scientific support for this position. We have thoroughly debunked this myth by providing facts based on scientific studies, the testimony of well-educated medical professionals, and qualified academic sources.*

- Religious ideology is no foundation for any law. *Apparently not! Through your argument, you have overthrown the validity of the sixth commandment to justify the murder of the unborn! Note that this argument effectively achieves its true aim, which is to change the narrative by putting the Christian on the defensive.*

- The vast majority of women who have an abortion do so in their first trimester. *If the vast majority of thefts occur between midnight and 3:00 a.m., should we legalize robbery during these hours? If the vast majority of people speed on the freeway, should we simply increase the speed limit to accommodate those operating outside of the confines of the law? The true aim of this argument is to function as a false pretense, diverting attention away from the true issue at hand.*

- Laws against abortion do not stop abortion; they simply make it less safe. *The premise here is that we should legalize abortion to promote a safer procedure. Interestingly, this position is incompatible with another held in the secular community. Replace the word "abortion" with the term "gun violence." In the name of promoting the public welfare, how can a person support unfettered abortion access while concurrently supporting a legal prohibition against the possession of firearms? These are completely contradictory viewpoints.*

- Women who are raped or victims of incest should not be forced to carry out a pregnancy. *Sometimes the best means of validating a claim is to seek input from the individuals most closely related to the underlying circumstances. To validate this claim, we should ask the surviving children of a rape or incest related pregnancy if they believe they should have been aborted.*

- A young woman may be too poor to cope with a child, especially in the event the father no longer remains in the picture. *Behind this claim is a tacit admission that the impoverished should not be entitled to the same privileges as the wealthy. This is a dangerous premise, especially coming from the same group that may be sympathetic to the "rights of the 99 percent" against the "evil 1 percent." Secondly, if the woman of a two-year old son subsequently loses her job, should she be encouraged to murder her son since she no longer can provide for him?*

- In the case of underage pregnancy, the girl may not have really understood what she was doing, and should not lose her education and career opportunities over one mistake. *When a society begins referring to life as a mistake, could there be any limits to their potential depravity? Might this be the necessary foundation for establishing a market for the exchange of body parts of aborted children?*

None of these arguments are grounded with even a shred of scientific evidence. Each appeal attempts to sway the impulses of the heart as opposed to the reason of the mind. Can any person claim to be a man of science while rejecting the scientific method, the binary nature of gender, or the sanctity of human life, all of which are central tenets to the "settled science" of biology? Lending a compassionate ear to these emotional appeals causes Christians to be unplanned accomplices in the genocide of millions of children of unplanned pregnancies. Lest the heart of the believer remain sympathetic to them, I implore the reader to open the Bible to Proverbs 14:8 and 12:

> "The wisdom of the prudent is to give thought to their ways, but the folly of fools is deception . . . . There is a way that appears to be right, but in the end it leads to death."

It is as if this passage was tailor-made for our "enlightened" progressive, secular culture. I will return to my sentiments at the outset of this discussion: I, too, believe in a woman's civil right to control her own body. The problem is that both science and the Bible confirm that a fertilized egg, equipped with its own unique set of genetic coding, is not part of a woman's body. Just as she would have no legal right to assassinate any other living member of our society, she also has no right to murder the God-given life forming inside of her womb.

Dr. Ravi Zacharias is one of the leading apologists of Christianity today. During one of his recent lectures, he presented an observation that is piercing in its profundity:

> "We live in a culture today that listens with their eyes and thinks with their feelings."[36]

Perhaps no field makes a greater appeal to the new American mindset than the science of economics. The arguments of many economists are bathed in emotional appeals, preying upon the heart of a culture reluctant to subject comforting rhetoric to empirical testing. Take, for instance, the minimum wage. Despite initially being ruled unconstitutional by the US Supreme Court in the 1905 *Lochner v. New York* Supreme Court case and "a violation of the commerce clause" in the 1935 *Schechter v. U.S.* proceedings, the minimum wage has become a fixture at both the federal and state level.[37,38] What changed? Have we progressed as a society because of this change?

In our present day, activism surrounding the subject has become so strong that we have moved from debating the need for a minimum wage to the necessity of a "livable wage." The International Labor Rights Forum, a human rights organization advocating for workers globally, broadcasts the following statement in bold font on its website[39]:

A LIVING WAGE IS A HUMAN RIGHT.

Before we have the luxury of subjecting any arguments supporting a minimum wage to economic testing, we must prevent the material spiritual issue underlying this discussion from being pushed into the periphery. Does a man have a civil right to receive a minimum level of compensation as determined by government administrators, regardless of the industry to which he is exerting his labor? Must this wage be sufficient to cover all basic living expenses, including food, shelter, clothing, and other incidental expenses?

To promote simplicity in our argument, we will simply address the concept of the minimum wage (although for all intents and purposes the reader may substitute the words "minimum livable wage" in its place). If we accept the premise that the minimum wage is a civil right, then we have unwillingly woven flexibility into the very fabric of what we consider to be our basic human rights. The very definition of flexibility insinuates a susceptibility to influence or persuasion. This susceptibility was already exploited twenty-two times in the roughly seventy years following the initial adoption of a federal minimum wage under the Fair Labor Standards Act of 1938. As believers in Christ, does it stand to reason that the

God we revere as being the same yesterday, today, and forever would confer a series of rights to human beings that may vary from yesterday to today, with the expectation of change in the future? If so, one of the following two statements must be untrue:

God is absolute in nature. The minimum wage is a basic human right.

An absolute God would not bestow two separate human rights that directly violate each other. Forbidding two parties from reaching any labor agreement below an arbitrary floor of compensation violates the liberty of both parties. Such a law would infringe upon a worker's right to set the price of his own labor. Conversely, if the minimum wage is indeed a basic human right, God cannot be absolute in nature considering the prospect of adjusting the rate based on changing economic conditions.

As beautifully inviting as the ocean may appear, those ignorant of the undertow shall soon disappear. Experience has regrettably washed many lifeless bodies ashore during a rip tide, giving us a healthy respect for the power of the ostensibly calm waters. This danger pales in comparison to the frightening undercurrent lurking behind the minimum wage debate. Carelessly dabbling in these waters risks the drowning of something far more valuable than our physical life.

The undercurrent of which I speak is the gradual usurpation of divine privileges befitting the supplier of human rights. Do these rights originate from God or from the governments of men? When we succumb to any impulse to validate the minimum wage as a basic human right, we effectively supplant ownership of human rights from God in favor of centralized administrators. Not only does this help explain why the issue has become a mainstay in domestic political discourse, it also sets a frighteningly perilous precedent. A government powerful enough to grant basic human rights is also powerful enough to take these rights away. We are merely left with the hope that such a government possesses the virtue necessary to respect our other rights to life, liberty, and the pursuit of happiness. We are left with the hope such a government is comprised of morally upright citizens dedicated to rendering equal justice under the law and promoting the domestic tranquility. Is this what comes to mind when you think of Washington, DC? The believer would be wise to recall the teachings of Solomon in Proverbs 11:7:

"Hopes placed in mortals die with them; all the promise
of their power comes to nothing."

The spoken words and the true intentions of the politician are typically poles apart; however, the man presiding over the adoption of the federal minimum wage, President Franklin Roosevelt, demonstrated an eager willingness to embrace his new role as supplier of human rights while arguing in favor of the platform in 1933:

"No business which depends for existence on paying less
than living wages to its workers *has any right* to continue
in this country."[40] (emphasis mine)

Unlike the minimum wage, civil rights have not, are not, and never will be provisional in nature. We must reject any notion that our rights are provided by government administrators and recognize such attempts as reminders of why we must remain deeply skeptical of centralized power and its ability to restrict personal liberty to achieve its own despotic ends.

Having explored the spiritual aspect to the minimum wage argument, we can now return to the science behind the economics. Mark Wilson, a former deputy assistant secretary of the US Department of Labor with nearly thirty years of experience as an economist, examined the empirical evidence from the primary types of economic models used to analyze minimum wage policy. His conclusions provided a grave warning against pursuing the economic policy of raising the minimum wage:

> "Seventy years of empirical research generally finds that the higher the minimum wage increase is relative to the competitive wage level, the greater the loss in employment opportunities. A decision to increase the minimum wage is not cost-free; someone has to pay for it, and the research shows that low-skill youth pay for it by losing their jobs, while consumers may also pay for it with higher prices. Moreover, evidence from a large number of academic studies shows that, even if there were no negative employment or other affects, minimum wage increases don't reduce poverty levels."[41]

Fightfor$15 is an organization that has enticed thousands of low-wage workers to advance a mission of raising the minimum wage to $15 per hour. Its website proudly boasts that they are an international movement in over 300 cities on six continents of fast-food workers, home health aides, child care teachers, airport workers, adjunct professors, retail employees – and underpaid workers everywhere.[42] As of December 2016, their landing page contained one simple justification for raising the minimum wage:

Fast food workers deserve $15 an hour *and a union* so we can pay our rent and support our families. (emphasis mine)

This simple statement proves that the movement has no interest whatsoever in elevating the lifestyle of fast food workers. By including the phrase "and a union," the pressure group reveals its true aim of opportunistically siphoning monies away from an industry filled with millions of employees. While this is not the appropriate forum to delve into the destructive nature of unions, I encourage the reader to simply direct attention to the city of Detroit, Michigan. Once the wealthiest city in the world, the city boasted the highest crime and poverty rates in the United States in 2014.[43] The city achieved this disgrace on account of decades of experience with unions siphoning money and resources away from a productive industry, without any effective check or balance coming from city officials. In fact, these officials only emboldened the union, accelerating the city's demise!

Returning to the matter at hand, take a moment to evaluate all of the support for why the minimum wage should be raised to $15 per hour, according to *Fightfor$15's* website:

1. As low wage workers we know what it's like to struggle to get by.
2. Because our pay is too low, we struggle to pay our bills and put food on the table. McDonald's answer? Go on food stamps.
3. We're robbed on the job by our employers looking to cut corners. Employers that are multi-billion dollar corporations.
4. Even though we work hard, we're forced to live in poverty.

5. On top of it all, even McDonald's knows it takes $15 to get by.
6. It's not right. That's why we strike.[44]

Is there even a trace of qualified, tested, empirical economic analysis behind any of these supporting factors, or are they entirely substantiated by the feelings of those individuals they are looking to manipulate? This poorly fabricated list of reasons to increase the minimum wage confirms that, at best, we are dealing with an unproven hypothesis. I'll leave the reader to imagine what we might be dealing with if we took a more cynical approach to these factors. As for me, I find it curious that the text on their website is red, the same color of communism, socialism, and Marxism; however, I'm sure that is just coincidental.

Remember, scientifically proven arguments always trump emotional appeals. In the absence of any scientific data from their website, we have the responsibility to conduct our own research. Since the pressure group prominently identifies quick-service ("fast-food") restaurants as "multi-billion dollar corporations looking to cut corners," it only makes sense to begin by analyzing such a business.

Yum! Brands, the parent company of KFC, Pizza Hut, and Taco Bell, is the nation's largest employer of workers in the fast-food industry.[45] How would an increase in the minimum wage from $7.25 per hour to $15 per hour impact this company? *Fightfor$15* would suggest this multi-billion dollar company could easily absorb these costs since it would force them to stop "cutting corners." What does the economic data reveal?

Yum! employed 505,000 individuals as of year-end 2015.[46] After accounting for all expenses, including salary and benefits; general and administrative costs; legal expenditures; research and development costs; food and beverage outlays; transportation expenses; energy costs; property taxes; insurance; compliance costs; corporate income taxes; and other miscellaneous expenses, the "heartless corporation" reported net income of $1.293 billion. Contrary to popular belief, when Pizza Hut sells a medium pizza for $10.99, the company does not report a profit of $10.99. The actual number is closer to $1.09.

Calculating the ability of the entity's net profits to absorb any increase to the minimum wage is a relatively easy calculation. We simply need to divide the total net profit by the total number of hours per employee. Assuming that each employee works an average of 2,000 hours per calendar year, we are left with the following equation: net profit ($1,293,000,000) divided by employee hours (1,010,000,000) equals $1.28. In other words, net profits would be sufficient to absorb a $1.28 increase to wages across the organization. Let's make the exceptionally liberal assumption that the average hourly worker receives a wage of $10 per hour. Using this data, the company would only have the ability of raising its average hourly wage to $11.28 before being forced to devise a strategic plan to either drastically raise prices or reduce employees to remain compliant with federal law. Let's evaluate the extreme approach to both options, where management either decides not to raise its prices on any of its product offerings (recouping all of these costs through employee attrition) or the alternative option where management decides not to release any employees (recouping all of these costs through price increases).

If management determined that the market would likely be unwilling to purchase any of the Yum! product offerings if prices were to increase, the compassionate appeal to raise minimum wages in this industry would force the company to reduce its workforce. Carrying forward the $11.28 hourly rate as a starting figure, the company would have to absorb $3.72 per hour through reductions in staff to reach an ability to pay its employees $15 per hour. The only way management would be able to do this would be to lay off 125,233 employees. This action would reduce the overall work force by nearly 25 percent!

On the other hand, if management determined that the market has such a voracious appetite for chicken, pizza, and tacos that they would absorb any price increase, what would the price of a medium pizza have to be in order to remain profitable as an entity? Assuming the business' net profit margins remained unchanged from the 9.9 percent figure reported at year-end 2015, they would have to raise the price of a medium pizza from $10.99 to over $40. Do you believe it is likely that the market would willingly absorb this price increase? If your answer is that you would simply move to Taco Bell, you can kiss that dollar menu good-bye. The price of a taco would be nearly $5! Keep in mind if our assumption of a $10 per hour average employee wage was higher than the actual figure, these prices would only increase!

Also keep in mind that this is measuring the impact to only *one business*, and it does not even account for the franchise model of the enterprise. Reacting to this potential legislation leaves Yum! with the challenge of finding the right ingredients to stay in business on a scale ranging from reducing its workforce by 25 percent to raising prices as high as nearly 300 percent. Assessing the industry-wide impact would cause national unemployment figures to surge! And for what reason? To merely remain compliant with an empty, biblically antithetical, promise to fast-food workers that they will never again have to feel "what it's like to struggle to get by?"[47]

There is no compassion or benevolence in pursuing a course of economic destruction. Loathing prosperity with such fervor that one would suggest "pulling down" as opposed to "lifting up" a society is evidence of bad fruit. Remember, we are all an indiscriminately fertile field that cannot help but produce fruit in concert with our actions and ideas. Even if our intentions were pure, we must comprehend that intentions do not comprise the root structure of a tree. Once the actual root structure of a tree (it's faith, values, and principles) becomes compromised, it becomes venomous and cannot help itself from producing bad fruit.

For those fast-food workers fortunate enough to retain their positions following the achievement of a $15 minimum wage, how far could they stretch their dollar? Today, a Yum! employee making the $7.25 minimum wage could afford a medium pizza from Pizza Hut after working roughly an hour and a half on the job. Following the increase, the same worker would have to labor twice as long to make the same purchase. Whereas they can purchase roughly six tacos from Taco Bell for every hour worked today, that number would quickly deflate to three.

When we introduce scientific data into the argument, the $15 minimum wage becomes downright laughable in its folly. Yum! could not possibly absorb these costs without making substantial adjustments to their business model that would include some combination of reducing staff and increasing prices. In all likelihood, the wage hike would cause a number of stores to close their doors. Lest the reader think I have cherry-picked this business, the same numbers were run for McDonald's and Wendy's. These businesses would similarly be unable to absorb the minimum wage more than doubling with existing profits. Is it any wonder why there is no empirical data whatsoever on the *Fightfor$15* website?

This organization should be ashamed of itself for taking advantage of good, hard-working young Americans simply looking to develop entry-level experience and strengthen their core aptitudes. When Marxist front groups reveal their parasitic character and ogle profitable entities with the insatiable thirst of a vampire, the culture must comprehend the risks facing future employment. Profits drive business expansion, and business expansion produces employment opportunities for tomorrow's young worker. Not only will raising the minimum wage reduce jobs from the existing worker pool, it will significantly impair the creation of future jobs by cutting the primary source (profits) supporting business expansion!

On its second quarter 2015 earnings call, the Wendy's Company management revealed a series of initiatives in the wake of potential minimum wage hikes. The primary proposal centered on the technological development of self-order kiosks to facilitate a simpler, more accurate ordering process. When asked about his company's propensity to simply increase menu prices, Wendy's CEO Emil Brolick explained in a separate call:

> "[O]ur franchisees will likely look at the opportunity to reduce overall staff, look at the opportunity to certainly reduce hours and any other cost reduction opportunities, not just price. You know there are some people out there who naively say that these wages can simply be passed along in terms of price increases. I don't think that the average franchisee believes that."[48]

In May of 2016, the company confirmed that self-service ordering kiosks will be made available across its fleet of over

6,000 restaurants in the second half of the 2016.[49] When government meddles with the free market to determine an arbitrary floor for the cost of labor, companies are incentivized to substitute for labor with capital costs. *Fightfor$15* would have you believe this decision is reflective of their evil nature. Perhaps they would better appreciate the decision if we translated the action into their pseudo-scientific language by saying it is merely evidence supporting a Darwinian "survival of the fittest" element alive and well in the business world!

Contrary to the secular humanist, modern believers do not fear or loathe science. If I, as a believer in Christ, was hostile to science, would I really be elevating the psychoanalytic discoveries of Freud, one of the leading atheists of the twentieth century? Would I remain steadfast in my adherence to the scientific method or the rigid tenets of the science of biology? Would I prefer independently validated conclusions as opposed to empty petitions pleading for emotional support, discouraging me from looking beyond how I am encouraged to feel?

This brief examination reminds us that the deductive reasoning applied by the world produces the following conclusions:

1. The scientific method begins and ends with the formulation of a hypothesis.
2. Life cannot begin at conception for a woman who is either too poor or too young.
3. Biology falls outside of the core curriculum for undergraduates pursuing a bachelor of science degree in biology.
4. Men's restrooms should be fully equipped to accommodate men who are experiencing their monthly menstrual cycle.

5. The national health department compassionately orders doctors to violate the Hippocratic Oath.
6. Even though all men are created equal, basic human rights come from bureaucrats, implicitly suggesting that some individuals are more equal than others.
7. The most benevolent technique one can employ to deal with low wages is to eliminate employment altogether.

The church of scientific development is nothing but a modern-day temple to Baal. On account of its foundationally paradoxical structure, it permits countless deviations from its own doctrine to address the inevitable logical quandaries experienced by its adherents. Only an Olympian like Mary Lou Retton could genuinely appreciate its tolerance for logical and intellectual flexibility. As for me, I am left with only one conclusion, and it comes from the Apostle Paul in 1 Corinthians 3:

"For the wisdom of this world is foolishness in God's sight."

FOUR

An Abstract
Social Construction Project

"I am absolutely convinced that the gas chambers of Auschwitz, Treblinka, and Maidanek were ultimately prepared not in some Ministry or other in Berlin, but rather at the desks and in the lecture halls of nihilistic scientists and philosophers."[1]

~ Holocaust Survivor Viktor Frankl

If the wisdom of the world is so foolish in the eyes of the Lord, logic would suggest there is a structural weakness in the primary process used to promote and develop intelligence in our culture. Could this weakness be the conviction that over the course of time, man persuades himself that any reliance upon an unseen God is primitive and ignorant, ultimately concluding that he is better equipped to pursue knowledge outside of a greater spiritual framework? By failing to unite (or even develop) a platform to restore prayer in schools and instruction from the divinely inspired Word of God, we will be pronounced accountable for sanctioning the removal of this spiritual seed from the minds of our children. While we may offer defenses of financial hardship or demanding time commitments, how could we possibly refute the words of our Lord and Savior from Luke 6:49?

> "But the one who hears my words and does not put them into practice is like a man who built a house on the ground without a foundation. The moment the torrent struck that house, it collapsed and its destruction was complete."

When we migrate away from an absolute standard in education, we cannot help but replace a concrete foundation with mere timber pilings, laying the foundation for the eventual evisceration of wisdom from our culture. If we believe that the fear of the Lord is the beginning of wisdom, how can wisdom even be garnered if God is completely unwelcome in our public schools?

The new foundation of education features an appointed panel of academic officials tasked with creating and uniformly delivering a set of proficiency standards across a vast network of primary and secondary schools. Before discussing the conception of these standards and the values upon which they are based, it is important to understand the ideological culture to which these officials may ascribe. After all, how these officials perceive their role in the education of our children can reveal whether their motives are compatible with our greater desire to preserve and strengthen our society, passing along a better standard of living to future generations than that which we so providentially inherited.

Woodrow Wilson, the twenty-eighth President of the United States, was the first true academic to reach the nation's highest office. After graduating from Princeton University in 1879, he spent the next thirty years of his life in academia before entering the political arena. Prior to serving an eight-year term as president of Princeton, he was a professor for 17 years. By all modern accounts, Wilson was a highly educated intellectual. With all of these years of education in such a highly-regarded, Ivy League institution, what did he have to say about education during this period representing the forefront of the progressive movement? In a newspaper article published by the Philadelphia Public Ledger in 1909, this holder of two doctorate degrees wrote the following:

> "The purpose of a university should be to make a son as unlike his father as possible. . . Every man of established success is dangerous to society. His tendency is to keep society as it is. His success has been founded upon it. You will not find many reformers among the successful men . . . . Society cannot progress without change."[2]

A life spent in academia helped Wilson conclude that societal upheaval was the primary objective of higher education. A father dedicates his life to carefully instilling values and principles in his children for eighteen years. As a father, I consider this to be my true life's work, in accordance with the dedication at the front of this book! Wilson's stated ambition, however, was to nullify all of these efforts by revolutionizing the primary methods of instruction. Is this action more reflective of a desire to preserve the fabric of a society or to uproot it?

Surely these sentiments are no longer commonplace in our culture, and they simply represent an antiquated lapse in judgment from which we have recovered and improved. Unfortunately, the evidence would suggest otherwise. President Wilson's scattered seeds sprouted a striking declaration from the Associate Director of the Michigan Elementary and Middle School Principals Association over one century later in February of 2012. When providing testimony before the Michigan House Education Committee, Associate Director Debbie Squires seemed to double down on the thoughts shared by President Wilson. When asked to opine on the parent's role in school operations, Ms. Squires explained:

> "[Educators] are the people who know best about how to serve children; that's not necessarily true of an individual resident. I'm not saying they don't want the best for their children, but they may not know what actually is best from an education standpoint."[3]

These quotations suggest the academic community is skeptical of the ability of biological parents to fully grasp what is in the best interests of their children. Why else would we need to unravel years and years of dedicated nurturing from the minds of our progeny, other than to rectify the harmful effects of what is secularly branded as such a colossal miseducation? What kind of mindset actually concludes that the instruction provided to a child by his parents is likely detrimental to his development? Yet this is precisely the supposition taken by President Wilson and Ms. Squires, and it is a dangerous precedent.

You may say these are merely anecdotal illustrations unreflective of our wider scholastic outlook. However, the

Draft Policy Statement on Family Engagement from the Early Years to the Early Grades, jointly issued by the US Department of Education and the US Department of Health and Human Services, should erase any doubt that we are actively sowing destruction into the very fabric of our society. While the policy is spuriously filled with what appear to be homages to the family unit, the following excerpts fortuitously unveil the true objectives of our highest academic officials:

> "It is the position of the Departments that all early childhood programs and schools recognize families as equal partners in improving children's development, learning and wellness across all settings, and over the course of their children's developmental and educational experiences. (The term *family* is used to include all the people who play a role in a child's life and interact with a child's early childhood program or school. This may include fathers, mothers, grandparents, foster parents, formal and informal guardians, and siblings, among others). States play a critical role in promoting family engagement."[4]

Not only does the policy blithely redefine the most fundamental building block of society, it divulges the haughty posture of our central planners in Washington. They envision their role as being identical to the role of parents in a responsibility as broadly categorized as childhood development, far beyond the limited reach of simply educating children.

Why make so much out of a harmless draft policy? Surely it just represents a plan of action seeking to achieve what is in the best interests of our children! Be keenly aware that we are dealing with the infancy stage of the wisdom of man, a process that upon maturity derives some of the conclusions witnessed at the close of our previous chapter. For this reason, we must remain on high alert and vigilant when evaluating the merits of the policy. Part of this due diligence process entails looking beyond the stated benefits to our children to identify the specific benefits granted to the federal agencies and administrators involved in the process of childhood development. Regrettably, our study will conclude that this document could very well be the caption used to depict the phrase "wolf in sheep's clothing."

The *Draft Policy Statement on Family Engagement from the Early Years to the Early Grades,* as initially proposed, accomplishes two monumental legal victories for supporters of a centralized education platform. The most significant of these achievements features the assumption of a 50 percent interest in the lives of all American children. By diluting the interests of parents by placing them on par with "all the people who play a role in the child's life," the policy effectively creates a new seat at the dinner table of families everywhere, the central location from which all significant family decisions are discussed and applied. The problem is that this chair is not just filled with one person; rather, it is wide enough to seat a number of individuals, including bureaucrats, administrators, legislators, social workers, and "others" claiming to have an interest in your child's development.

Anybody with the most basic business acumen understands the value of a 51 percent controlling interest in the business world. The party exercising the majority of the company ownership ultimately steers the organization in a direction consistent with his vision, even if the remaining 49 percent of the company prefers to chart an alternative course. For nearly all of the recorded history of western civilization, societies have recognized and appreciated the role of parents to exclusively discharge their parental duties with relative autonomy. This policy effectively reduces the interest of parents in their child-rearing responsibilities from 100 percent to 50 percent. This equal partnership prevents either party from exercising authority in the decision-making process without the full consent of the other. As an aside, this is precisely why there is so much hostility to the concept of homeschooling. The Federal government recognizes the limitations homeschooling would place on its mission to fully centralize all education in this country. To covertly address these limitations, this policy gets the Department of Education one step closer to its long-term goal of abolishing homeschooling from sea to shining sea. Does destroying the liberty of parents to educate their children as they best see fit constitute a win for the follower of Christ, particularly after giving consideration to the conspicuous absence of any biblically-based instruction whatsoever from the preferred curriculum?

As a believer in Christ, should I be forced to grant parental privileges to an entity that ardently rejects the central tenets of my faith construct? While the policy arrogantly "recognize(s) families as equal partners in improving children's development," I have not observed any evidence worthy of conferring such an elevated privilege to this federal department in any fashion. I do not want them involved in raising my children, nor do I value their opinion on my nurturing obligations as a father. Yet my stated objections are irrelevant to this draft policy statement. Legally, I am now forced to place them on par with me as a parent.

What defense do I have against an agency insistent on crowbarring its way into my house, assuming an unwelcome seat at my dinner table, and rendering unsolicited opinions under the semblance of parental assistance? For assuming such an outwardly altruistic visage, the policy sure seems to aid and abet actions that are commonly associated with the crime of larceny. Not only are these individuals taking ownership of what does not belong to them (the blanket parental rights of the non-ruling class), but they are engaging in the more heinous act of supplanting the God-given rights of the individual. It is rather curious that this continues to be a theme when dealing with progressives in a position of power.

If you believe allegations of larceny are unsubstantiated, consider the following scenario: who would be the ultimate arbiter in a situation in which neither party could persuade the other to the merits of his viewpoint? Would it not be the American court system, an entity that has demonstrated an increasing propensity to stand opposite the side of Christianity, as we will further explore in chapter seven? In other words, while ostensibly exalting the "critical role" of parents, the draft policy categorically undermines their very sovereignty by providing the federal government with the ultimate say in the upbringing of a child. This is, without question, the hallmark achievement of the draft policy from the vantage point of the Department of Education.

Lamentably, these developments constitute cultural progressions to previously observed trends both in education and the court system. In 2001, the Palmdale School District in California opted to survey[5] its elementary students aged seven through ten for the purposes of psychologically testing children who were later referred to as "subjects" in court documents. Under the guise of evaluating childhood exposure to trauma and identifying behaviors such as anxiety and depression, the survey included highly-charged sexual inquiries that would otherwise generate charges of pedophilia were it not to transpire within the protected walls of a governmental education facility. Among the questions *posed to children as young as seven* were queries on how often they thought about sex, whether they were "touching . . . private parts too much," and whether they wanted to kill themselves. Although the school provided consent letters for parents to sign, these forms neglected to disclose the sexual nature of the survey.

Upon learning the truth of the experiment, a group of parents brought legal proceedings upon the district for violating their right to privacy and their right "to control the upbringing of their children by introducing them to matters of and relating to sex." After an initial dismissal of the case by a lower court, the parents appealed to the Ninth Circuit Court of Appeals. This higher court unanimously held that "the defendants' actions were rationally related to a legitimate state purpose" and included the following excerpts in its official legal opinion, issued in 2005:

- "There is no fundamental right of parents to be the exclusive provider of information regarding sexual matters to their children."

- "Parents have no due process or privacy right to override the determinations of public schools as to the information to which their children will be exposed."

- "[Parents] have no constitutional right . . . to prevent a public school from providing its students with *whatever information it wishes to provide*, sexual or otherwise, when and as the

school determines that it is appropriate to do so."
(emphasis mine)

- "[O]nce parents make the choice as to which school
their children will attend, their fundamental right
to control the education of their children is, at the
least, substantially diminished." [6]

Remarkably, the court held that the survey was an action
consistent with the state's broader mission of protecting
the mental health of the children. Apparently this mission
encompasses introducing seven-year-olds to the wholesome and
nourishing concepts of masturbation and suicide. Seemingly
without a trace of irony, the verdict later references that "the
rearing of children" is one of the higher social functions of
education, and "(public education) is a principal instrument in
awakening the child to cultural values." This is the same Ninth
Circuit that previously opined[7] that the phrase "under God"
was unconstitutional with respect to the Pledge of Allegiance.
At the conclusion of the opinion, they arrogantly state that
they reached these conclusions with "little difficulty." It would
be difficult to find a better example to uphold the prophetic
truth of the words of the Apostle Paul in the first chapter of the
book of Romans[8] when he wrote that although they claimed to
be wise, they became fools.

Returning to our discussion of the draft policy, the paramount
achievement of usurping consecrated parental privileges does
not represent the sole victory for central administrators. The
document accomplishes the secondary goal of incorporating
vague language into the definition of family. The term used to
narrow the criteria for eligibility as a family member is "all the
people who play a role in a child's life." Apparently "all of the

people who have an actively beating heart" would have been too much of a dead giveaway. As if to add insult to injury, the definition also includes the ambiguous "among others" as a catch all. Taken together, these two clarifications introduce a new interpretation of family. This interpretation features the undesirable attribute of infinite elasticity, a trait not generally associated with the concept of private assembly.

What is noticeably absent from the policy statement is definition of the term "playing a role." For example, if I were to pick up your son on the way to taking my son to soccer practice, would this constitute playing a role in his life? The absence of a legal definition restricts us to the literal meaning of the word "role," which would simply mean a function performed in a particular operation. With the assistance of a savvy lawyer, this would not be a difficult position to sustain, particularly in the event these court proceedings began on account of your demonstration of a lapse in judgment of some sort.

This trivial illustration highlights the complications that legal flexibility can introduce into a culture. Blurring the lines of family, a term that featured broad consensus for virtually all of human history until the advent of communism, is one of the preliminary structures that must be cemented to facilitate acceptance of the idea that children belong to the community at large. Unfortunately, this idea is now widely accepted in American culture. Former Tulane professor and MSNBC television host Melissa Harris-Perry explained with pitiful eloquence that, "[W]e have to break through our kind of private idea that kids belong to their parents or kids belong to their families and recognize that kids *belong to whole communities*"[9] (emphasis mine). Hillary Clinton famously wrote a book entitled *It Takes a Village* to accentuate and embellish the impact individuals outside the family have on a child's well being.

Do these sentiments have any commonalities with earlier episodes in world history? As a matter of fact, they do. They are, in fact, quite similar to the views expressed by a certain world leader in 1937:

> "When an opponent declares, 'I will not come over to your side,' I calmly say, 'Your child belongs to us already. . . What are you? You will pass on. Your descendants, however, now stand in the new camp. In a short time they will know nothing else but this new community. This new (government) will give its youth to no one, but will itself take youth and give to youth its own education and its own upbringing.'"[10]

The leader is none other than Adolf Hitler, a man widely regarded as one of the most evil characters in human history. In fact, in an earlier speech from 1933, Hitler said, "Your child *belongs to us* already"[11] (emphasis mine). Here we have historical and contemporary examples suggesting that embracing a collective approach to raising children is a demonstration of our cultural progress. In reality, it represents the height of cultural regression, since these quotes all suggest that human beings belong to other human beings. That is the very definition of slavery.

The family is the most basic, fundamental, and foundational unit of society. Although the institution represents the earliest form of human social relationship and has existed since the beginning of time, the leaders of the Department of Education are unequivocally incapable of finding direct value in this private social group. Rather than assess the agency by its meaningless and empty rhetoric, judge them by their actions. Why else would they impose foreign interests that are diametrically opposed to the concerns of a child's mother or father, but not to fundamentally change the structure of society? Would a general contractor purposely build cracks into the foundation of his own home? The desire to fundamentally change something does not overflow from feelings of love and appreciation; it stems from a heart filled with disdain for the culture in which it finds itself.

As we now appreciate from our first chapter, these feelings of scorn did not originate overnight. The policy represents the ripened fruit resulting from the scatter of a range of intellectual seed. Clearly the seed is not grounded in biblical truths, since those would overwhelmingly reinforce the virtue of an intact nuclear family unit. What is the underlying belief structure supporting the ideas that children belong to the state and that civil servants are an integral component of the family?

While these philosophies have existed for centuries, they were first mainstreamed into western civilization upon the publication of the most significant text of the nineteenth century, *The Communist Manifesto*. In this work, Marx and co-author Friedrich Engels jubilantly pen the most significant, albeit underappreciated, tenet of communism with these words:

> "Abolition of the family! On what foundation is the present family . . . based? On capital, on private gain. Do you charge us with wanting to stop the exploitation of children by their parents? To this crime we plead guilty."

As members of society, our duty is to support and implement an education policy that will enhance our general welfare. Wisdom would never dictate prudence lay in blind obedience to an official suggesting "educators are the people who know best." We must perform independent due diligence to follow the evidence to its logical conclusion, impartial of our preliminary hypothetical speculations.

It is only after exercising this due diligence that we find irreconcilable differences between the policy statement and the core values and principles of Christianity. First and foremost, the proposed policy has more in common with *The Communist Manifesto* than it has with the Bible. By publicly proposing this policy, those tasked with framing education strategy have formally acknowledged they believe society benefits from a gradual erosion of the nuclear family. Launching attacks against the family is directly in line with Marx's ultimate goal of complete abolition. As Marx himself wrote, "[B]lessed is he who has no family."[12] Second, there are inconvenient similarities between the policy and the failed totalitarian regimes of Nazi Germany and fascist Italy. Benito Mussolini said "[I]t is the State which educates its citizens in civic virtue, gives them a consciousness of their mission and welds them into unity."[13] Here is yet another example of an authoritarian assuming ownership of the citizenry to provide them with a greater sense of purpose. Sound familiar?

Is it really reasonable to overlook these similarities or discard them as anecdotal, considering we are dealing with the literal framework of our national education program? These are *systemic structural deficiencies* that compromise the very integrity of our academic foundation. It is awfully difficult to "progress" or "move forward" as a culture when the primary methodology employed to improve the plight of our youth involves the willful suspension of reason.

Not content to simply scatter the seeds of communism throughout our public school system, bureaucrats are now deploying a seemingly limitless funding source to provide an infinite supply of sunlight and water in order to reap a bumper crop of socialist fruit. The Organization for Economic Cooperation and Development produced an annual report in 2013 which found that the United States spends over $15,000 per student on education, highest among the 34 industrialized countries comprising the group.[14] In addition, first-year high school teachers received an average salary approximately 22 percent higher than their peers from other countries.[15] Despite ample funding, students continue to lag their international counterparts in terms of scholastic aptitude.

How have we elected to remedy the problem of deteriorating academic performance? By and large, we offer seemingly limitless support to supplemental education spending bills, "budget override" legislation, and county bond issuances designed to invest the proceeds into local schools. This is illogical. If public schools' demonstrate a general hostility to Scripture, communist underpinnings, and a disdain for parental rights, does it really make sense to equip them with more and more of our hard-earned resources?

The fact of the matter is that we remain powerless when faced with the typical argument that *it's for the kids*. This is an argument that appeals most heavily to the emotions and feelings of an individual, and it contains no independently tested or validated scientific conclusions whatsoever. By falling prey to the empty emotional arguments of secular humanists, we are simply ignoring the science of economics. Such actions demonstrate that we largely assess our parental approach to educating our children by using a measuring stick of financial investment. Does a man measure distance with a thermometer or time using a tire pressure gauge?

The academic crisis has nothing to do with finances; it has everything to do with an absence of values. The most significant issue facing our public school system in 2016, according to the Obama administration, had nothing to do with activities transpiring in the classroom, despite a shocking report confirming that the average college freshman reads at a seventh-grade level.[16] Instead, they chose to spotlight the bathroom by fabricating perhaps the most preposterous issue ever mainstreamed into American culture. In May of 2016, the Obama administration issued guidance directing public schools to allow transgender students to use bathrooms matching their "gender identity," ensuring that "transgender students enjoy a supportive and nondiscriminatory school environment."[17] In fact, six months earlier, the Obama administration sued a high school in Illinois for refusing to allow a teenage male to use the girls' locker room, restroom, and shower facilities.[18] Do these concerns have anything to do with instruction, intellectual empowerment, spiritual development, character growth, or the pursuit of wisdom?

Obviously not. However, does this directive align to the *Draft Policy Statement on Family Engagement from the Early Years to the Early Grades*? Absolutely! Similar to the evolved definition of family, transgenderism is a term clouded in legal haze. It is visually impossible to determine the truthfulness of an adolescent claiming to identify as a member of the opposite sex. In the spirit of inclusion, this directive provides license to any student to use any bathroom without restriction. The move also represents a surprising divergence for President Obama; in fact, it might constitute the first time in his political career in which he has concluded that the absence of regulation is a prudent course of action!

Enabling limitless access to high school bathrooms endangers the safety of our daughters. Might a group of teenagers pressure a boy into using the girls' locker room before gym class as a form of social hazing? Is it feasible that a teenage boy would feel compelled to "transgender" after witnessing an attractive girl walk into the ladies' room alone? Is it really pragmatic to facilitate an environment removing the barriers to sexual harassment or even rape? Let's make the unreasonably unrealistic assumption that this edict will have no impact on the number of rape crimes. What about the fact that universal bathroom access now provides a means for adolescents to discreetly engage in all forms of sexual behavior, including intercourse? For being so vocal about a "war on women," it sure is surprising that legislators are so eager to jeopardize the safety of our underage daughters!

Sadly, we do not have to theorize these potential outcomes. In the rural town of Virginia, Minnesota, in September of 2016, a biological male high school student self-identifying as "transgendered" allegedly engaged in highly charged, sexual behavior in the girls' locker room. Rather than simply use the locker room to change clothes, the student elected to use this time to dance in a sexually explicit manner (twerk), lift his skirt to reveal his underwear, and comment on the girls' bodies and bra sizes. The behavior left female students in tears, most likely out of the threats of vulnerability, insecurity, horror, and the thievery of their innocence. In a lawsuit that was subsequently filed by at least eleven families, the representing attorney alleged that the school district turned a blind eye to previous complaints raised by the girls and their parents.[19]

While the directive is completely asinine if assessed on its ability to improve test scores or overall college readiness, it makes complete sense when viewed through the communist prism of weakening or damaging the family. Universal bathroom policies will directly lead to an increase in teenage pregnancy. Administrators, bureaucrats, and those in a position of power win regardless of how these pregnancies progress. If they end in the birth of a child, there is an overwhelming likelihood the baby will have been conceived outside of wedlock. If the girl elects to terminate the pregnancy, it represents a business opportunity for Planned Parenthood. If the girl visits a Planned Parenthood facility, she likely does so without discussing the situation with her parents. No matter the scenario, the true victim of this "inclusive" policy is the family, and there is nothing a true proponent of a communist ideology would prefer more than fostering conditions that would place the family under assault.

To further understand the true values behind our current education platform, we need only review the words of Michelle Obama as she was campaigning for her husband in May of 2008:

> "Barack knows that we are going to have to make sacrifices; we are going to have to change our conversation; we're going to have to change our traditions, our history; we're going to have to move into a different place as a nation."[20]

When we fail to embrace the progressive side of zealous cultural objectives such as the public bathroom emancipation project, we are warned that we are "standing on the wrong side of history." As opposed to prostrating ourselves before our leaders in hapless submission, perhaps we should discern what the Scriptures dictate when framing an education curriculum. The eighth chapter of the book of Job provides us with the following insight:

> "Ask the former generation and find out what their ancestors learned, for we were born only yesterday and know nothing, and our days on earth are nothing but a shadow. Will they not instruct you and tell you? Will they not bring forth words from their understanding? Can papyrus grow tall where there is no marsh? Can reeds thrive without water? While still growing and uncut, they wither more quickly than grass. Such is the destiny of all who forget God; so perishes the hope of the godless" (Job 8:8–13).

It is impossible to "ask the former generation and find out what their ancestors learned" when our national objective is to change our traditions and history.

In an effort to conform to these new standards of education, California Governor Jerry Brown signed a bill in July of 2011 requiring public schools in the state to teach students about the contributions of lesbian, gay, bisexual, and transgender Americans.[21] One year later, Broward County School Board members in Fort Lauderdale, Florida, unanimously passed a formal resolution recognizing October as LGBT History Month.[22] The resolution empowered educators to develop lesson plans completely grounded in the sexual proclivities of certain cultural figures.

Following a lengthy cultural growing period spanning from the sexual revolution of the late 1960s, the LGBT movement has finally reached the time for national harvest. In

June of 2016, Washington state public schools announced that "gender expression" will begin to be taught to *kindergartners* in the 2017–18 academic school year.[23] Under newly approved state standards designating sexual health as a "core idea" of public education, Washington schools will incorporate "self-identity" education to children as young as five years old with the expectation that students will understand there are many ways to express gender.

The above examples represent just the first fruits of this new national harvest. Although these advances are widely perceived as victories for tolerance and inclusion by the secular community, they are nothing of the sort. Sadly, leaders in the Obama administration are merely using current LGBT activists and sympathizers as a means to their ultimate end of "changing our history."

The central purpose of studying history is appreciating that certain inescapable human tendencies lead to total devastation if left uncontrolled. History shares countless lessons warning us against the impulsive pursuit of such destructive behavior. On an individual level, history can teach a man that the pursuit of an extramarital affair will threaten his marriage simply by observing the divorce proceedings of his adulterous neighbor. As a society, history can warn a nation that the mixture of eroding traditional values with central government corruption is the very recipe that led to the fall of the Roman Empire, the greatest civilization in the history of man at its time.

Sexual preference falls completely outside of the framework of studying history, and exaggerating the importance of these inclinations is not doing any service to our children. Actually, it diverts their attention away from the hard lessons learned by prior generations, and it also obscures the central theme of the subject matter. As a student, is it more important to remember a historical figure for his role in history, or simply because he was gay? Most importantly, any such instruction repurposes how children perceive their role as citizens. History can be hard to appreciate because so few of us believe we will ever be placed in a situation of historical significance; however, we all can immediately grasp the temptation to "make a cultural statement" in hopes of attaining fame and recognition. This directive incentivizes students to be pioneers of depravity by stretching the boundaries of established norms by engaging in increasingly boorish behavior.

Nevertheless, with the assistance of our idleness, the scope of history has indeed expanded. Just seven years after Ms. Obama shared her heartbreaking contempt for America's traditions and heritage, educators in Atlanta, Georgia, began the process of founding a national prototype institution catering exclusively to the education of students identifying as lesbian, gay, bisexual, transgender, queer, questioning, intersex, asexual, or otherwise allied with these groupings. On its website, The Pride School promises students, families, and educators a safe, fun, and rigorous learning environment free of homophobia and transphobia. The leading founder of the school self-describes on the school's website as "a formerly heterosexual cisgender woman who is now a queer-identified transman (male pronouns, FTM) with a wife and 2 wee ones, one of whom is gender fluid."[24]

The school formally opened its doors in August of 2016, with parents of full-time students coughing up a tuition of $13,500 per year. Pride's website indicates that applications for the 2016–17 school year continue to be accepted on a rolling basis for approximately fifteen full- and part-time students.

Curiously, the school operates out of the Unitarian Universalist Congregation of Atlanta, a church whose mission statement is "to foster a community of faith that encourages and supports our individual spiritual quests out of which we act together for social justice."[25] The setting houses the perfect matrimony between church and state, two entities committed to pursuing a faith that acts harmoniously in their pursuit of social justice. Whereas the Christian church is the bride of Christ, this secular house of worship functions as the bride of the State, receiving its seed to cultivate a new American family. Irrespective of each entity's comprehension, when this new bride and groom became equally yoked in August of 2016, they actually united using the traditional husband-and-wife marriage format!

Man cannot cast a pebble into a lake that does not cause the water to ripple. Similarly, administrators cannot overhaul the purpose of history without impacting the greater standards of academic proficiency. Consider that the school's Twitter feed proudly boasted as of May 24, 2016, that the President of the United States formally invited two Pride School scholars to an upcoming White House Summit.[26] This was quite an honor, especially after giving consideration to the fact that the school had yet to formally open its doors to the general public. (In fact, there are probably thousands of schools that have been open for centuries that have never sent a scholar to the White House). This invitation suggested that modern academic proficiency had nothing to do with reading comprehension, the satisfaction of examinations, or written essays on subject matter. Apparently, one day in the classroom was not even necessary to achieve the esteemed honor of "scholar." Scholarship was solely determined by a student's ability to make social progress toward advancing an agenda. Misleading a child into believing he has achieved scholarship in this fashion is a form of criminal academic abuse to both the child and society at large.

Redefining the family, providing unrestricted bathroom access, limiting the influence of Christianity in schools, and changing our approach to history are all strategies that would align with former President Wilson's goal of greater social upheaval. They are also each aligned to the goals of communism. It is evident by now that this continues to be a recurring, cautionary, theme, but what makes these matters such a serious concern? For this, an actual lesson in history is required.

Leonid Sabsovich was a high-ranking urban planner and economist working for the State Planning Committee (Gosplan) during the infancy of the Soviet Union. He worked under the Lenin and Stalin regimes. This was a man actively developing the framework of a communist society in the middle of the 1920s, the first decade following the Russian Revolution of 1917. If our ultimate aim is to discover the true intent of a disciple of Marxist communism, we would be hard-pressed to find a better case study due to his position of influence. What seeds was he attempting to scatter over society? Here are a few excerpts from his writings in the 1930 publication, *The Socialist Cities*:

Everything that currently creates the need for an individual household and binds a man to a woman should be completely eliminated in the Socialist way of life . . .

In the socialist city, houses should be constructed in such a way that they provide the greatest convenience for the worker's collective life, collective work, and collective recreation. They should also provide the most comfortable possible conditions for individual work and individual leisure. These houses should not have separate apartments with kitchens, pantries, and so forth, for individual domestic use, since all of the worker's everyday needs will be completely socialized. In addition, they should not include space for private family life, because the idea of family, as we now know it, will no longer exist. In place of the closed, isolated family unit we will have the "collective family" of workers, in which isolation will have no place . . . .

The question of joint dwelling for children and their parents can only be answered in the negative. Infants are best located in special buildings where the mothers can visit for feeding. . . . Pre-school and school-age children should spend most of their time in spaces designed for their learning, productive work, and leisure. It is clearly pointless to provide space for them in the same dwelling as their parents, where they would return at night. Therefore, house-communes should only be built for adults.[27]

These writings suggest a philosophical desire in the communist ideology to completely separate children from their parents as early as possible (infancy). If we weren't so busy as a society repurposing history, this would be the information our children would otherwise be learning! When we integrate behavioral sexual psychology into the curriculum of studying history, we sever the opportunity of our children to learn the perilous lessons of the past. The hundreds of millions of deaths attributable to communism, in less than one century of recorded human history, prove the ideology to be the most venomously cancerous disease ever mainstreamed throughout society. Developing a school system hostile to truth and history literally prevents this disease from being diagnosed, treated, prevented, and ultimately eradicated from the lives of our posterity. Regardless of how we *feel* about our efforts to educate our children, these *actions* constitute a treasonous indifference toward their future prosperity. While this would be bad enough, a true survey of modern academic policy actually detects a national sympathy to the communist philosophy. Again, this is nothing short of willfully criminal, academic child abuse.

Dyed-in-the-wool communists salivate at the opportunity to gain access to children at an increasingly earlier age, for reasons which by now should be obvious. Earlier education not only limits the instructional influence of parents, it also provides an avenue to alleviate any financial hardship resulting from considerable childcare expenses. Starting children earlier in the academic process promises to provide preschoolers with a head-start in their learning careers, and who could possibly object to that?

Our inquiry began on the premise that we are failing our children by suppressing the ultimate source of wisdom from their primary curriculum of academic instruction, and we have since confirmed our initial fears by identifying structural weaknesses in the tools used to depose our once time-tested wellspring of instruction. Having observed the breakdown of this relapsed academic approach, does it really stand to reason that the solution to improving education for our children involves starting the process earlier? Wouldn't this be akin to suggesting that a restaurant offering low quality food could solve its problem by simply increasing its portion sizes?

According to New York City Mayor Bill de Blasio, developing a program to universalize pre-kindergarten instruction in his city was "literally mission critical for the good of our schools" in a move that would "fundamentally change the nature of the school system."[28] A careful listener can easily identify two red flags from these excerpts. De Blasio's intended beneficiaries of these program proposals are not the children; they are the schools. This is of paramount importance, since progressives always value the art of their abstract social construction projects with far greater zeal than the precious children they claim to benefit. Secondly, his desire for fundamental change reveals the more malicious emotions on his heart. And where did these emotions originate? Mr. de Blasio is a man who honeymooned in the communist country of Cuba, toured parts of the Soviet Union during the height of the Cold War, and physically supported the ruling socialist government in Nicaragua in the late 1980s. Upon his inauguration as mayor, People's World, a website associated with the Communist Party USA, reported that "the air was filled with the joy of a new day for New York."[29] As you watch the roots and influence of communism expand throughout our country, do you feel a similar joy in the air for the Kingdom of God?

Just as a house featuring a compromised foundation lacks the structural ability to prevent penetration from unwelcome visitors, our refurbished education model features an environment wholly conducive to all forms of infiltration. A prudently constructed framework would feature natural defenses to repel foreign exploitation from agents attempting to introduce antithetical values. Not only does our poorly assembled replica lack any security software, it practically features Las Vegas style billboards inviting malware on account of its endless supply of federal, state, and local funding sources.

Enter the Common Core State Standards Initiative, a curriculum designed to fundamentally transform education in our country. According to the official Common Core website, the standards are designed to "ensure that all students graduate from high school with the skills and knowledge necessary to succeed in college, career, and life."[30] The mission statement intimates academic fulfillment can only flourish through the pursuit of college and career. Can this statement be relevant to the student pursuing enrichment from a career in the trades, professions which do not require a college education? How about women embracing the traditional role of stay-at-home mother? Additionally, while the statement appears admirable, the key to truly analyzing its merits lie in the definition of the word "succeed." Although no definition is provided on its page, even unbelievers would acknowledge the wide range of technical differences between worldly and spiritual success. How could God's definition of success possibly be synonymous with the world's definition of success if the Bible notes that the wisdom of the world is foolishness in God's sight?[31]

To help determine the motivating drive behind these standards, we must understand why they were developed. To address this question, the website is quite helpful, since the developers prominently disclose their formal diagnosis as the decentralized nature of the American school system. Although the group suggests this is merely one reason for the strategic change, it is the only reason stated. In other words, the entire reason we are overhauling our academic approach is to eliminate the problem of intellectual diversity.

This diagnosis only leaves us with a plethora of questions. As it is a broad, sweeping generalization lacking any criticisms to the existing standards in place, what are these specific deficiencies? What were the research parameters applied in the comprehensive study concluding the only way to improve the process was through a complete overhaul? Since the general public funds these school systems out of their hard-earned tax dollars, why was this report not made available to assist them in determining the need for these standards? Is the report being shielded from taxpayers because their input is not valued, because the report does not exist, or both? Is this merely another progressive social science experiment beginning and concluding with the formulation of a hypothesis?

Why would a group of people vocally praising the values of diversity, tolerance, and inclusion frame educational standards that promote conformity? This course of action is completely incoherent from the vantage point of their stated value system. What is clear from the approach, however, is that we are dealing with at least some degree of dishonesty with the proposal of these new standards. This is why character is so important. Knowing that the transgender movement used duplicitous means to achieve their more foreboding ends, it is well within the realm of possibility that these new academic standards could also be little more than a means to an end. If that were indeed true, it would confirm the strategy has no concern whatsoever about the improvement of our children.

Common Core represents a first-of-its-kind attempt to nationalize education in the United States of America. Again, this lofty aspiration places the curriculum in the not-so-elite company of China under Chairman Mao, Nazi Germany under Hitler, and the Soviet Union under Lenin and Stalin. All of these regimes actively sought to control education nationally. These centralized ambitions are agonizingly ignorant of yet another lesson in history, this time from the pen of nineteenth century British philosopher John Stuart Mill, a man who lived through the onset of the communist ideology:

"A general State education is a mere contrivance for moulding people to be exactly like one another; and as the mould in which it casts them is that which pleases the predominant power in the government . . . it establishes a despotism over the mind, leading by natural tendency to one over the body."[32]

Loosely translated, centralized education is the most efficient means of transforming schools into assembly lines capable of mass producing ideological slaves to the state authority. And while I am doing everything possible to ring the warning bell with my pen, I cannot possibly match up to the testimony of someone who actually lived through the horrors of national education. Lily Tang Williams was born in the Sichuan province of China and lived under Chairman Mao for the first 23 years of her life before immigrating to the United States in 1988. Listen to the words from her heart after living through the type of education toward which our country is progressing:

"I am strongly opposed to Common Core. I cannot sugar coat it. In my eyes, Common Core reminds me of the Communist Core I went through in China. When I was growing up under Mao's regime during the Cultural Revolution, starting with first grade, we were told to chant every day in the government run public schools; "Long Live Chairman Mao, Long Live the Communist Party." We were required to write in our diaries every day and turn them in for our teachers to review. In the diaries we were supposed to confess our incorrect thoughts to Mao or do self-criticism, or report anything bad we heard or saw about other students, family, and friends. We would memorize Mao's Quotations and recite them aloud during class. For school fun activities, we would dress up as Chinese minority people in their costumes to sing and dance, thanking Mao and the Communist Party for saving them from poverty, or we dressed up like soldiers to fight for the new China. Mao was like a god to me. I would see him rising from the stove fire or talking to me from the clouds. We all truly believed in Mao and Communism because we were completely indoctrinated and did not have any other information. We had nationalized curricula, one of the subjects we were required to study was Politics (Communist Party history, Karl Marxism, Mao Zedong Thought, etc.). Our teachers had to comply with all the curriculum and testing requirements, or lose their jobs forever. Parents had no choice at all when it came to what we learned in school. The government used the Household Registration and Personnel File system to keep track of its citizens from birth to death."

She went on to issue a dire warning to her new countrymen:

"If you forget the past, you will repeat its mistakes and you won't know who you are. The first step of Communism was to take away your parental control of your children and indoctrinate them."[33]

Can nobody hear the desperate outcry of history? Most Americans have been chillingly unable to connect these parallels simply because we have been ignoring the importance of history now for decades. To immigrants, however, the resemblances are impossible to overlook since they have lived through the misery from which we have thus far been spared. Should we willingly insist on remaining ignorant, it will not be our leaders who shackle the chains on our wrists. The bondage will be of our own volition!

With the publication of the Common Core *Next Generation Science Standards* we finally have conclusive evidence of a double standard that we know has been in effect for years. Progressives live in constant fear of an educational environment in which the central tenets of the Christian faith are integrated into scientific lesson plans; however, they have no concerns with promoting an agenda that demands uniform allegiance to their own secular doctrines. The new "science" standards require that children be instructed that biological evolution is supported by multiple lines of empirical evidence, despite the complete absence of any fossilized evidence confirming the capacity of one species to adapt into another. This is a direct violation of Genesis 1:24–26, which maintains that God made all of the animals each according to their own kind.[34]

Additionally, children will be instructed that human activities are "major factors" in global warming. Beginning in the sixth grade, classes will begin to emphasize that only a true understanding of climate science can result in the ability to reduce the impact of climate change.[35] This is a direct violation of Genesis 8:8, which maintains that day and night shall never cease as long as the Earth endures. The Bible is filled with references to the second coming of Christ. Would not the Earth have to remain intact in order to facilitate his impending return? Lastly, does it leave you with a sense of comfort knowing that students should be able to use proper names for body parts, including male and female anatomy, by the end of the second grade?[36]

The looming education reforms in this country are hostile to children, families, and Christianity. Does any Christian believe that the problem with education in this country is due to an uneven patchwork of academic standards? The removal of the Bible and prayer have *nothing* to do with a greater erosion of values? We have taken to an education system that instructs our children that their lives have no more meaning, worth, or purpose than that of any of the animals commonly found at the local zoo. We have taken to an education system that requires fourth graders to perform 108 steps to solve the problem of 90 divided by 18.[37] We have taken to an education system that has replaced Mark Twain's *Huckleberry Finn* with a bureaucratic policy statement entitled "Executive Order 13423: Strengthening Federal Environmental, Energy, and Transportation Management."[38] I am not making this up.

Academic performance has plummeted since we have thrown God out of the classroom in the early 1960s. *A Nation at Risk: The Imperative for Educational Reform* represented one of the first national undertakings to examine the state of public schooling in America. The report was issued by the National Commission on Excellence in Education in April of 1983, a group consisting of 18 members representing the federal government, private sector, and field of education. Consider two of the reports qualitative findings:

- The College Board's Scholastic Aptitude Tests (SAT) demonstrate a virtually unbroken decline from 1963 to 1980. Average verbal scores fell over 50 points and average mathematics scores dropped nearly 40 points.

- Between 1975 and 1980, remedial mathematics courses in public 4-year colleges increased by 72 percent and now (1983) constitute one-quarter of all mathematics courses taught in those institutions.[39]

The report concluded that our nation was at risk in the mid-1980s because "our society and its educational institutions seem to have lost sight of the basic purposes of schooling, and of the high expectations and disciplined effort needed to attain them." While the study was indeed insightful, the discoveries are actually superfluous to both the believer and the student of history. When God is displaced in a culture, academic performance suffers because of the natural erosion of values and discipline that are necessary to sustain long-term, inter-generational scholastic improvement. The SAT findings in this report are so relevant because the starting period of the measurement directly ties to the official eviction of God from the classroom (1963). Whether we like it or not, spiritual faith and academic performance are positively correlated variables. This is why we should now come to expect more frequent accounts like the March of 2016 *New York Post* report informing us of a town whose Planning Board voted down the Pledge of Allegiance in a 4-3 vote, with its vice chairman referring to the oath as a "total waste of time."[40] This action represents a logical progression that an elementary student likely could have anticipated from his lessons on cause-and-effect. Removing reverence removes values!

Since the founding of the Department of Education in 1979, academic performance has only continued to sour. The United States continues to lag its international competitors on the OECD Programme for International Student Assessment (PISA) survey, a triennial assessment given to 15-year-olds across 34 industrialized nations. The most recent data published in 2013 reveals United States students place twenty-sixth and twenty-first in mathematics and science, respectively.[41] Independent domestic appraisals also uncover ominous deficiencies. The ACT college readiness assessment was taken by over 1.9 million graduating seniors in 2015. After aggregating the results of these exams, the non-profit agency's annual report demonstrates a full 31 percent of test takers were unable to demonstrate aptitude for college coursework requiring English, reading, math, or science skills.[42] These results parallel a 2011 joint study by the Johns Hopkins University and the University of Arizona concluding that two-fifths of high school graduates are unprepared for college or the workforce.[43]

Although humility is unpleasant and difficult in our "advanced" society, at what point do we suspend our pride for the benefit of our children? In Psalm 10, David uses the term *wicked* to describe a man whose pride-filled heart has no room for God; however, James prominently notes that God opposes the proud but shows favor to the humble in the New Testament. Does the idea of prayer and biblical instruction in schools cause such discomfort that it would be preferable to witness steadily declining skills in our children as opposed to ingesting a mild degree of spiritual teaching? Did the removal of these two elements of faith really constitute a victory for our civilization after giving consideration to how critically unprepared many of our children now are for life beyond high school?

Due to the seeds they scatter, ideas and philosophies are never without consequence. The German people did nothing to halt the rise of the Third Reich, and their neglect led to this horrific quote from Holocaust survivor Viktor Frankl:

> "I am absolutely convinced that the gas chambers of Auschwitz, Treblinka, and Maidanek were ultimately prepared not in some Ministry or other in Berlin, but rather at the desks and in the lecture halls of nihilistic scientists and philosophers."[44]

We currently have the fingerprints of nihilistic scientists and philosophers all over our national curriculum, suggesting that we are pursuing modern enlightenment using the very blueprint of the apathetic German. Developing an educational platform that employs a complete disregard of a horrific episode as recent as the Jewish Holocaust is yet another example of the brutal ignorance that is the wisdom of the world. Should we continue in this pursuit, there could be no better demonstration of our hatred for our children.

To truly appreciate the strength and sophistication of this ignorance, however, we must turn to the state-of-the-art technologies helping to shape a world that continues to drift beyond the confines of reality.

FIVE

Reconstructing Reality

"I need to watch things die from a good safe distance
Vicariously, I live while the whole world dies
You all feel the same so why can't we just admit it?"
— *Tool*, song lyrics from *Vicarious* (2006)

By their very nature, abstract solutions are limited in their capacity to service the practical needs of the real world. Real-world problems require pragmatic remedies that do not ignore the distinguishing characteristics that shape human nature or the rigid attributes unique to our surrounding environment. Whereas a real-world solution proposes to address the unchanging weaknesses woven into man or the greater needs of the community at large, an abstract solution can only become practical by first attempting to alter natural law or human nature.

Today, we live under a system of governance whose stockpiles overflow with abstract solutions to meet the challenges of the real world. Some of these abstractions include the idea that we can prevent obesity by capping the size of fountain beverages, the thought that we can halt casualties related to firearms by prohibiting law-abiding citizens from practicing self-defense, and the previously discussed belief that we can improve education by separating children from their biological parents. These proposals are a mere sampling from volumes and volumes of regulations and policy directives that violate natural law and completely ignore human nature.

When a culture reaches the point where policy-related deficiencies are so well-defined as to be commonly observable by the general populace, an opportunity arises to evaluate the backbone of a nation by observing which of the three strategies it pursues to address its present circumstances. The first and preferred option would feature a change in the general direction of government on account of its development and promotion of policies that are utterly incompatible with human nature. Prudent men would then return to the third step of the scientific method to determine a new hypothesis for addressing the greater needs of their community. If we were indeed a nation comprised primarily of prudent men, for example, we would have long since exercised this option.

Lamentably, prudent men now meet the technical definition of an endangered species in twenty-first-century America. While many would likely chide me for displaying the deplorably judgmental temperament so typically attributed to Christians, is this not the logical conclusion to draw from the July 2016 Rasmussen poll showing that only 21 percent of Americans believe our country is headed in the right direction?[1]

When nearly four in five of us believe we are bequeathing a decaying republic upon our children, yet by and large we refuse to be inconvenienced by the hard work necessary to reverse the trend, can there be any other deduction? (We will take a deeper dive into parenting in our next chapter). The science of economics is a study of supply and demand, surpluses and shortages. It's simply a statement of fact to acknowledge that we have a shortage of individuals willing to suspend their own comfort and exhaustively toil for the benefit of their posterity.

The second potential course of action would be to maintain the status quo, an option that is almost never recognized as being viable. While the general public and administrative officials may disagree with which direction to shift government, both parties identify adverse societal conditions warranting some degree of action. The reason that there will never be a season in which the field of government lays fallow is because bureaucrats simply do not believe they are adequately doing their job unless they are proposing solutions to advance society.

Since the general shortage of virtuous men prevents our ability to pursue the strategy of correcting government and the pervasiveness of problems forbids continuation of the status quo, we are largely powerless to prevent our fruitless pursuit of the last remaining option. This terminal strategy features the willfully ignorant belief that previously identified weaknesses persist due to an insufficient dosage of governmental interference. This flawed logic recommends doubling down on the volume of abstract solutions imposed upon the people. Making this strategy feasible requires the multi-faceted approach of making an all-encompassing appeal to hope (demanding faith), developing a compelling marketing strategy (propaganda), excessively relying upon platitudes and rhetoric (shifting the lens from results to intentions), and punishing dissenters for their opposition (ridicule). Whereas the prudent man would change any policy pursuits that are incompatible with human nature, this lethal option attempts to change human nature to remain compatible with currently broken policies. Since the distinguishing characteristics of men can never be changed, the only means of accomplishing the desired end of power and control is to pursue the three-pronged strategy of reconstructing reality, redirecting worship away from their traditional outlets, and redefining the very purpose of life.

It is impossible to change reality, plain and simple. For example, there is nothing we can do to suspend the laws of gravity or eliminate natural disasters. Similarly, the persuasive power of the various vices of man can never be legislated out of a culture due to man's inherent predisposition to sinful behavior. This was one of the painful lessons learned during the prohibition experiment of the 1920s.

Since altering reality for nearly 325 million Americans is an impossible undertaking, central planners and their supporters must pursue an alternative route in their quest to change human nature. While reality may be frustratingly absolute, the relativity of perception provides an inviting gateway through which the opinions and values of men can be attuned. If likeminded humanists could infiltrate the medium of television to portray the conditions most favorable to their ideology, changing the perception of reality would become possible. If they could simultaneously penetrate those stations branding their image as credible news sources, the process of reconstructing perception would be complete, save for one critical assumption: the majority of the citizenry must demonstrate a steadfast commitment to consuming the wide array of programming made available by the television. Fundamentally transformative cultural efforts, whether they be through government, education, or social issues, are not possible in a nation of this size without first having an unwavering loyalty to the inanimate object that is the television.

As a people, we have an insatiable appetite for entertainment, and the majority of what we find entertaining flows through a television set. According to Nielsen ratings, the average American watched more than five hours of broadcast television every day in 2014, with that figure increasing to over seven hours for those who have reached the age of 65.[2] Regardless of intent, this statistic shows that Americans have ideologically committed to the philosophy that obtaining information through a television is preferable to conversing with their fellow men. For this reason, television now wholly controls the flow of public discourse in America.

Lessons in finance explain that all investments produce a return. Wise investments can yield portfolio appreciation, while poor investments can place the entire amount of funds at risk of complete loss. When a culture invests over 20 percent of its time complacently seated in front of a television, what type of return is reasonable to expect? This first ratio does not account for the time required to work or sleep. Assuming an eight-hour workday and six hours of sleep per evening, we are actually investing half (*half!*) of our discretionary time into the "entertainment" provided by a television!

What if the television actually amounted to a poor investment? What if the device was the human equivalent of an electrical discharge insect control system, more commonly referred to as a bug-zapper? Both devices feature a glow captivating to their target audience. Both devices serve as a surrogate source of light absent the presence of the sun. Each device has the ability to distract its onlookers for extended periods of time, reducing their dedication to the pursuit of more productive, life-sustaining activities. The purpose of one of these items is to fully expunge life. *At a minimum*, the other possesses the ability to fully expunge critical thought.

Even though the television was created long after the completion of the Bible, the Scriptures provide a constant reminder for believers to remain vigilant in their mission to seek purity and discipline through their everyday affairs. Consider the following excerpts:

> "Do not conform to the pattern of this world, but be transformed by the renewing of your mind. Then you will be able to test and approve what God's will is—his good, pleasing and perfect will" (Romans 12:2).

> "Do not be misled: 'Bad company corrupts good character'" (1 Cor. 15:33).

> "I will not look with approval on anything that is vile" (Psalm 101:3).

> "The eye is the lamp of the body. If your eyes are healthy, your whole body will be full of light. But if your eyes are unhealthy, your whole body will be full of darkness. If then the light within you is darkness, how great is that darkness" (Matt. 6:22–23)!

Can we sustain and preserve the overall health of our eyes while allocating a 50 percent discretionary time investment into a television set? Considering the quality of available programming, we are currently in the process of fervently dimming our inner lamp. Television is a highly competitive industry, and many television executives have become smitten with the idea that stretching the boundaries of socially acceptable behavior is the most effective method to remain "cutting edge" in their quest to continually hypnotize the American public.

Our viewing behavior should give pause for reflection, as the programs we most highly cherish tend to feature values completely antithetical to those we claim to profess. In 2013, the Guinness World Records required revision for the category of "most critically acclaimed show of all time."[3] The new award recipient featured a series in which a terminally ill high school teacher develops a lab with a former student to sell crystallized methamphetamines in order to secure his family's financial future. The entire plot is grounded in the philosophy that the most important thing you can do in life is attain financial security at any cost, even if that security destroys the lives of others living within your community. Should we choose to ignore the symbolism of this new distinction, it will be at our own peril.

The Parents Television Council (PTC) is a non-partisan education organization of over 1.3 million citizens advocating responsible entertainment. The PTC most recently examined the fall 2013 season of every major broadcast network and every primetime show featuring a family unit central to its storyline. The major findings of the study revealed that 99 percent of the shows contained some form of adult content, 94 percent contained profanity, 81 percent contained sexual content, and 33 percent contained violence.[4] The study describes an example of an NBC comedy show airing on a Thursday night in which an 8-year-old walks into the main hallway completely naked with his private parts pixelated for the viewing audience. The youngster explains to his father that this behavior is acceptable because he observed his aunt walking around the house naked earlier in the day, a mouthy retort likely written to elicit laughter from the audience.

These findings hardly suggest that viewers are engaging in a process of renewing their mind by flipping on the television. As a matter of fact, they strongly suggest a conformity with the world that would threaten any ability to discern God's true will. The PTC report concludes by listing seven "helpful tips" to ensure television viewing remains consistent with the values parents attempt to establish in the home. The guidance includes such tips as encouraging parents to promote critical thinking skills in their children, reminding their kids that these shows do not represent reality, and teaching them to appreciate that media messages contain values and ideologies that produce social and political consequences. Isn't it curious that these findings and recommendations never reached the airwaves of a national nightly news program?

Network television has become little more than a vehicle that secular humanists use to advance their worldview under the illusory façade of entertainment. Network titan FOX kicked off the 2017 calendar year by promoting a nihilistic family sitcom dubbed *The Mick*, in which a responsibility-phobic woman assumes the parental responsibilities for three spoiled children growing up in suburban Connecticut.

Within its first several episodes we are given the following exchange between Aunt Mickey and Sabrina, the eldest teenage daughter:

Sabrina: "I'm going to go to a fundraiser for Planned Parenthood . . . . Maybe you don't know this, but Planned

Parenthood provides healthcare to over 3 million women in this country."

Aunt Mickey: "Oh, sweetie, I know all about Planned Parenthood. I should have one of those punch cards that gets you a free sub every 10 visits!"

Sabrina: "Gross."

Aunt Mickey: "No, I just meant . . . I-I never got, like . . . uh . . . I just had a bunch of bacterial infect- you know what?"

Sabrina: "Ew."

The show then features a separate exchange between Aunt Mickey and a 7-year-old boy who is outfitted in a dress as he is headed off to school. Aunt Mickey compliments the little boy by saying, "You look really good in that dress!" The boy responds with the zinger: "Thanks. It kind of breezes on my vagina."

The show is graphical proof of the indiscriminately fertile field of network television executives. As they continue to spiral down the rabbit hole of total depravity, their fruit only becomes more and more poisonous, toxic, divisive, and harmful to society. Sadly, the remarks of at least two of the show's critics indicate that the show falls short of gratifying what appears to be an insatiable appetite for totally depraved content. When providing their respective reviews of *The Mick*, these two reporters lament the restrictions that the prime-time network structure will likely place upon the show. One critic notes that the show is "too soft and squishy," while the other explains that "this wannabe-badass sitcom could really earn its stripes by shedding its leash."[5,6] These comments prove that future content will only become more debauched and depraved with the passage of time.

The internet non-profit LifeSiteNews described *The Mick* as "a smorgasbord of the crude one-liners, immature sexual humor, vulgarity, promiscuity, binge drinking, perversion, and left-wing social activism—much of it involving children."[7] As a culture, why do we exempt television networks and their executives from child abuse when it is presented within the confines of a 23-minute weekly sitcom?

Television also has an uncanny ability to change the perception of a nation. In 2013, the Centers for Disease Control and Prevention produced the first comprehensive study measuring the sexual orientation of Americans. The study revealed that 2.3 percent of Americans self-categorize as gay, lesbian, or bisexual.[8] If network executives had any interest of accurately reflecting reality, this statistic would result in LGBT themes surfacing on roughly 1 of every 50 shows. GLAAD, an organization choosing to identify by the acronym as opposed to its former Gay & Lesbian Alliance Against Defamation, comprises an annual report entitled *Where We Are on TV.* GLAAD's 2013 report noted that FOX led all network programmers by including LGBT-themed content on an astounding 42 percent of its primetime shows, a figure that exaggerates reality by more than 1,700 percent.[9] The ABC Family network led all networks with a remarkable 50 percent ratio. When pressed on his company's content evolution at the time, former ABC Entertainment Group President Paul Lee explained:

> "We set out to make the modern family in all its passion and dysfunction, and reclaim that word for what it really is for our audience."[10]

Is it purely coincidental that this network's desire to redefine the family is in complete harmony with the educational policy objectives addressed in our previous chapter? Or could this perfectly reflect the causality between the perception of television and the reality of national policy? Either way, the initiatives have achieved their desired results. In May of 2015, Gallup reported that Americans estimate 23 percent of adults are either gay or lesbian.[11] The same survey reported that the percentage of Americans who deemed gay and lesbian relations to be "morally acceptable" increased from 38 percent in 2002 to 63 percent just thirteen years later. None of the national discourse emphasizing LGBT "civil rights" or "inclusive" bathroom policies could have been possible without the misleading influence of television.

While the gender narrative is one example of how perception can become reality, television makes a heavier contribution to society through its chronic over-representation of criminal activity. According to the Senate Committee on the Judiciary report issued in September of 1999, an American child will have seen an average of 16,000 simulated murders and 200,000 acts of violence by the time he reaches the age of 18.[12] This immersion directly causes our children to be less trusting of their fellow man by the time they reach adulthood. Even worse, this is precisely the prescription necessary to desensitize a nation to the point of nurturing bystander apathy, a psychological term used to describe situations in which individuals do not offer any means of help to a victim when other people are present. Neither of these outcomes are in the long-term interests of a healthy culture.

With homicide-themed shows airing on television now for nearly twenty-five years, we no longer look upon the outside world with a healthy degree of joyful optimism. Instead, we now live with a greater suspicion towards our fellow man and cynicism toward the world at large. Due to this distorted perception, a whopping 68 percent of Americans now believe it should be illegal for children aged 9 and under to play in a park unsupervised.[13] This jaded distortion helps explain how "justice" was recently applied to a South Carolina mother after allowing her 9-year-old daughter to play unsupervised at a public park. For this heinous crime, she spent seventeen days in jail, temporarily lost custody of the girl, nearly lost her job, and initially faced up to ten years in prison for potential felony child neglect.[14] Who could possibly believe we are progressing as a culture amidst such a pervasive fear and distrust of our fellow man? These are the ripened fruits of our insatiable appetite for depravity and destruction.

Perception and experience are the two primary factors that shape public opinion. When we elect to substitute our actual experiences with senseless fabrications, it is only natural that we would begin to perceive men as being largely unworthy of trust or respect. Television largely represents men as either bumbling idiots or sex-crazed animals. If an increasing number of women were to ascribe to these depictions, what would be the point of marriage? If a woman wanted to experience motherhood, would it not be preferable to simply use a man to fall pregnant as opposed to having to manage both the child and the imbecile that is his father?

Could this perception potentially be the reason why men have no rights whatsoever when it comes to restricting the abortion of their children, or why men lose full custody of their children 91 percent of the time, even though women originate 80 percent of divorce proceedings? [15,16] While perception suggests that men are worthless, scientific data confirms that children living in fatherless homes commit 72 percent of adolescent murders and are almost four times more likely to be poor.[17,18] A Princeton study concluded that boys raised apart from their fathers were up to three times more likely to wind up in jail before they tuned 30.[19]

Is a father insignificant to the welfare of his family? If so, why are girls whose fathers have left the picture by the time they enter first grade five times more likely to wind up pregnant as teenagers?[20] Why are 85 percent of all children exhibiting behavioral disorders produced from homes lacking a father?[21] The empirical data simply rejects any conclusion that men are superfluous entities in the family unit. Why do we cast men in such an unfavorable light?

Embracing perception at the expense of reality produces the environment necessary to stifle basic human interaction through constant legislation, since crime *must necessarily increase* with a concomitant devaluation of adult men. Is this the type of behavior we should really be looking to harvest?

Despite the overwhelmingly negative contributions television bestows upon our culture, we refuse to even consider the prospect of turning it off. A Nielsen survey identified that 98.9 percent of American households owned a television set in 2010.[22] The television has become our primary means of emotional expression, as it is where we go for entertainment, information, comfort, laughter, relaxation, and even wisdom. Most importantly, however, it is where we go to escape reality. Contrast this level of consumption with a recent Barna survey revealing that although 80 percent of people believe the Bible to be "sacred literature," only 13 percent of Americans read it daily, and 40 percent of participants responded that they "never have enough time to read it."[23] Just as there is no room for God in the core curriculum of our schools, our private actions demonstrate a similar apprehension from even welcoming Him into our living rooms. This mindless response affirms a complete conformity with the world, as well as the immeasurable value that our culture places on television. Do we really lack the flexibility to trim even a portion of the five hours of daily average television consumption to accommodate the reading of Scripture? If not for the sake of the Kingdom, how about for the sake of our culture and our children's future?

Television possesses the immense power to change reality because of the vast strength of its root structure. We have spent the last sixty years recklessly and diligently scattering seed into this medium, and now the weed has fully matured into a behemoth capable of fully suffocating our culture and shielding our eyes from the true sunlight we so desperately need. Despite its principal contribution of accelerating our depravity, television remains the most vibrant feature of American culture. Our passion for television was best captured in the 2006 song *Vicarious* by the American rock band Tool, and its lyrics retain a striking clairvoyance more than a decade after first hitting the airwaves. Copyright restrictions prevent me from quoting more than one line of this song, which I have already done at the beginning of this chapter. I strongly encourage the reader to pause at this point to read the entire words of the song, as it could no more effectively encapsulate man's infatuation with his television.

The first step in the addiction recovery process requires the admission that we are currently powerless over the influence of television on our culture. Just as alcohol consumes the thoughts and desires of an alcoholic, television drowns any hopes for cultural sobriety in the midst of tumultuous domestic and world affairs. Until we take the courageous first step of admitting the problem, we have no choice but to remain in this national state of impairment as we watch the greatest civilization in the history of humanity carelessly slip from the grasp of our fingertips.

Thus far, our survey into the power of the television has consisted entirely of outside observations without regard to those taking ownership of content creation. Prudence would advise the thinker to consider the perspective of those living inside the bubble to confirm or refute our ultimate suspicions. Might one of the purposes of television in fact be the distortion of reality?

Vanity Fair caught up with Bill Pruitt, one of the producers for the first two seasons of *The Apprentice*, a reality television show in which contestants competed for an apprenticeship to New York billionaire Donald Trump. The magazine's correspondents were curious to solicit the perspective of Mr. Pruitt regarding the election of Mr. Trump to the highest office in the world. On December 21, 2016, *Vanity Fair* released the following email from Mr. Pruitt, and his remarks reveal the grotesque underbelly of the foremost agent of distortion in American culture:

> "The Apprentice *was a scam put forth to the public in exchange for ratings. We were "entertaining," and the story about Donald Trump and his stature fell into some bizarre public record as "truth." This is nothing new . . . We are masterful storytellers and we did our job well. What's shocking to me is how quickly and decisively the world bought it. Did we think this clown, this buffoon with the funny hair, would ever become a world leader? Not once. Ever. Would he and his bombastic nature dominate in prime-time TV? We hoped so. Now that the lines of fiction*

*and reality have blurred to the horrifying extent that they
have, those involved in the media must have their day of
reckoning. People are buying our crap.* "[24]

As an executive producer for some of the nation's most
popular television shows, Mr. Pruitt has made a living out of
blurring reality for the last fifteen years. Having witnessed the
full maturation of the reality television concept, he confesses
that, at least in this instance, his "masterful" efforts were nothing
but a "scam" to produce "crap" that resulted in "horrifying"
consequences.

Shortly after the election of Donald Trump, MSNBC
correspondent Mika Brzezinski all but tipped the hand of the
news media. During a *Morning Joe* segment in which the network
unsurprisingly advocated the sudden need for compromise
in Washington, Brzezinski brazenly suggested that it was the
media's "job" to "control exactly what people think."[25] Perhaps
even more stunning than the arrogance of her confession was
the complete absence of any dissenting viewpoint from the four
other panelists on the program. Not only did they not walk her
statement back, but host Joe Scarborough went on to compare
President Trump to Benito Mussolini and Vladimir Lenin
simply for mistrusting the news media. Pruitt's comments
show how a Donald Trump presidency could not have been
possible without the powerful influence of the television, while
Brzezinski's comments reveal a media agenda that stretches far
beyond the mere reporting of news. We would be wise to learn
from their respective confessions.

With the reconstruction of reality achieving completion
through the power of television to alter perception, progressives
have now accomplished Phase I of the three-pronged strategy

to create the abstract world necessary to absorb their broken policy pursuits. Phase II features the equally challenging task of redirecting worship away from their traditional outlets, a feat seemingly impossible to any community embracing the first two commandments engraved on stone tablets on top of Mount Sinai:

> "You shall have no other gods before me. You shall not make for yourself an image in the form of anything in heaven above or on the earth beneath or in the waters below. You shall not bow down to them or worship them; for I, the Lord your God, am a jealous God, punishing the children for the sin of the parents to the third and fourth generation of those who hate me, but showing love to a thousand generations of those who love me and keep my commandments" (Exod. 20:3–6).

Honoring the first two commandments has caused an increasing degree of discomfort for many Christians because of the impact that our spiritual wandering has had on our overall human composition. As human beings, when God breathed into us the very breath of life, we were born with both an instinctive tendency for worship as well as a deep need for community and social engagement. When our society featured a healthy Christian influence, the church and our various cultural institutions displayed a complementary relationship. Neither would actively seek to suppress the influence of the other, leading to the harmonious promotion of values and purpose to all members of the community. As we have drifted away from God, these two previously symmetrical human attributes have naturally come into conflict. To briefly digress, this is precisely the reason godless societies are so prone to death and destruction. They first create these types of irreconcilable fissures within the human spirit that later mature into an uncontrollable element of civil unrest if left uncorrected.

Since we lack the capability of suppressing our personal need to worship, and we similarly cannot disregard our need for social acceptance, we are now faced with the choice of which element to prioritize. Shall we remain firm in our adulation for our Creator and suffer the rejection of an increasing amount of our peers, or should we make compulsory alterations to our worship practices in a greater search of worldly appeasement? This is precisely the type of faith test alluded to in the first chapter of the book of James:

> "Consider it pure joy, my brothers and sisters, whenever you face trials of many kinds, because you know that the testing of your faith produces perseverance. Let perseverance finish its work so that you may be mature and complete, not lacking anything. If any of you lacks wisdom, you should ask God, who gives generously to all without finding fault, and it will be given to you" (James 1:2–5).

By tolerating the expulsion of God from nearly all of our cultural institutions, we have elected to pursue a policy of cultural appeasement to address this modern day trial. To preserve the acceptance of our fellow men, we have willingly withdrawn the great majority of our outward demonstrations of traditional faith from the public square. Rather than engage in the Great Commission on account of our faith in Christ, we have practiced this Great Omission to remain in the good graces of man.

The impact of this "evolution" in our worship practices has only served to cement a new perception of secularism in our culture. Whereas the television *overstates* what it would have us believe by exaggerating the value of sin and depraved entertainment, the distinct retreat of Christian believers to the safe walls of their respective churches *understates* the life-changing power of the Gospel of Jesus Christ. How powerful could the message really be if Christians are so willing to sacrifice their faith at the feet of an earthly throne?

Our propensity to worship cannot change, so when we elect to moderate our reverence for our Creator, we walk through the enticing corridors of idolatry in search of a suitable replacement. History and experience suggest that the door most commonly chosen in this tragedy conceals a small room featuring the presence of an unaccompanied mirror. Our culture has replaced this outer door with a turnstile, and the endless toil of millions has now refined and modernized this object using the wonders of technology. This new mirror is simply breathtaking in size and scope, capable of reflecting a vanity never before seen within a culture.

Our new cultural looking glass is the platform of social networking. Although we largely use this new medium to remain close with friends and family, we never paused to initially consider if there might be any long-term risks to this new means of communication. Our current behavioral patterns show a scattering of virtually limitless seed into Facebook, Instagram, Twitter, Snapchat, Flickr, Vine, Reddit, and countless other social media websites. While we are exuberantly fertilizing these channels with robust investments of time, we are overwhelmingly avoiding eye contact with strangers, withholding greeting gestures from shoppers at the grocery store, screening our doorbell through the peephole on the door, demonstrating road rage in the car, and even holding back a friendly wave from our neighbors. Though few would admit to it, our behaviors affirm a general comfort supplanting traditional interpersonal exchange in favor of refining these trendy, new outlets. Before we cement our embrace and cast aside the merits of face-to-face contact, we should at least develop a basic understanding of the structural differences between these two methods with which we pursue dialogue.

The paramount difference between the various forms of web-based communication and traditional face-to-face contact is that the former creates an intermediary to facilitate basic human contact, resulting in a greater decay of emotional fulfillment as these platforms gain in strength. This "cyber-middleman" now provides people with an ability to spend hours engaging in virtual communication from a crouched position of physical isolation. Herein lies the principal risk of migrating towards social networking. Rather than engaging directly with our family, friends, or acquaintances, we are channeling our innermost feelings into a handheld device or computer screen that has no capacity of returning these emotions.

Is it reasonable to expect that we can continue to experience love with such boundless authenticity, friendship of staunch loyalty, or even laughter filled with the power of spiritual rejuvenation after we downgrade the conduit of human interaction from its current high-speed, two-way arrangement to a deeply delayed system characterized by isolation and proxy? Can the advent of video chatting or instant messaging offset the tenderness of a touch or the warmth of an embrace?

Quite frankly, whether or not we have ever paused to consider these questions is highly debatable. Nevertheless, our actions demonstrate a voracious appetite for electronic expression. Consider the growth of Facebook since its initial launch in February of 2004. At that time, the site reported one million monthly active users. On its 2016 first-quarter earnings call, founder and CEO Mark Zuckerberg remarked that total users have now swelled to 1.65 billion worldwide and the average user spends an average of 50 minutes per day on the social media site.[26] Nearly five out of every seven online American adults use Facebook, and at least one independent source reports that the site is now responsible for roughly 20 percent of total internet page views in the United States.[27,28] This is merely one form of social networking!

There is little evidence to suggest that we have approached Facebook or any of the other social media platforms with any degree of moderation or restraint. As we have investigated throughout this chapter, television now controls our national discourse, while handheld devices will soon dominate interpersonal relationships, if they do not already. To best appreciate the social impact and consequences of these changes, we need to evaluate the perspectives of college students and young professionals. These are the very people who have fully adapted to the social media, and they will soon be raising the next generation of Americans in accordance with their customs, values, and experiences.

To understand how this group of people views the technological advancements to how we communicate, the *Cisco Connected World Technology Report* is quite useful. This study is conducted periodically and highlights the mindset of this very group of people. The 2011 report surveyed over 2,800 participants between 18 and 29 years of age, in part to determine the value they place on social media and the internet.

This report revealed that nearly one-third of those surveyed consider the internet to be "as important" to their life as water, food, air, and shelter, while another 48 percent responded that it is not as important, but it is "pretty close" in importance. In other words, four-in-five respondents believe that the internet has ascended to the status of fulfilling a basic human need. Even more alarming, only 7 percent of these young adults declare that they could live without the internet absent an accompanying degree of anxiety. A full 65 percent responded, "I could not live without the internet, it is an integral part of my daily life," and 28 percent responded, "I could live without the internet but it would be a struggle based on my lifestyle." When given the choice between the internet, social activities, romance, and music, college students indicated that the internet was most important in their daily life.[29]

To understand how the internet could possibly be this important, we just need to understand its role as the middleman in facilitating basic human contact. The Cisco survey shows that approximately 77 percent of college students and young professionals access their Facebook page on a daily basis.[30] Millennials do not crave connectivity because they prefer to be anti-social or simply do not like public engagement. *They crave connectivity because social media is their primary method of public engagement.* When they are responding that they cannot live without internet, they are really professing that they, like the rest of humanity, cannot live in a world without social interaction. Do their responses really merit criticism when properly viewed through this prism?

As we learned from chapter one, ripened fruit will sprout from our diligent scatter of seed, and heavier planting will only bring about a more vigorous harvest. Whether or not social media has already become our primary means of communication is a moot point; considering the fervency of our planting over the last ten years and the absence of any noticeable headwinds, it is inevitable that it will. As we have increased the frequency of our electronic correspondence, we have begun to develop a slight discomfort with the idea of openly conversing without our newfound intermediary. What is most concerning is that this development does not discriminate based on the seasoning of a relationship. As we have substituted conversation for connectivity, spontaneous dialogue with a stranger is substantially more difficult considering the increased likelihood at least one of the parties is actively engaging with their handheld device. A metro ride during rush hour that once sparked chemistry between two young professionals exchanging playful glances is now much less likely since that commute provides a more compelling opportunity to "catch up" with their social media accounts.

In the increasingly difficult event that we do land a date with a member of the opposite sex, these challenges do not subside. The info graphic on the front page of the *USA Today* from February 8, 2017 presented the following statistic: 33 percent of people on a first date say they had to compete with an electronic device for attention.[31]

At the other end of the spectrum, it is now common to observe married couples sharing dinner at a public restaurant with their eyes transfixed by the glare of their cell phones. Lastly, simply attempting to capture the attention of somebody interacting with the cyber-middleman produces that same look our mother used to give us when we were five years old, asking for her attention: *Can't you see that I'm talking to somebody? Let me finish my conversation and then you can ask me your question!*

Do you have any idea how rude you are being right now? If these early manifestations are already observable today, how will our culture look in five or ten years? At our current pace, I fear we may be looking back to the current day with a sense of nostalgia!

Our evolving communication practices leave many of us with falsely negative impressions of people who are not already members of our inner circle. By observing the high degree of engagement between man and machine, we assume these strangers are likely unapproachable and would only be irritated by interruptions on our account. This is an unhealthy and divisive cultural progression, the exact opposite of the desirable environment in which public discourse would help unite the community. While the framework of discourse is rapidly changing, our innate human needs have and will always remain constant. We continue to possess a desperate need for the emotional intimacy that only comes from genuine reciprocal dialogue with another human being. Virtual surrogates will never be able to primarily meet these needs, since they do nothing to alleviate the first situation labeled in the Bible as *not* being good:

> The Lord God said, "It is not good for the man to be alone" (Gen. 2:18).

Although social media represents an incredible technological development that can make the world smaller by rekindling lost friendships or promoting social causes, these benefits are also accompanied by the substantial drawback of a presumed barrier to entry for those lacking previously established access to one's existing friend group. This obstacle is why we can feel so alone despite being surrounded in what appears to be a sea of humanity while standing in line, walking down the street, or even riding the elevator. Giving in to that temptation to remain "connected" while we wait erodes our most basic human need for contact by replacing potentially genuine interaction with isolated, artificial engagement. As this behavior increases, we begin to perceive each man as an island.

The great tragedy of modern communication is that we are intentionally choosing to create millions of these islands of seclusion despite living in the most abundant civilization in the history of mankind. Much like our homes when we hear the doorbell or our phones when we see an unrecognized number, these islands are in process of becoming impenetrable. It is in this fashion that we are promoting conversational dehydration in our culture. To analogize, the sea of technology is very similar to the salt water that fills the ocean. The water appears clear and suitable for consumption; however, the salt levels in the water are far beyond what can naturally be processed by the human body. When we drink the water from the ocean, we are only left with a greater thirst for refreshment. Similarly, when we drink from the sea of technology, we are only left with a greater thirst for attachment. Nevertheless, many of us are drifting out to sea without the requisite rations to sustain either ourselves or our community, oblivious to this unmitigated risk of conversational dehydration. Have we become so blind that we cannot see that what we need lies not within a device, but in our fellow man?

The onset of dehydration is marked by loss of appetite and fatigue before leading to impaired vision and a greater sense of confusion. Newton's third law suggests that for every action, there is an equal and opposite reaction. Thus, it is only logical that as we engage in simulated exchange with increasing frequency (action), we would begin to adjust our outward focus (reaction). Whereas the best means of being "others focused" is to actively seek opportunities to engage in the community, the best method of being self-absorbed would be to gradually disengage from the public square. Might there be symbolism in the fact that this isolation customarily features adult men and women attempting to communicate from the fetal position as they adjust their broader focus?

As we gaze and gaze and gaze upon our very profiles with intensifying regularity, we are voluntarily redirecting our acts of worship upon ourselves, which plays right into the hands of those seeking to double down on the defective policies proposed by those in power. Remember, Phase II of the formula to reformat human nature to ensure compatibility with secularism is to redirect worship away from their traditional outlets. The worship of God cannot be tolerated because a selfless populace takes responsibility for the neighbor who has fallen on hard times, usually through the greater church community. Thriving churches create competition for a federal government otherwise dedicated to expanding dependency in the culture, which is a partial explanation for why Christianity is so hated to the man in power. The best way we can serve the Lord is to serve our fellow man; the best way we can serve the state is by serving ourselves. As our selfishness matures, we begin to greedily look to Washington for our daily provision without giving consideration that the state can never give what it has not first taken from another man.

Despite living on these metaphorical islands and suffering from this emblematic dehydration, we continue to crave the affirmation of our fellow man. As we are gradually losing the ability to freely obtain this validation, we must turn our attention to an undertaking that can at least partially quench this need. If we could just find a means of constructing a glorified representation of our lives, that would seem to achieve the twofold aim of procuring the acceptance we so desperately seek while improving our own feelings of self-worth.

Amidst this backdrop, it is quite easy to understand the appeal of social media. Albeit fruitlessly, the platform attempts to fill the void of insufficient human contact. Through it, we can erroneously measure our self-esteem through the amount of positive feedback we receive on a post. Like Dorian Gray, we can exaggerate our self-image by creating the person we wish other people to see, at the expense of actually experiencing the precious life we have been given. Our culture's obsession with paying hard-earned money to attend a concert or similar live event, only to record the experience through a cell phone, is nothing short of tragic. Why else engage in this behavior but to refine our image or impress our contacts? Through social media, we can project the semblance of a perfect life, devoid of worry, stress, or adversity. With the new object of our affinity being none other than ourselves, has our excessive pride in our appearance, image, and accomplishments ever been on greater display? In this fashion, our overindulgence is nurturing a cultural narcissism that is spiraling out of control.

Lastly, social networking lends itself to envy. As we continue drinking this water that never quenches, the ensuing visual impairment comes in the form of the illusion that we are surrounded by people living perfect lives as we struggle to achieve basic acceptance of who we are. There is no positive in comparing yourself to another person, since it will either result in arrogance or jealousy. If your analysis concludes you are superior to your peer, you adopt the role of the snob, while if you feel you cannot measure up to your contact, you begin to grow restless. Envy and personal satisfaction can never coexist.

With television helping to stretch a fresh, new canvas over creation and the allure of social media interfering with the authenticity of our interpersonal relationships, we now find ourselves living in the very abstract world necessary to absorb the wildest ambitions of those in power. This parallel universe is replete with division, rampant distrust, and the glorification of the desires of the flesh. The more connected and technologically "advanced" we become, the more our reality becomes virtualized. What is "virtual reality" but a creative slogan used to rebrand the oldest plight known to man? The phrase technologically markets isolation as exciting, innovative, and cutting-edge, even though it produces the same empty desolation experienced by our ancestors, long before the advent of any type of handheld device. As Solomon wrote:

"What has been will be again, what has been done will be done again; there is nothing new under the sun" (Eccl. 1:9).

Virtual reality is and will always be an illusion. If man cannot touch water without getting wet or fire without getting burned, how can he submerge himself into this setting without risking absolute corruption?

This is where the third and final phase of cultural destruction becomes inevitable. Bound by intensifying darkness, we begin to concoct a new meaning of life that is congruent with our perceived surroundings. The shift constitutes a spiritual disconnect from our initial makeup. We were called to worship God and serve our fellow man, but this reconstructed reality has produced the perception that our fellow man is increasingly unworthy of our concern. With people appearing to possess primarily negative attributes, the invisibility of God only grows more noticeable and concerning. Why would an allegedly loving God allow tragedy and suffering to be such a prominent part of the world? If God has firmly washed His hands of the world, might He not exist? If God does not exist, what is the point of serving other people? If heaven is not real, why not simply live for the moment? Where else shall we cast our ambitions but upon ourselves?

These disparate reflections contravene our nature and promote inflated feelings of self-worth and a desire to have a greater control over our surrounding environment. Stated alternatively, they are vulnerably fertile to the aims of the statist while practically lying barren to the message of the Gospel. In this fashion, refusing to moderate our engagement with our electronic mediums expedites the kingdom of man at the expense of the Kingdom of God.

Virtual reality ascribes to all of the hedonistic values of narcissism, which venerate affluence, fame, beauty, perpetual youth, sexual enticement, extravagance, materialism, entitlement, reckless irresponsibility, and various other forms of debauchery. By and large, our culture remains interconnected by means of virtual reality. Consistent with the transitive property of congruence, if virtual reality is grounded in narcissism, and our culture is becoming grounded in virtual reality, then our culture must ultimately become grounded in narcissism.

Twenty-first-century America features sporadic occurrences of virtue and benevolence that are largely overshadowed by the near ubiquitous reverence to selfishness and vanity publicized by our chosen methods of basic communication. These mediums enable contemporary idolatry to now travel at the speed of light, accelerating the spread of narcissism throughout our culture. It makes sense that we have directed the majority of our ambitions into the pursuits of wealth, comfort, and pleasure because we all possess an indiscriminately fertile field. Soil has no choice but to produce fruit following the scattering of seed. That which we consume, we shall produce. We have no choice!

Consider the latest example of progress with respect to basic human relationships. The June 2016 issue of *Men's Health* peers into the future by examining the first fruits lying at the intersection of virtual reality and human intimacy. The magazine contains an article entitled *Why This Guy Fell in Love with a Sex Robot*, and it chronicles the experience of a man inviting a $7,649 sex doll into his single-occupant residence to function as his companion. Despite the man expressing that "if (he) could press a button right now and have the choice of being with a sex robot or a real woman, (he'd) pick the real woman every time," the author acknowledges the intensifying allure that synthetic human relationships will produce in the near future:

> " . . . the sex robots of tomorrow might just embody everything you want from a woman. For the right price, you could have a partner that thinks exactly like you and shares your beliefs and interests. She'll be tailor-made to your tastes, with none of the compromises that come with having a relationship with a real woman."[32]

This article follows an August 2014 Pew Research report in which one of the lead researchers predicted that "robotic sex partners will be a commonplace" by 2025.[33] This prophecy accurately integrates the concepts outlined in chapter one with respect to the fertility of the human heart. The fully ripened fruit of virtual relationships feature a man becoming one flesh with a machine. This is not evolution and progress; it is devolution and degeneration!

Rather than reconstructing reality, redirecting worship away from our Creator, and redefining the very purpose of life, we should be exhausting all efforts to starve any plant that causes our bushels to overflow with such destructive cultural fruit. The initial step in this process requires having the fog-penetrating faith to understand that we are currently living through a deeply deceptive illusion. For many of us, we are simply unable to exercise this first step having already made such substantial investments into the television, social media, and our mobile devices. Collectively, these outlets have only hardened a conviction that people are stupid and worthy only of manipulation for personal gain, even though these opinions are pernicious hallucinations more aligned to the desires of the enemy. We must refuse such lies that sprout from the rapacious root structure of our technological idols.

Alas, all men do sin and fall short of the glory of God. For this reason, the best means of assessing our true values lies not in the evaluation of our own actions. Have there been any changes to human nature since these writings were expressed by the Apostle Paul shortly after the death of Christ?

"We know that the law is spiritual; but I am unspiritual, sold as a slave to sin. I do not understand what I do. For what I want to do I do not do, but what I hate I do. And if I do what I do not want to do, I agree that the law is good. As it is, it is no longer I myself who do it, but it is sin living in me. For I know that good itself does not dwell in me, that is, in my sinful nature. For I have the desire to do what is good, but I cannot carry it out. For I do not do the good I want to do, but the evil I do not want to do—this I keep on doing. Now if I do what I do not want to do, it is no longer I who do it, but it is sin living in me that does it" (Romans 7:14–20).

To identify the authenticity of what we value in twenty-first-century America, we need to examine our approach to guiding and raising our children. While the deep roots of sin may have compromised our personal fortitude as best exemplified by the sentiments of Paul, we possess the full capacity to protect the impressionable minds of our children from the undue influence of secular humanism. If we cannot fix ourselves, we can at least attempt to sever these destructive root structures from taking hold of our descendants. For in them, we place our deepest hopes, dreams, and aspirations, and we hold complete control over their upbringing, education, and media intake. Much to the dismay of those in power, we are the ones who are most influential in instilling values into them, and we have the responsibility of dispensing discipline to keep them within the boundaries of healthy development.

To truly understand whether we have indeed redefined the very purpose of life, we must explore our administration of this next generation of individuals, and this will be the subject of our next chapter.

SIX

A Shameless, Parental Derelíction of Duty

"Don't handicap your children by making their lives easy."

~ Robert Heinlein

The biblical purpose of parenting is absolute. Contrary to conventional wisdom, it does not change with the times, and it cannot be altered by technological developments. The standards are culturally and geographically blind. The expectations do not increase for the wealthy to account for their surplus resources, and they do not relax to alleviate the pressures facing the impoverished. The responsibilities of a mother are identical whether the pregnancy befalls her as an unwed teenage girl or as a woman who has been married for 40 years at the time of conception. The true purpose of parenting is outlined in Psalm 78:

> ". . . he commanded our ancestors to teach their children, so the next generation would know them, even the children yet to be born, and they in turn would tell their children. Then they would put their trust in God and would not forget his deeds but would keep his commands" (Psalm 78:5–7).

The simplicity of this charge enables its application to transcend age, wealth, culture, and even technology. We are instructed to raise our children to put their trust in the Lord and keep his commands. According to the Bible, this is the sole requirement necessary to be a competent parent.

Even though we already hold the guidebook in our possession, many in our society decry the injustice of our children not coming with an owner's manual at birth. Since the Bible has been all but silenced by today's culture, we have opted to take more of an "on-the-fly" approach to shepherding our posterity. In so doing, we have traded the unseen favor of God for the observable validation that can be provided by a peer group of child development experts, friends, and family. Their guidance has provided us with the conventional wisdom that now guides the contemporary approach to parenting that we will soon address. Subscriptions to this alternative approach have become widespread across all demographics, as the actions of a majority of Americans suggest they believe this new method will provide their children with the resources necessary to pursue comfort and prosperity as they mature within our culture.

From an academic perspective, efforts to refine purpose and direction generally fall under the purview of self-improvement and life coaching. This is an industry that heavily relies upon testimonials to substantiate the legitimacy of new approaches to the unchanging complexities of life. Without question, any deviation away from the biblical standard of child-rearing would constitute a material change. Thus, before we dissect the intricacies of our fashionably novel approach to parenting, reviewing the testimonials associated with this change would be of extreme importance. Thankfully, the American polling company Rasmussen can provide us with insight into the prudence of our evolved approach.

As it pertains to parenting, Rasmussen provides two relevant surveys highlighting how our departure from the biblical standard has affected our societal welfare. The first of these surveys was conducted in February of 2013. Participants were asked a series of nine questions under the theme of "Looking Ahead." The survey found that only 15 percent of American adults believe today's children will be better off than their parents.[1] Lurking behind this response is the suggestion that our national priorities are in disarray, a trend that threatens the overall viability of the culture. There is only one possible method in which a generation can convey an inferior way of life upon their posterity, and that would be to wholly neglect their custodial responsibilities. Consider that the results of this poll follow decades of cultural efforts to delegitimize traditional marriage as well as the essential contributions of women in the home.

These poll results are the logical outcome of a culture that disparages tradition, and the statistical relevance of these correlated variables cannot be overlooked. Tradition and prosperity are positively correlated variables; therefore, when a culture attacks tradition, it unknowingly also assaults its own prosperity. There is no element of coincidence behind this opinion poll. Additionally, what does it say about a culture when an overwhelming majority of its citizens assert that they find more optimism in yesterday than tomorrow?

While this survey certainly paints a gloomy picture of the future, the results merely highlight the perspective of Americans at a certain point in time. There is always the possibility that it could represent an inconsistent data point, so to strengthen our understanding of our collective outlook, we would need to consult a secondary metric.

The same company has been assembling a *Right Direction or Wrong Track* survey dating back to 2009. Every week, Rasmussen surveys 2,500 likely voters to gauge their opinion of the general direction of the country. For example, only 21 percent of respondents believed that the country was headed in the right direction during the week ending on July 14, 2016.[2] This number has hovered in the twenties for most of 2016, after reaching a low of 13 percent in October of 2013. In fact, in the 408 weeks in which the survey was administered, the "Right Direction" response has only exceeded 40 percent five times. It has never eclipsed 50 percent. In other words, Americans have been pessimistic about the future for every single week dating back to January 2009, without exception.

This survey is simply a rolling testimonial about our modern approach to parenting. Every week that Rasmussen conducts a new outreach, a new crop of 2,500 Americans is unintentionally affirming the inadequacy of our child-rearing techniques. Looking into the future of a nation requires only a gaze upon its children, for they will soon mold society into a shape that best fits their values and principles. Remaining perennially pessimistic about the years to come is simply an unwitting confession that we have failed to suitably ingrain moral standards into our posterity.

Even worse, there is no evidence whatsoever to support that we have attempted to make any personal sacrifices to reverse course, despite remaining convinced that the future for our children will be bleak. In fact, there has only been one material development that has surfaced since the turn of the century. This has been the creation of the previously discussed Common Core State Standards Initiative, a scheme that features communist underpinnings, an underhanded assault on the nuclear family unit, and a decreased emphasis on traditional learning methods. This cartoonish solution attempts to depress the accelerator in hopes of simply driving over the cliff with enough speed to safely land on the other side without the vehicle plummeting into the ravine.

Our fashionably novel, contemporary approach to parenting has overhauled the biblical standard in favor of an unwritten methodology that is now supported by four primary pillars: the outsourcing of supervision, the rejection of work, the suppression of discipline, and the promotion of poverty. These pillars serve as evidence that we have indeed redefined the very purpose of life, since none of them groom our children for a life of serving God by serving our fellow men (the actual purpose of the Christian life). Instead, they overemphasize the comfort and entertainment of our children, resulting in a new paradigm that has unconsciously institutionalized our idealism in a fashion that will assuredly usher poverty upon our posterity.

Motivated by a rigid idealism that childhood should be a twenty-five-year daydream wholly devoid of personal responsibility, we have erroneously erected these distinct structures while we were busy insulating our children from the harsh realities of life. Nowhere in the blueprint of this evolved approach to parenting do we seek adversity as a developmental opportunity for our children. In fact, we exhaust all possible measures to prevent them from ever tasting the sting of defeat, despite the fact that the literal foundation of success is failure. Preventing the next generation from ever experiencing failure is the surest method of inhibiting their future success. The epitome of ignorance is taking the culturally fashionable position that the "Millennials" are somehow to blame for the demise of western civilization. In reality, our actions have translated to nothing short of a shameless, parental dereliction of duty.

The first of these pillars is the outsourcing of supervision, a principle that begins with the seemingly harmless introduction of our children to the world of educational programming. Television has long monopolized this market through the delivery of programs that use cartoon characters and furry monsters to dispense informative content to our kids. This medium had previously been limited to the home, but the advent of "smart" technology has granted children limitless access to this programming through the development of applications and games. It is now common to see little ones interacting with iPhones and tablets in public settings from churches to restaurants and all points in between.

Am I really suggesting that educational programs delivered through an electronic medium for the benefit of children are detrimental to their health? You bet I am, though the damage does not actually come from a content perspective. The actual harm lies in the introduction of our children to these mediums several years before they attain the cognitive development to think logically or engage in operational thought. According to renowned Swiss psychologist Jean Piaget, the second most quoted twentieth-century psychologist for his instrumental work in the field of developmental psychology, children lack the propensity to acquire these skills until age seven.[3]

Familiarizing children with the notion that the television or Smartphone is a primary source for information gathering and ethical instruction distorts and substantially impairs their cognitive development during a time in which the human brain is most vulnerable. Toddlers learn normalcy through repetition and observation, and they have no ability to distinguish imaginative depictions from reality at this point in their lives.

Nevertheless, we continue to pursue an unspoken domestic policy of issuing practically unrestrained licenses for our toddlers to indulge in these illusions. According to a 2013 Common Sense Media Research Study, the average child will have logged over 5,000 hours into screen media (anything delivered via television, Smartphone, tablet, or computer) by age seven.[4] To put that into perspective, the average American full-time worker logs just over 2,000 hours per year. In other words, by the time our children reach the age to think logically or engage in operational thought, they will have logged the equivalent of two-and-a-half years of full-time employment into some sort of electronic programming. In this fashion, efforts to outsource or supplement the basic instruction of numbers, letters, colors, and animals to cheerful actors or lovable puppets comes at a steep price. The true cost of this introductory stint into the realm of entertainment is to retrain the mind of a child to look beyond parents and disproportionately value the perspective of the media when faced with matters of consequence. This lesson is critically important to the long-term aims of secularism.

As we've previously explored, the principal longstanding contribution of the television has been to distort reality by preventing basic human contact, genuine conversation, and authentic interaction between the members of our society. Yet in many instances, whether out of choice or necessity, this same device serves as a surrogate parent to toddlers. By nurturing an environment that promotes binge media consumption, we are teaching our children that the values and messaging of electronic platforms are trustworthy during their most critical stage of cognitive development. The first several years of a child's life serve as the moral foundation upon which everything else will be constructed. By deeply embedding a trust in the media into this foundation, the majority of our children have a natural crack built in their moral fabric. The complications resulting from this crack are typically revealed during their teenage years, when the messaging of the once trustworthy media begins to pursue its own ulterior motives.

Consider the value of educational programming from the vantage point of media executives. Providing this content enables them to take the moral high ground of caring for early learning development while simultaneously exploiting the intellectual immaturity of our youth. Keep in mind that this is the same industry that has graced us with six seasons of *Toddlers and Tiaras*, a "beauty pageant" series that openly sexualized little girls as young as three years old before a viewer base of millions of American households on a weekly basis. The show featured toddlers dressing as hookers, sporting fake breasts, donning padded push-up bras, and pretending to smoke cigarettes while strutting down the catwalk.[5] Like all children under the age of seven, these little girls also lacked any ability to reason at the time they were paraded down the runway.

The secularist worldview thrives on a mind predisposed to emotional appeals, and television has mastered the art of enticing empathy through artificial simulation. Whether the vehicle is reality, situational comedy, drama, romance, or myriad other genres, the robust arsenal of content overwhelms the young mind that has been hardwired to trust its ethical standard. Unbeknownst to them, however, this standard soon becomes substituted for one that is morally bankrupt and fully resigned to depravity once they enter the hyper-impressionable stage of adolescence.

In this fashion, there would be little difference between placing a toddler before the glare of a television set and embarking upon a quest to domesticate an African lion. The charming naiveté of the friendly cartoon characters would match the cuddly innocence of a five-pound lion cub. Both would elicit the idealistic possibilities within the imagination with a complete disregard to potential risks that lay beyond the horizon. As they age, however, each of these life forms will develop a fierce ability to mercilessly strike the vulnerable member of the herd who has isolated himself from his peers. The instinctive attack will momentarily placate the insatiable appetite of the beast, striking its victim without any discrimination before proceeding to its next conquest. Any exercise aiming to fully understand the power and strength of the media must begin by analyzing the marriage of technology with the embryonic brain. Who among us has not logged countless hours into the television during our formative years?

Outsourcing supervision to various electronic outlets emboldens youthful idealism at the expense of reality, ignorant of the biblical proverb that the one who chases fantasies will have his fill of poverty.[6]

Many of the messages portrayed by the media through its young adult programming are fully immersed in fantasy, and this is precisely what adolescents observe on a daily basis. By championing philosophies that simply do not work, such as sex without consequence, luxury without productivity, and status without tenure, the new generations are entering adulthood with a mindset grounded in complete intellectual fantasy. This whole process starts with that fateful decision to partially outsource supervision to the small screen.

Of course, color television has been around now for over sixty years, plenty of time for the device to fully mature into an instrument of secular instruction. Smartphones, on the other hand, have only been around for the last ten years. In spite of this youth, however, its potential as an agent of influence in our culture is unparalleled. A 2015 Bank of America consumer trends study revealed that 71 percent of respondents sleep with or next to their phone.[7] One year earlier, the market research firm Harris Interactive issued an eyebrow-raising report that Americans consider mobile phones more important than sex.[8] A Pew Research Center study, also released in 2015, found that nearly half of Smartphone users said they "couldn't live without" their phones.[9]

Given its paramount importance, it was only a matter of time before the Smartphone writhed its way into the administrative repertoire of the everyday parent. In addition to the various features of making phone calls, sending text messages, checking emails, and browsing the internet, many parents have discovered an unadvertised feature of critical importance. The device has the ability to function as an electronic pacifier to their children. And unlike traditional pacifiers, the Smartphone works on children every single time.

Just as our comfort with television has taught our children to completely trust the media, the relaxation of our resolve when it comes to Smartphones is also instilling a dangerous lesson in our children. When we make the decision to hand them our devices to appease their impatience, we are sending them a clear message that an attention span is a completely worthless behavioral attribute. A healthy attention span is a foundation of basic societal engagement! Even so, we all too often disregard its lasting value to solve the short-term irritation of whimpering children. This trend is doing critical damage to our culture. From 2000 to 2013, the time frame featuring the exponential surge in "smart" technology, a Microsoft study found that the average human attention span decreased by 33 percent.[10] The study found that a goldfish now has a longer attention span than an adult human being.

To understand why this matters, consider the overwhelming influence of the basic internet meme, a term used to describe the attachment of a witty caption to a culturally-relevant image. Primarily through their uncanny ability to portray the opposing position as utterly ludicrous, memes have emerged as effective tools of political influence that put forth the illusion of an enlightened, consensus opinion. While their mass appeal, specifically among the younger generation, certainly stems from a call to humor within popular culture, the political ability of this vehicle exposes the perils of a people who have lost their ability to focus.

To those who find it preposterous to suggest that people rely on memes to support their political persuasion, consider the popularity of comedy shows masquerading as news programs among the younger generation. During the 2012 election, Mitt Romney's face was portrayed alongside the caption, "Nothing says I believe in America like using a Swiss bank account to avoid paying taxes."[11] During the 2016 election cycle, perhaps the savviest politician in American history, President Barack Obama, publicly compared the Republican Party to the popular Grumpy Cat meme during the 2016 election cycle.[12] By making the association that the GOP is always "so down on America" and believes that "everything is terrible," he is astutely making the heartfelt pitch to young voters that it is the Democrat Party who supports the platform of optimism and hope. In this fashion, memes have developed a unique ability to truncate all of the complexities of a presidential election into one humorous witticism.

This tactic can only work on a culture that has no intellectual stamina. A culture that cannot focus places little value on deductive reasoning, opting for peer validation as a suitable replacement. Behind a façade of humor, memes prey on a people who have grown overconfident with the outsourcing of their minds to the whims of entertainers. Like a magnet, they pull the thinker away from cautious reason, returning his mind to its primitive form of instinct and impulse. It will not be long before an entire generation will be able to pinpoint this lack of intellectual stamina all the way back to that fateful first decision of being handed their parent's Smartphone.

Additionally, we are teaching them that there is no value in time spent developing an imagination or engaging in deep thought. Raising our children with no capacity of staying focused when encountering the proverbial passing squirrel gives them no chance of tackling the problems they shall soon encounter. How can you solve a problem that you can neither recognize nor remember? The media commonly exploits this emerging phenomenon by pursuing what is commonly referred to as the "Friday News Dump." Since more and more Americans have lost the ability to pay attention, the federal government and its agencies tend to release politically uncomfortable news on a Friday afternoon. Between a Saturday typically filled with leisure activity and a Sunday filled with football, the weekend is typically sufficient to ensure this news is quickly forgotten by the ensuing Monday. Was it any coincidence the FBI released documents on the investigation of Hillary Clinton the Friday before the Labor Day weekend in 2016? The move attempted to conceal the outright incompetence and dishonesty of Mrs. Clinton. This is a process that only works with a developmentally impaired electorate, and we are inadvertently promoting this prerequisite each time we choose to hand that Smartphone over to our children. Why must we so mindlessly deploy these parental tactics that are so instrumental to furthering the kingdom of man?

The second of these pillars is the rejection of work, a general principle that is antithetical to the teachings of the Bible. By contrast, work is so heralded by the Bible that both Testaments consider it to be a basic prerequisite for living:

> "By the sweat of your brow you will eat your food until you return to the ground, since from it you were taken; for dust you are and to dust you will return" (Gen. 3:19).

> "It is good for a man to bear the yoke while he is young" (Lam. 3:27).

"All hard work brings a profit, but mere talk leads only to poverty" (Prov. 14:23).

"For even when we were with you, we gave you this rule: 'The one who is unwilling to work shall not eat'" (2 Thess. 3:10).

Work is so highly regarded in the Scriptures because there is no better method of civilizing a society than through productivity. Furthermore, there is no better means of instilling respect, responsibility, and work ethic into an individual than to provide him with employment. The inverse of work is sloth, a characteristic so castigated by the Bible that it warrants classification as one of the seven deadly sins. In fact, Proverbs 12 proclaims that laziness is so perilous to a culture that it will end in forced labor!

Since the Bible has lost the power of persuasion in American culture, the countless endorsements for hard work that scatter this holy book have given way to an emergent, idealistic commitment to providing lives of leisure and entertainment to our children. To persistently echo the central theme of the book, this new parental paradigm is yet another piece of ripened fruit to sprout from our refusal to live our faith. Failing to live our faith removes its influence from the public school system and nearly all forms of media. As a result, the secular influence over both of these cultural institutions has surged, only helping to solidify our compromised system of values. Although schools, television, and the internet are convenient scapegoats for our valueless culture, the real perpetrator for the demise of the culture is the Christian. These points have been exhaustively explored in prior chapters and do not require restatement.

What has yet to be explored, however, is a matter that has impeded parents from instilling work ethic and industry into their children for over seventy-five years. Despite promising to protect our children, the practical application of this mechanism has become so perverted that it has actually grown to be the most effective method of creating the culture of dependency that now suffocates our way of life.

The mechanism of which I speak is our general framework of laws. When it comes to knocking out any measurable element of productivity from our children, the federal government is a figurative Goliath. Using its one-two punch of arbitrary age restrictions and ludicrous permit requirements, children need far more than a basic sling to accomplish something as scandalous as earning a few dollars. The arbitrary age restrictions effectively make it illegal to provide even the most insignificant of employment opportunities to any person under the age of fourteen, with the limited exceptions of agriculture and babysitting. In other words, we now live in a country in which 13-year-olds cannot be trusted to ring a register, but children as young as the age of four have sufficient cognitive development and aptitude to transition from their biological gender to the one in which they identify. How does that work? Secondly, the business license requirement extends the might of the oppressive arm of Goliath to prevent the most likely entrepreneurial efforts for any child, regardless of age. The extent of underage commerce is charming in its naiveté, yet the central authority has no tolerance for these edifying exploits. Between these two components, the federal government has concluded that the most effective means of instilling respect, responsibility, or work ethic into our children actually threatens their welfare.

This is not hyperbole. Consider a scenario in which a 13-year-old aspiring photographer desperately sought an introductory employment opportunity and was fortunate enough to find a professional willing to take her under his wing to shoot a Saturday wedding. Let's assume the photographer elected to compensate the amateur $10 per hour for six hours. The value of this proposal from the vantage point of the apprentice is incalculable, far in excess of the $60 stipend. A more gallant gesture from an employer would be hard to find, since it would be highly unlikely that the output of the trainee would match the compensation provided. It is much more likely that he would be selflessly entering the arrangement as a mentor to nurture her interest in the field. This mutually beneficial arrangement is illegal in our society, and it would expose the photographer to a fine for violating the Fair Labor Standards Act. Had he demonstrated a pattern of mentoring aspiring photographers (aka "exploiting child labor"), the viability of his business could be threatened in the event an upstart reporter got wind of the story.

Sound preposterous? It should. If authorities were to intervene to either fine the photographer or otherwise prevent the apprenticeship, their actions would only serve to stifle independence, initiative, and entrepreneurship from being cultivated in the mind of an impressionable youth. It would be challenging to argue that this development constitutes progress, or "moving forward."

Before we cast aside this contention as an unlikely hypothetical, consider a concrete example from Overton, Texas.[13] In June of 2015, two sisters (aged 8 and 7) wanted to do something special for their daddy in anticipation of Father's Day. They agreed that going to a local water park would provide the perfect setting to make for a magical day. Realizing that they would need to raise just over $100 to take the family to the park, they assembled a lemonade stand to work eagerly toward their goal. After earning $25 during their first hour, the girls were soon confronted by local city officials seeking to verify that they had the necessary permit and health code clearances to operate the stand. When the officials learned that the girls overlooked these requirements, they forced them to shut down the business. This incident is far from isolated. Six kids running a lemonade stand were fined $500 for failing to obtain a vendor's permit in Montgomery County, Maryland.[14] Iowa police shut down the lemonade stand of a 4-year-old girl after it had only been open for 30 minutes, and Georgia police sacked the efforts of three girls operating a stand in the summer of 2011.[15,16]

These episodes provide an opportunity to evaluate our cultural priorities. In one simple action, closing the lemonade stand reinforced the secular values of discouraging work ethic, responsibility, enterprise, initiative, self-sufficiency, and community. If our central authority truly had the best interests of our children at heart, wouldn't they promote legislation that was compatible with the following biblical call to parenting?

"Start children off on the way they should go, and even when they are old they will not turn from it" (Prov. 22:6).

Instead, they have classified something as harmless as a neighborhood lemonade stand as a legitimate business endeavor that should be regulated in the same fashion as the local Applebee's. Requiring a permit for such an undertaking is asinine. In reality, stretching the reach of permit and health code standards to cover the fleeting fancies of children is nothing more than a measure taken to ensure that children remain relegated to their proper place of uninterrupted leisure and entertainment.

Efforts to repress the work ethic of young people are not limited to the lemonade industry. In January of 2015, two New Jersey high school seniors sought to capitalize on a snow day by soliciting their snow removal services door-to-door.[17] While canvassing the neighborhood to drum up business, an unidentified neighbor contacted the police to alert them of the solicitation. Shortly after receiving the call, the police advised the two students that a license costing upwards of $450 would be required in order to engage in their desired business. Upon hearing the story from local media, one resident flawlessly articulated his outrage on the community events Facebook page:

> "Are you kidding me? Our generation does nothing but complain about his generation being lazy and not working for their money. Here's a couple kids who take the time to print up flyers, walk door to door in the snow, and then shovel snow for some spending money. And someone calls the cops and they're told to stop?"[18]

The hard truth is that our culture is downright hostile to the idea of an enterprising minor, and the evidence lies in the fact that we have practically codified youthful sloth into the federal register. In the juvenile permit requirement, progressives have found the perfect tool to douse any budding entrepreneurial fires since its scope is sufficiently wide to engulf virtually any potential business endeavor. Between the permit and the minimum age restrictions outlined in the Fair Labor Standards

Act, these hurdles practically guarantee outright idleness from any individual under fourteen years of age. If idle hands are the devil's workshop, why are central administrators so eager to cultivate this new form of truancy within our youth?

If childhood indeed ends when a person turns eighteen, parents are essentially sacrificing three-quarters of the available time with which they have to instill a healthy work ethic, simply on account of this smothering, discriminatory legal framework. Keep in mind that supporters of Goliath are only seeking to strengthen the beast. If the *Fightfor$15* pressure group is successful in doubling the federal minimum wage, this will add the devastating left hook of completely pricing adolescents out of the labor market. Private-sector employers are seldom in the habit of paying workers a salary in excess of their productivity; thus, the principal benefit of legislating an artificially high minimum wage will be the extension of outright idleness in our children all the way through age eighteen, if not higher. These are the fruits of our well-intentioned quest to "protect" our children from work, and they are completely foreign to the biblical approach to parenting.

Of course, many will deride this viewpoint as regressive and desirous of returning our children to an assembly line for 60 hours a week, leaving no time for schoolwork. Please do not fall prey to the progressive tactic of changing the narrative by making a sensationalized appeal to your emotions. Nobody is advocating full-time employment for school-aged children. The true question to resolve is why the governing authorities are so desirous of cultivating dependency that they will hastily descend on our kids within a matter of hours to prevent them from partaking an applied lesson in free enterprise. Running a lemonade stand for one hour a month is hardly sweatshop labor.

Failing to mobilize and make a national issue out of our wide-ranging hostility to self-sufficiency only substantiates our complicity to this injustice. Since we have chosen to systemically mandate sloth in our children, our kids have no concept of the fundamental value and necessity of business. Can there really be any wonder why we are dealing with the spreading plague of socialism? We have been nurturing this broken philosophy now for nearly a century!

The third pillar of modern parenting is the suppression of discipline. As was the case with the rejection of work, this voguish guideline is also antithetical to the teachings of the Bible. When it comes to discipline, the Old Testament does not mince words. In fact, warnings from the book of Proverbs are so severe as to suggest that parents who relax or otherwise fail to discipline their children are willing accomplices to their demise:

> "Discipline your children, for in that there is hope; do not be a willing party to their death" (Prov. 19:18).

> "The evil deeds of the wicked ensnare them; the cords of their sins hold them fast. For lack of discipline they will die, led astray by their own great folly" (Prov. 5:22).

The New Testament promises that the benefits of discipline will not only sustain the individual, but the society at large:

> "No discipline seems pleasant at the time, but painful. Later on, however, it produces a harvest of righteousness and peace for those who have been trained by it" (Heb. 12:11).

The Bible declares that the road to life and peace is painstakingly paved using the asphalt of discipline. Conversely, the loose gravel of disobedience composes the untenably bumpy road leading to a certain death. If all we are saying is give peace a chance, wouldn't enduring the occasional discomfort of discipline be a small price to pay for such a magnificent reward?

Although the Bible clearly sings the praises of discipline, our culture approaches this instruction with fear. Much of the fear is structural on account of our litigious culture, and this dynamic all but eliminates discipline from the public square. For example, numerous stories have surfaced over the past several years in which public school teachers have neglected to intervene while students were actively fighting in class. In one such instance in Palm Beach, Florida, a teacher did not try to physically stop an altercation in which a 13-year-old student was pummeling one of his peers during class.[19] The alleged reason? School policy holds that staff may only intervene after undergoing training, since any injury resulting from teacher intervention could introduce a lawsuit that would threaten the career of the teacher. Similar stories have emerged from schools in Texas, Washington, and Oklahoma, signifying that the trend is on the rise.[20,21,22]

The inaction of teachers in critical situations such as these is bewildering at first glance; however, it is merely an offshoot from the compromised structural environment in which they operate. These teachers likely receive mixed messages from their administration, the teachers' union, and their personal conscience. Following an episode from a high school in Dallas, Texas, a local teachers' union president shared the following remarks that appeared to defend the noninterventionist approach:

"Teachers have intervened in the past. They have been injured. They have not been able to return to work.

They have been reprimanded for intervening. So there is a huge question mark as to what's truly appropriate. In today's society which is a violent society, you do not touch the student. That should be left up to the administration."[23]

After the incident in Florida, another teacher shared the following comments:

"It's his job to teach remedial math. I'm not trained (nor) paid to intervene in fights. If I don't, I'm negligent. If I do, I'm abusive. There is no way to do the right thing."[24]

Is it a sign of progress when "the system" paralyzes educators to play the role of idle bystanders during a fight between two (or more) minors? Can our fear of discipline be so strong that we refuse to protect our children in their most desperate time of need? Cross reference these reports with our earlier discussion in chapter four. These are the same school authorities who our central government advocates should be included in the contemporary definition of family, essentially granting them the parental rights previously restricted to a mother and father. Is this how you would react if your son or daughter was on the ground? Would you refuse to act?

While the fear of legal reprisal has virtually removed discipline from the public square, basic parental rights to practice discipline in the private domain is similarly under assault. One of the more illuminating cases demonstrating this development comes from Corpus Christi, Texas, in which a mother was fined and sentenced to five years of probation after spanking her nearly two-year-old daughter.[25] The whole case was despairingly prompted by a blood relative electing to have this private family matter settled by an otherwise disinterested and potentially agenda-driven court system. In fact, the public statement of the judge seems to suggest an irresponsibly dangerous approach of pontificating his personal ethical standard from his position on the bench. To support his ruling, Judge Jose Longoria made the following statement:

"You don't spank children today. In the old days, maybe we got spanked, but there was a different quarrel. You don't spank children."

A more disconcerting legal statement would be hard to find, as there is nary a trace of common-law heritage anywhere in these three nakedly prejudiced sentences. As expected, this legal determination from the secular authority is utterly incompatible with biblical teachings, particularly the oft-quoted verse from Proverbs 13:

"Whoever spares the rod hates their children, but the one who loves their children is careful to discipline them."

What Judge Longoria and his academic enthusiasts fail to recognize is that the purpose of discipline is not to punish our children, but to correct them. This is one of many examples depicting how emotion can paralyze reason. A man cannot associate discipline with punishment unless he has first committed to think with his feelings. When a man thinks with his feelings with respect to rearing children, he joins the community of pragmatically blind individuals promoting the cognitive and behavioral impairment of our national posterity. This is why the Bible confirms that an undisciplined child is an unloved child.

Returning to the matter at hand, the reader should pause to contemplate the significance of these two separate accounts. In a truly stunning display of thoughtless inconsistency, our legal system looms with threats to prevent authorities from intervening when somebody else is physically assaulting your child. *At the very same time,* these same adjudicators openly punish parents who choose to discipline their children by means of spanking. Alas, this is the wisdom of the world.

Figuratively speaking, Judge Longoria and disciplinary abolitionists across the country have been picketing at the curb of the traditional American household for years. Standing next to their SHAME ON THE AMERICAN FAMILY banner, their aims to curb discipline have been veiled behind a mantra of making the world safe for children. By employing an effective emotional appeal, their perpetual nagging has granted them slow access inside the homes of many families. Whether it be due to these appeals, rulings such as the aforementioned, or some combination of the two, parents are slowly warming to the idea that local authorities should indeed be consulted prior to pursuing disciplinary measures.

One such example emerged from a town in southeastern Florida near the end of 2014. Upon returning home from a trip to Wal-Mart, a father found his two daughters fighting over a tablet. One of the girls had allegedly locked herself in her bedroom with the device, but her sister was soon able to gain access to the room by picking the lock with a knife. Amidst the bickering, the father resolved to discipline one of the girls using a paddle; however, he was mindful of the changing climate and potential legal ramifications of pursuing this action. For this reason, he elected to call the local sheriff's office to request that a member of law enforcement supervise the paddling, and the punishment was indeed administered under the supervision of the deputy.[26]

A second report surfaced from Belen, New Mexico, in June of 2016. In this occurrence, parents were dealing with an unruly teenage son whose behavior did not improve following a number of earlier efforts to restrict his electronic privileges. After admitting she had "tried everything else," the mother decided to punish her son by making him live in a tent outside in the middle of the New Mexico summer. She and her husband indicated that their son was welcome back into their home to shower, get water, and use the restroom only after obtaining prior permission. The mother went on to say that her son "has to knock on our door just like a visitor would because he disrespected our home and he disrespected rules. And like we told him – here, it's disrespect and out there it's a felony and you go to prison." They opted to pursue this disciplinary measure *after* calling the New Mexico Children, Youth and Families Department to obtain their prior permission.[27]

Let us be clear at the outset: the chosen disciplinary measures enacted by both sets of parents are admirable. Regardless of their individual faith construct, they both are in tune with biblical instruction. The danger, however, lies in the growing tacit acceptance of the state as the ultimate parental authority in modern culture. When it comes to correcting our children, we should not be surrendering judgment to an entity that is otherwise chiefly concerned with cultivating dependency within them.

Solely out of fear of the swelling federal leviathan, good parents are now electing to outsource final disciplinary responsibility to the whims of the state. By seeking this permission, it stands to reason that each set of parents would have reversed course in the event the local authorities objected to their targeted pursuits. There will come a time when the secular winds are of such strength as to preclude any disciplinary measures whatsoever. That time has not yet come, which explains the temporary endorsement in both cases. But nowhere in the Bible is there any suggestion that parents should first consult with the secular authorities when it comes to instructing and correcting their children.

It is certainly a bold contention to suggest that American parents will soon lose any rights to discipline their children. Many would find this claim preposterous, but this is precisely what happens to nations who fully abandon the ways of the Lord. Consider the aims and ambitions of the United Nations, the largest intergovernmental organization in the world. Nearly every sovereign nation in the world belongs to the UN, a conglomerate touting that its membership extends to "all peace-loving states."

In September of 2015, the UN brazenly adopted an initiative known as the 2030 Agenda for Sustainable Development.[28] The plan states ambitious goals of ending world poverty, ending world hunger, taking "urgent action" on climate change, achieving gender equality, and fostering peaceful societies that are free from fear and violence. On this latter point, the UN has moved to attract and direct financial resources through a Global Partnership to End Violence Against Children.

The global partnership website prominently notes that it "will bring together stakeholders from across the world to end *all forms of violence against children*, turning the belief that *no violence against children is justifiable* and all violence is preventable into a compelling agenda for action."[29] (emphasis mine). This language is the international, parental equivalent of a zero-tolerance school policy, the same type of ideology that suspends children for biting their Pop-Tarts into the shape of a gun.[30] In short, the UN has made it a priority to rid the entire world of discipline by the end of 2030.

Curiously, just four months following the grandiose unveiling of this global agenda, the UN publicly affirmed infanticide (abortion) as a basic human right.[31] Progressives simply cannot help but run up the score in the game of hypocrisy. There is no legitimacy to any child safety concerns from an entity that openly sanctions the murder of children. Of course, this is par for the course for an organization that welcomes notorious human rights violators into its hypocritical tent of peace loving states. UN membership extends to the state of Iran, the leading state sponsor of terrorism and world leader in child executions according to Human Rights Watch; China, whose own government confesses to the prevention of 400 million births on account of its one-child policy; and Somalia, a nation that has allowed 98 percent of its women to undergo female genital mutilation according to a 2005 World Health Organization estimate.[32,33,34]

Naturally, the single-spaced, twenty-eight-page blueprint to utopia makes a grand total of zero references to God, Jesus Christ, the Holy Spirit, Christianity, or the Bible. In other words, in its quest to transform Earth into heaven by reformatting human nature and seizing the divine powers of the Creator, Agenda 2030 is doomed from the start. Nevertheless, the United States of America is an ardent supporter of the endeavor, with President Barack Obama delivering remarks at the closing session of the conference. Can any independent thinker honestly claim that parental rights to exercise discipline are not under assault in the United States of America?

These are the intellectual seeds being scattered over not just ours, but nearly every developed country in the world. By embracing Agenda 2030, the leaders of these nations are agreeing that any efforts to physically punish children should be criminalized, including right here in our backyard. By placing such a short time frame on the agenda, the UN is predicting quite the harvest in less than 15 years. If they are correct, we will soon have the honor of leading virtually every child astray on a multicultural march to death.

Ever the pioneer of secular thought, National Public Radio (NPR) reacted to the UN initiative by blending a few investments within its academic thought portfolio. After obtaining the perfect mix to meet the intellectual demands of its stake holders, the organization ran a truly stunning "thought" piece entitled *Should We Be Having Kids in the Age of Climate Change?* on one of its radio programs in August of 2016.[35] The piece employs a form of passive-aggressive alarmism, drawing heavy influence from Dr. Travis Rieder, a philosopher and Assistant Director for education initiatives at the Berman Institute of Bioethics at Johns Hopkins University. Mr. Rieder proposed that it "seems unfair" that people in the world's poorest nations suffer severe climate impacts due to the carbon emissions of rich nations. He went on to suggest that "maybe we should protect our kids by not having them." This is certainly a curious perspective coming from the proud father of a two-year-old daughter.

While it certainly is not the actual subject matter, there is an important lesson to learn from this piece. By broadcasting this perspective nationally, the mindset of the progressive comes into focus. Secular disciples are well aware that it is never too early to scatter ideological seeds into perpetually impressionable minds. Deploying the false gospel of climate change to cause people to second guess procreation is only possible because of the general public's reverence for institutions of higher learning. What a wonder it would be if we held the same veneration for the ageless positions of the Bible.

Yet here we find another of the countless examples of the wisdom of the world. The best way we can end violence against children is to prevent them from ever being born. Bear in mind that NPR receives nearly half a billion dollars of taxpayer funding per year to make these types of contributions available to the culture through its far-reaching frequencies. Just how far on the wrong track is our culture? Our colleges and universities have traveled so far down the rabbit hole of obscurity that they are diligently theorizing supportable justifications to extinguish life. To their credit, though, curtailing human reproduction would indeed save future generations the occasional discomfort of having to administer discipline from time to time.

These first three pillars of modern parenting pose devastating limitations to the development and future success of our children; however, it is only after the accompaniment of the fourth that we officially enslave them to the ways of the world. This final pillar is an unavoidable byproduct of our larger national denunciation of discipline, bringing a contemporary light to the following biblical proverb:

> "Whoever disregards discipline comes to poverty and shame, but whoever heeds correction is honored" (Prov. 13:18).

The fourth pillar is the promotion of poverty. The overwhelming majority of colleges and universities have maneuvered to sculpt a modern, albeit imbecilic form of enlightenment that disregards science, truth, human experience, and even life. Even after witnessing countless examples of how their efforts have either perverted or distorted academic expansion, we remain unfazed in our devotion to secular academia. Our public reverence is so strong, in fact, that we continue to mindlessly instruct our children that there is but one principal method of achieving success: spend at least four years of life navigating these increasingly unscrupulous marshlands in search of a college diploma. The fallout of this parental technique has been the financial, moral, spiritual, and intellectual bankrupting of our children.

As a society, we now place a higher value on an adorned piece of paper than the independence of our children. The proof is in the costs of these institutions and our behaviors when these young adults complete their post-secondary studies. The College Board reported that the average annual costs for students enrolled full time at a private university was $43,921 for the 2015–16 academic year.[36] This equates to a cost and potential debt load of over $175,000 over the span of four years, a figure that exceeds the median price of a home in Kansas City, Missouri.[37] Since Pew Research identified that the median annual earnings of a college-educated young adult totals $45,500 as of its most recent study in 2013, an increasing percentage of these graduates simply cannot afford to provide for their most basic human need of shelter.[38]

In yet another demonstration of progressivism fomenting cultural regression, young adults are returning to their parents' quarters in droves. Nearly one-third of adults aged 18–34 now live with their parents, the highest percentage in over 75 years.[39,40] Nevertheless, a full 94 percent of parents, when surveyed, respond that they "expect" their child to attend college.[41] This robotic response is most likely given from the idealistic mindset of what higher education ought to be, as opposed to its current function as a means to the ultimate end of a high paying job. After considering that college is becoming the quickest method of providing our children with all of the anxieties of a mortgage without any of the satisfaction of freedom or advancement, we should all take time to reevaluate these expectations. The costs of post-secondary education are now so burdensome that they threaten to stunt the independence of an entire generation.

Considering the financial outlay, one has to imagine the rigorous demands of a college or university-level education pose quite a challenge to the aspiring student. Unfortunately, this is hardly the case. The Heritage Foundation recently found that "the average *full-time* college student spends only 2.76 hours per day on all education-related activities."[42] The fact that students can satisfy these academic requirements *while allocating almost 90 percent of their typical day* to leisurely pursuits is downright embarrassing. If this was the type of output an employer received from a full-time employee, he would most certainly terminate the employment relationship. In the university setting, however, this part-time effort merits the esteemed conferral of a diploma. At best, this statistic reveals that our system of higher education has become severely watered-down, lending support to the previous "means to an end" allegation. After taking time to contemplate this information, how could a college education possibly be worth such an exorbitant financial investment?

Despairingly, the cultural damage produced by college is not limited to the harmful financial impact on an individual.

These institutions are imposing disastrous social damage by commoditizing human relationships and indoctrinating the student body into extremist secular thought. Consider the University of New Mexico, whose Sex Week event in 2014 featured workshops entitled "Negotiating Successful Threesomes" and "How to be a Gentleman AND Get Laid." When prompted for the purpose of this event, the UNM Women's Resource Center Director Summer Little explained that the overall strategy was to "provide . . . information on healthy relationships, consent, healthy communication, as well as respect within relationships."[43] By using such racy themes, however, it would be hard to argue against an opposing viewpoint suggesting the goal may have been to provide strategies to advance the male sexual conquest ethic and create a palatably novel method to subjugate women.

UNM is not an isolated example in its promotion of this carnal exhibition, as the University of Maryland, Harvard University, Yale University, Brown University, the University of Tennessee, the University of Chicago, the University of Kentucky, the University of Michigan, Lafayette College, Northwestern University, and Emory University have also experimented with a University Sex Week platform, just to name a few. By sanctioning these events, these universities willfully ignore the countless references to the importance of sexual purity in the Bible, despite some of them being founded specifically to advance the Gospel of Jesus Christ!

Our societal migration away from a biblical standard has only intensified the resolve of these institutions to evangelize the gospel of secular humanism. Recent cultural victories have emboldened many of them to amplify their reverence for the worldly creeds of diversity, inclusion, acceptance, and social justice. In the event traditional academic instruction gets in the way of this evangelism, it is a small price to pay for the greater good of achieving cultural progress.

Perhaps the most blatant example of this evangelism was on display at Wayne State University in the summer of 2016. As its faculty was reviewing its course offerings between semesters, an internal committee moved to add a three-credit hour requirement in diversity to the general education curriculum at this Michigan establishment. In a report to the administration, these instructors explained that creating a menu of diversity courses would "provide opportunities for students to explore diversity at the domestic level and consider the ways in which it intersects with real world challenges at the local, national and/or global level." To make room for this social good, the educators recommended that Wayne State remove the general requirement for students to pass at least one mathematics course before earning a degree. The university accepted the motion, becoming one of the first schools to offer degrees without students having to demonstrate any mathematical proficiency whatsoever.[44]

Oregon State University has sprouted another thistle from this troublesome vine. Proudly listed at the top of its *Spring 2016 Town Hall – Feedback Session*, the university has charged a group of faculty, staff, *and students* to develop a training initiative "to provide all students entering Oregon State University an orientation to concepts of diversity, inclusion and social justice and help empower all OSU students to contribute to an inclusive university community."[45] Generally speaking, students typically possess a limited amount of "real-world" experience. If a university brands this collection of uncredentialed individuals as expert voices capable of developing an academic framework for a university program, how can it make any sense to consider the resulting courses as worthy of college credit? Does this action not invalidate the whole notion of a college education, questioning the larger purpose of the university? Regardless, the desire to preach the secular gospel has become so strong that the university apparently is willing to risk its reputation by employing this "all hands on deck" approach to enlightenment!

These brief examples show that many colleges and universities are dealing with a pandemic outbreak of ethical and academic cracks in their foundation. Rather than directly addressing these budding liabilities, however, many officials have chosen to divert the attention of future applicants to the beauty of their lavish construction projects. Thus far they have been successful in these efforts because we have rewarded their behavior by foolishly encouraging our children to attain their coveted credentials *at any cost*. This has provided administrators with a virtually limitless budget with which they can improve their outward appearance, a dynamic that will only intensify the long-term pain experienced by our society due to the ongoing spread of toxic ideas throughout the culture. By tolerating and blindly promoting this system for so long, we have largely lost the ability to discern the merits of the most basic societal virtue: right and wrong.

Just how have we fallen this far? Much like the public school system, colleges and universities have a near-universal acceptance of any piece of literature as a potential instrument of learning . . . with the sole exceptions of the Bible and the United States Constitution. It is not an accident that poverty has befallen our children and our culture. These establishments largely ascribe to the cultural ideology of the left, integrating Marxism, progressivism, and secular humanism into the basic core curriculum. This is a logical outcome considering a recent George Mason University study found that the percentage of college professors ascribing to either atheism or agnosticism is 26 percent higher than the general US population.[46] It is long overdue that we reevaluate our propensity to encourage our children to mortgage their future in pursuit of a potentially godless education.

In this chapter, we have seen how enlightened secularism prefers death to discipline, idleness to work, fantasy to reality, and worldly credentials to independence. But just how have we plummeted so far so fast? We have already seen how the legal system can ensnare our efforts to raise our children, but this is just one offshoot of judicial governance. To understand the true speed and tenacity of our freefall, we will need to develop a greater appreciation for our constantly evolving system of courts. Progressives have fully infiltrated the judiciary and are now deeply indebted to a legal system that has unapologetically advanced their agenda to the detriment of the American people. This study will help explain perhaps the most significant consequence of failing to live out the Christian faith.

SEVEN

The Weathervane on the High Court

"I tremble for my country when I reflect that God is just; that his justice cannot sleep forever."

~ Thomas Jefferson

I n the early 1960s, Christians granted security clearance to a Trojan horse outwardly dressed as a vessel in search of religious inclusion. The premise was simple: the rights of the vocal minority of parents taking offense to facets of our education system that were grounded in religious heritage must be protected. Shortly after reaching interscholastic soil, however, the ravenous wolves dwelling within quickly abandoned this false pretense to malevolently impair the minds of children and their yet-to-be-born descendants by removing prayer and the Bible from all public schools. This historical episode represents the seen element of the infiltration, for we are in possession of the legal opinions and transcripts chronicling the respective court cases. But like most mechanisms in life, the significance of the unseen typically carries a greater weight than what can readily be observed by the naked eye. In this instance, the standard vision of the typical adult living in 1960 simply could not see the potential threats of granting progressives unrestricted access to the complex network of fields housing tens of thousands of educational establishments. The true unseen element represented the secular seed that was scattered over each of these respective institutions.

Fifty years have transpired since we've welcomed this Trojan horse inside our gates. These seeds have now had plenty of time to deeply ensnare the once-healthy root structure of public education, and the true implications of what was unseen in 1960 become glaringly evident when we observe the enthusiastic reception nearly all schools and universities provide to the aims of the modern progressive. Trojan horses only need to be dispatched once, for there is no need to infiltrate something you to which you've already been granted free access.

The cultural concern of our day is being publicized as gender identity inclusion, a concern affecting 0.3 percent of the US population, according to a 2011 study produced by The Williams Institute.[1] To meet the needs of these individuals, our universities are constructing safe spaces to promote the free expression of all forms of sexual orientation, including but not limited to the open rejection of biological gender. Owing to the successful infiltration of academia over fifty years ago, this epidemic has spread throughout the United States. Campuses overflow with apologetic, albeit gullible, viewpoints of good-hearted individuals convinced they are partaking in a positive historical movement in support of this latest aim of "inclusion."

While they are correct that this movement is indeed historic, they fail to recognize the identical bait-and-switch sales tactic from recent history. We are being encouraged to focus on the pretty (rainbow-colored!) packaging of this bill of goods without giving any consideration to its contents or ability to nourish and sustain our culture. We similarly receive no warning on the presence of any unintended consequences of consumption. After recently being fleeced by a similar bill of goods arriving by means of a Trojan horse, are we so naïve as to accept this new cultural product at face value? Lying before us is an opportunity to learn from this recent history to preserve one of the most precious liberties essential to a free society.

The fancy packaging of gender identity inclusion cloaks the naked ambition of today's progressive, which is the predatory desire to abolish the free speech rights of believers. While this claim undoubtedly seems far-fetched, if not downright conspiratorial, I implore the reader to take an open-minded approach to history, recent developments on college campuses, and the brazen remarks of high-ranking officials who will be tasked with hearing the "social justice" cases that will inevitably surface from this movement. The only missing element from the contemporary progressive formula is a community of apathetic Christians. Should they find this missing ingredient in our culture, we shall soon find that it will be impossible to retain the First Amendment rights that literally took thousands of agonizing years to attain.

Having already touched on history and the fertility of college campuses, we have a natural segue into the setting that is campus life. Let's begin with one of America's elite, Ivy League institutions. Yale University currently benefits from its perception as one of the most prestigious academic institutions in the country. According to its admissions website as of June 2016, average SAT scores for incoming freshman ranged from 2,140–2,400, with the upper limit of the range representing a perfect score on this standardized test.[2] The school admitted only 6.3 percent of applicants for its Fall 2014 term.[3] Of the more than 4,000 colleges and universities spread throughout the United States, this acceptance rate makes Yale the third most difficult school to gain admission in the country.[4] Without question, our culture considers the minds of those roaming the campus to be the most prodigious our society has to offer.

Near the end of 2015, an individual attempted to garner the support of these intellectually gifted students for a petition designed to reduce their exposure to uncomfortable opinions.[5] The petition also carried the benefit of limiting the ability of people to "make fun" of other people. These idealistic ambitions won resounding support from Yale students. During the hour of time the petitioner spent on campus, he was able to accumulate over fifty signatures, and endorsing students provided the following comments as they were lending their support:

- "I think this is fantastic. I absolutely agree."
- "Excellent – love it!"
- "I appreciate what you're trying to do."
- "I totally agree with where you're at."
- "Thank you for doing this."

So what action was proposed to usher a greater degree of comfort and acceptance upon the culture? Nothing other than getting rid of, blowing up, or otherwise repealing the First Amendment to the United States Constitution, the very document providing us with the precious rights of speech and assembly! In a masterful display of technical incompetence, these highly educated individuals failed to recognize that signing this petition advocated that no American should ever have the right to make a petition before the government. This episode is not just an indictment of Yale, but also the SAT examination and the overall public school system. How can this test have any integrity when such a high number of students potentially acing this examination cannot make this most basic connection?

As we've thoroughly addressed, the wisdom of the world is foolish to the Lord; therefore, it is only logical that such an episode would transpire at one of the most highly esteemed secular institutions in America. Yale University represents low-hanging fruit, so it may be a little unfair to reach an assessment from an institution so near the summit of secular wisdom. Perhaps the traditional state university system takes a more sensible approach to the First Amendment. After all, aren't colleges heralded as beacons where ideas and beliefs are openly challenged to promote free expression and dialogue?

One of the top priorities for the University of California system of colleges entering the 2015–16 academic year was to educate its professors on the subject of microaggressions.[6] This term is defined by Merriam-Webster as "a comment or action that is subtly and often unintentionally hostile or demeaning to a member of a minority or marginalized group."[7] The sensitivity training program was launched to plant the concept of microaggressions in the minds of the roughly 190,000 faculty and staff in the UC system. Upon completion of the training, the hope was that all staff would be proficient in removing any comments and actions that could cause discomfort to the student body.

Of course, this stated aim of the program only represented its pretty packaging. If we look underneath the wrappings, we will find the groundwork for the deliverance of the most cherished secular right upon twenty-first-century society: the right to never be offended. There is only one thing preventing this progressive "right" from being conferred upon the people in American culture, and that is the First Amendment right to free speech.

Microaggressions are a completely fabricated concoction geared to accomplish three secular aims. Principally, its adherents encourage people to embrace victimhood, which is the state of being most conducive to helplessness and dependence. By emboldening classes of people to take offense at the most subtle or unintentional of remarks, these intellectual elites are fostering a completely avoidable division within the culture. Do not overlook the symbolism in the fact that this ambition is being launched at the university level, the venue widely considered to be wellspring of civilizing enlightenment. Civility does not strengthen through the preponderance of victimhood and dependence.

Secondly, microaggressions empower chaos and lawlessness. By equating emotional pain with bodily harm, progressives are seeking to legitimize restitution for feigned wrongdoing in the same fashion as what we would expect from a physical crime. In fact, it introduces the even more dangerous precedent of soliciting "proactive" restitution since those feeling "triggered" can negotiate their demands from a position of leverage. Forcing the hand of a university, for example, would typically only require the threat that the marginalized group cannot be responsible for any damage in the event their demands continue to remain unaddressed. This is the tactic currently being engaged by the Black Lives Matter faction of society, and the strength of this movement simply would not be possible without the intellectual assistance of academia. It is not coincidental that the terms *microaggression* and *triggering* were launched into our culture simultaneously. Microaggressive theory holds that people cannot be held accountable for lapses in judgment that are "triggered" by the words or deeds of others.

Lastly, microaggressions emasculate the culture. Attacking the attributes of fortitude and accountability only helps to break the human spirit by teaching people that they cannot be expected to solve their own problems without the mediation of a third party. In 1944, our eighteen-year-olds were fearlessly storming the beaches of Normandy to sacrifice their lives for the betterment of the world. Seventy years later, our eighteen-year-olds are fearfully storming the dean's office in desperate search of conscience appeasement.

Despite these toxic contributions, microaggressive theory remains a top priority for the University of California at the directive of newly-appointed president Janet Napolitano. True to form, university leaders endorsed Ms. Napolitano as the most qualified candidate after reviewing a résumé showing twenty years of executive experience in the unaccountable bubble of state and federal government. Save her own academic pursuits, she held no educational experience whatsoever. Nevertheless, she was offered the presidency in July of 2013 with a first-year compensation package exceeding $720,000.[8] With her background, can any reasonable person act surprised that this divisive undertaking would be the first initiative she chose to spearhead?

So what types of speech are so heinous as to warrant censorship in our culture? Ms. Napolitano and the University of California provide a series of examples on the subjects of race, culture, and gender; however, the most telling are the following five expressions listed under the heading *Myth of Meritocracy*:

- "America is the land of opportunity."

- "Everyone can succeed in this society, if they work hard enough."

- "I believe the most qualified person should get the job."

- "Men and women have equal opportunities for achievement."

- "Gender plays no part in who we hire."[9]

These expressions plant an alluring trap for impressionable minds to follow down the rabbit hole of race and gender speculation. Before we eagerly run down this hole with torches and pitchforks, we should pause to first consider the greater meaning of this agenda. Take a second look over this list of "offensive" expressions. What is the foremost group of people that find these comments offensive? Blacks? Hispanics? Women? Homosexuals?

No, no, no, and no.

The group of people taking greatest offense to these axioms are the progressives. The most poisonous idea to a progressive is the notion that individuals can achieve success of their own volition. Meritocracy is thus presented as a myth because the concepts of self-determination, enterprise, innovation, ambition, and individualism are the kryptonite of the kingdom of man. The notion that people might not need the mighty arm of government for personal empowerment launches a dagger at the heart of the secular worldview; for this reason, it must be suppressed. Launching a university-wide initiative to inculcate the student body on the threats of microaggressions creates a new denomination of secularism tasked with regulating independent thought. The University of California is aided in its discipleship efforts by state university systems in New Hampshire, Wisconsin, Missouri, and North Carolina, just to name a few. [10,11,12,13,14] Efforts to promote victimhood, lawlessness, unaccountability, and cultural emasculation now permeate the American system of higher education, all in the name of progress. At our current pace, it will not be long until every freshman visiting student registration on their first day of college will be provided with an individual identification card and personal license to be offended. Do these trends better prepare students for a real or abstract world?

Perhaps in a move "triggered" by these cultural developments, the University of Cincinnati announced a new policy directive in the summer of 2016 to pioneer new paths on the road to idealism.[15] Beginning in July, its own website reports the university will now require a diversity and inclusion statement from all applicants seeking employment within the school network. Every new job application at the university will now pose the following question to aspiring candidates:

"[How do] your qualifications prepare you to work with faculty, staff and students from cultures and backgrounds different from your own?"

Historic American culture featured a tradition of asking citizens to hold their right hand on the Bible only when absolutely necessary. This practice was typically limited to the court of law when resolving disputes. In nearly all other cases, people would simply assume virtue and honor from their fellow man, presumably to promote a culture of trust and unity across the land. Juxtapose this custom with the emerging tradition of demanding a diversity pledge as a basic precondition of employment. Could there possibly be any more incriminating evidence that thought falls outside of the provisional scope of diversity? The administrators are basically shouting, *"If you refuse to kneel before our Asherah pole of sight-based diversity, then you have no place here in our establishment!"*

Studying history and the current university climate certainly raises a series of red flags in the realm of free speech. Nevertheless, these analyses cannot form a completely unqualified opinion that free speech is under assault due to the reliance upon deductive reasoning. Simply stated, any erroneous deductions in our cognitive process would threaten the validity of drawn conclusions. To eliminate this weakness, we must label our findings using the "preliminary" label while we seek alternative sources of information to solidify our position. To calculate whether the abolition of free speech might not just be achievable, but in fact probable, we need to develop an appreciation for modern judicial philosophy using the words of our judges. The best method of determining the true intent of the heart is through an evaluation of the spoken words. As Jesus spoke in Luke 6:45,

> "A good man brings good things out of the good stored
> up in his heart, and an evil man brings evil things out

of the evil stored up in his heart. For the mouth speaks what the heart is full of."

Our survey may just reveal that the only tolerance they truly seek manifests itself in the form of an orthodox conformity, a standard that cannot be achieved without the suppression of speech.

To understand how progressives can perceive free speech as a threat, we must return to their system of values. As explained in chapter two, the statist believes that human nature can be perfected, leading to the deliverance of heaven on earth in the form of a secular utopia. This philosophical worldview is wholly rejected, even pitied, by the two most influential texts shaping the United States of America: The Holy Bible and the United States Constitution. The first recognizes man's essential need for a Savior due to his inherently sinful nature, while the latter establishes a separation of powers to protect the basic rights and liberties of the people. For these reasons, their influence must ultimately be eliminated since they only serve as a barrier to secular progress. Historical texts that best address the brokenness of man have no value in our brave new world because they pose a direct threat to this core belief structure. The reader must grasp that this is the reason why fully devoted progressives have committed to this process of patient insurrection. As an aside, it also explains why the #AmericaWasNeverGreat hashtag was able to trend so easily on Twitter *on Independence Day* in 2016.[16]

Today, we find ourselves at a turning point. Now that the leaders of the kingdom of man have concluded that the evangelistic efforts of our cultural institutions have converted a sufficient volume of disciples to join their movement, political elites are comfortable turning up the pressure dial on the dwindling number of adherents to an antiquated religious worldview. While branding continues to make heavy use of catchy buzzwords like *tolerance, inclusion,* and *diversity,* a new condescension is emerging to expose the true thoughts that lie behind the jaded curtain of progressivism.

There is always a liberating joy in sharing a closely-held worldview without fear of reprisal. When the influence of the Bible and US Constitution were strong, a primarily secular worldview was not quite embraced by the general public with open arms. Now that the influence of these documents is waning and they can sense the finish line, statists are becoming quite evangelical in expressing their hostility to the old guard.

Richard Posner provides a compelling example of this modern evangelism. Mr. Posner is a highly educated judge on the United States Court of Appeals for the Seventh Circuit in Chicago, and he also functions as a Senior Lecturer at the University of Chicago Law School. He recently offered a "naked and without shame" view of his appreciation for our nation's founding documents:

> I see absolutely no value to a judge of spending decades, years, months, weeks, day, hours, minutes, or seconds studying the Constitution, the history of its enactment, its amendments, and its implementation (across the centuries—well, just a little more than two centuries, and of course less for many of the amendments). Eighteenth-century guys, however smart, could not foresee the culture, technology, etc., of the 21st century. Which means that the original Constitution, the Bill of Rights, and the post–Civil War amendments (including the 14th), do not speak to today.[17]

One has to wonder if Mr. Posner, a 77-year-old man, ever paused to consider the irony of suggesting that the value of old perspectives gradually lose their relevance over time solely on account of age. Nevertheless, his flagrant and blatant disregard of the Constitution is irreconcilable to the judicial oath he swore to uphold pursuant to Title 28 of the United States Code (28 U.S. Code § 453) prior to assuming his position. By attesting that the original Constitution, Bill of Rights, and amendments "do not speak to today," we can begin to appreciate how displacing God for the "wisdom" of the world inevitably lays the foundation for totalitarian style governance that can only deliver slavery upon the people. In this instance, we find a high-ranking judge explaining that the basic rights of free speech, a free press, the freedom to assemble, the freedom of religion, and the freedom to petition have no place in modern culture. And this is just the first amendment!

Our "enlightened" society now depends on the services of Mr. Posner, and other such judges who are openly hostile to the foundation of American law, to prudently administer justice. He and his ilk would be much more comfortable hurling our principal governing documents into the dustbin of history, and this process necessarily entails the rejection of free speech as a basic human right. What could possibly be the true motives of people who consider this to be progress?

Progressivism has systemically injected a judicial poison into American culture that is spreading like wildfire. The words of Mr. Posner on the Seventh Circuit Court in 2016 and the Ninth Circuit Court's 2005 decision to ultimately deny parental rights (as noted in chapter four) are not isolated departures from an otherwise reliable system of justice. They are the ideas and values cementing the foundation of a new justice system grounded in partiality and perversion.[18] This poison has even reached the Supreme Court of the United States. When pressed for her opinion on which influences the Egyptian people should consider while the country experienced great unrest in 2012, the governing documents Justice Ruth Bader Ginsburg most highly praised were not those of her own country that she has sworn to protect. Instead, she offered the following remarks:

> You should certainly be aided by all the constitution-writing that has gone on since the end of World War II. I would not look to the U.S. Constitution, if I were drafting a constitution in the year 2012. I might look at the constitution of South Africa. That was a deliberate attempt to have a fundamental instrument of government that embraced basic human rights, had an independent judiciary. . . It really is, I think, a great piece of work that was done. Much more recent than the U.S. Constitution—Canada has a Charter of Rights and Freedoms. It dates from 1982. You would almost certainly look at the European Convention on Human Rights. Yes, why not take advantage of what there is elsewhere in the world?[19]

Ms. Ginsburg provides two unique illustrations of disdain with these statements. First, she showcases the compulsory degree of self-absorption we should come to expect from a post-Constitutional Supreme Court Justice. Echoing Mr. Posner, she seemingly discards all human history leading up to the moment of her birth with a mystifying enthusiasm. By using this new lens, Ms. Ginsburg regards the distant annals of history as irrelevant to any problems we may experience in modern times. This is a devastatingly narcissistic perspective of human history that arguably constitutes a return to the days of Galileo. Just as the religious leaders of his day believed the sun revolved around the earth, modern political leaders believe the greater human experience revolves around the current generation. This is another of the many heretical positions of the secular church. Just as the earth revolves around the sun, a healthy appreciation of times gone by affirms that the current generation is merely orbiting the timeless sphere of human history.

Secondly, and perhaps of greater importance, her disdain puts forth an illusory comfort that we have simply evolved beyond the oppressive regimes that litter the chronicles of history. Academia has already taken the baton from the hands of the politician in this process by overhauling the curriculum of history at all levels of education. There is no value in history considering that progressives believe every step taken under their watchful eye represents a step forward in the human experience. If we are always "moving forward," looking into the rearview mirror provides no value. But how can this be possible when they reject the overarching authority of God? Every step "forward" is actually a step taken away from God and toward the unforgiving bayonet. History has already foretold the story! Has not this exact episode already been chronicled in the twelfth chapter of Ezekiel?

> "The word of the Lord came to me: 'Son of man, you are living among a rebellious people. They have eyes to see but do not see and ears to hear but do not hear, for they are a rebellious people'" (Ezek. 12:1–2).

An increasing number of judges have joined the swelling ranks of rebellious people who lack sight in our day. These hordes include central planners, administrators, and bureaucrats who possess a haste and zeal to write new rules and regulations to control nearly every aspect of basic human interaction. While they hold a rigid adherence to a technical architectural plan, they simply cannot see that they are methodically following the blueprint leading to the construction of a rudimentary weathervane. This mechanical device is unquestionably the most politically expedient instrument accessible to the statist. If all of human history revolves around our generation, it is quite useful to first know the direction in which the wind is currently blowing. If the reader will entertain an irresistible digression, it only makes sense that a world so enamored with the creation of a weathervane would become so obsessed with climate change.

While traditional weather patterns may have changed little over the years, the intellectual and political climates now blow a fierce secular wind through the culture. There is mounting evidence that these winds have infected the respiratory system of our judiciary. How else can we explain the following events? In 1996, the Bill Clinton administration enacted the Defense of Marriage Act (DOMA) with veto-proof support from both houses of Congress, legally defining marriage as the union of one man and one woman.[20] Just seventeen short years later, in the face of strong headwinds, the weathervane on the high court accurately identified the secular desire for gay marriage and overturned DOMA to redefine the institution principally responsible for supporting nearly all civilized societies for thousands of years.[21]

In addition to rejecting traditional marriage, the federal government also opted to reject its most elemental purpose of protecting citizens from invasion. When the state of Arizona attempted to take action to address the incessant influx of foreign trespassers in 2010, federal legislators quickly mobilized to side with the infiltrators by filing a lawsuit against the state.[22]

Lastly, our unsophisticated weathervane cannot even differentiate between an actual wind gust and the full-throated exhale of one influential person. Despite handling our nation's most confidential documents with reckless abandon, Attorney General Loretta Lynch appeared to collude with the husband of presidential candidate Hillary Clinton less than one week before she was ultimately exonerated of any criminal charges by the head of the Federal Bureau of Investigation.[23]

These episodes are covered in biblical significance. They reveal that our system of justice is unduly influenced by the impulses of the crowd . . .

> "Do not follow the crowd in doing wrong. When you give testimony in a lawsuit, do not pervert justice by siding with the crowd" (Exod. 23:2).

shows partiality to the wealthy . . .

> "Do not pervert justice; do not show partiality to the poor or favoritism to the great, but judge your neighbor fairly" (Lev. 19:15).

and ignores its basic purpose of punishing those who seek evil . . .

> "For the one in authority is God's servant for your good. But if you do wrong, be afraid, for rulers do not bear the sword for no reason. They are God's servants, agents of wrath to bring punishment on the wrongdoer" (Romans 13:4).

Psalm 82 explains that defending the unjust and showing partiality to the wicked is evidence of a people wandering about in darkness displaying a total lack of understanding. On the contrary, the university network, media, and Washington elites suggest that these judicial inclinations are evidence of progress.

To whom shall we listen? Would it be wise to side with those defending the position that there is nothing new under the sun, and our current generation revolves around the greater human experience? Or should we embrace the progressive mindset that holds that every generation represents a new center of the universe, even though there are no less than five active generations cohabitating today? The most basic measures of rational honesty and intellectual objectivity would identify the logical paradox inherent to the latter viewpoint. If the ultimate aim was to maliciously divide the society, this would be a pretty good philosophy with which to start.

Learning opportunities tend to reside at the intersection of competing world views, and we have a lot to learn from the actions of political officials when the only variable impeding their progress is a dusty, 2,000-year-old book. One such opportunity surfaced in the city of Houston, Texas. In May of 2014, the city passed an ordinance known as the Houston Equal Rights Ordinance (HERO).[24] Seemingly not content with Title VII of the Civil Rights Act of 1964, which made it an illegal practice for any American business to discriminate based on race, color, religion, national origin, sex, or pregnancy, HERO added the following eight characteristics as additional discriminatory protections to its residents: ethnicity, familial status, marital status, military status, disability, genetic information, *sexual orientation,* and *gender identity* (emphasis mine). The initiative was spearheaded by openly-gay Mayor Annise Parker, who confessed in an interview upon passage that "this has been on (her) to-do list for a long time."[25] Perhaps in anticipation of the backlash from the faith community, religious organizations were provided a specific exemption due to the conflicts HERO would present to their central faith tenets. This exemption was codified in Section 17–54 of the ordinance.

City officials began to feel the extreme heat of political pressure shortly after passage of the measure, and their subsequent actions speak volumes of their concern for our basic civil liberties. Less than two months following approval (and presumably to the chagrin of many Yale students), conservative groups and faith leaders exercised their right to petition, collecting over 50,000 signatures in an effort to bring the matter to a referendum for a potential repeal vote. The matter quickly became a legal affair when city officials challenged the integrity and validity of the signatures, and at this juncture, the two most pivotal city officials mistakenly revealed an ephemeral glimpse of their scorn for basic First Amendment rights.

In October of 2014, attorneys representing the city of Houston issued subpoenas to five local pastors who were involved in encouraging people to sign the petition.[26] Aside from this completely legal undertaking, the pastors were otherwise detached from the lawsuit. The subpoenas were seeking "all speeches, presentations, or sermons related to HERO, the Petition, Mayor Annise Parker, homosexuality, or gender identity."

The subpoena represented a blatant disregard of the freedoms of speech and religion; nevertheless, the city's senior legal officials, Attorney David Feldman and Mayor Parker, appeared to fully endorse these overstepping efforts in separate remarks. Mr. Feldman told reporters, "If someone is speaking from the pulpit and it's political speech, then it's not going to be protected."[27] Mayor Parker provided the following comment on her Twitter account: "If the 5 pastors used pulpits for politics, their sermons are fair game."[28] Within twenty-four hours, she walked back the demand for the sermons, but she will never be able to retract the raw emotions of her heart.

These comments prove that in at least this instance, those in search of social justice can act with surprising haste on their temptation to suspend the basic First Amendment rights of their own townspeople for the "greater good" of advancing a secular narrative. Rescinding the liberty of thought and speech is a predictable example of the wrath of the false gods of tolerance and inclusion. The referendum vote ultimately repealed HERO in a landslide vote in November of 2015, despite supporters outspending dissenters by a roughly four-to-one margin.[29] For the moment, religious liberty scored a brief victory in the city of Houston; however, this victory will prove to be short-lived. To understand why, we will need to turn our attention to the missing ingredient in the grand progressive recipe. Unusual as it may seem, the best way to search for traces of apathy among Christians is through an inquiry of our system of representative government.

The political representative is the most mistreated profession in America. There is currently nothing more fashionable in our culture than placing the blame upon these delegates for all of society's ills. When we grieve over the actions of our representatives, though, we tend to conveniently overlook their essential job function. Plain and simple, our elected officials exist to represent who we are and provide a proxy vote to save us the time and effort of constant policy engagement. Thus, when we choose to lament the current state of affairs by castigating our politicians, what we are essentially doing is rebuking ourselves indirectly since our policymakers are merely doing what we likely would do if we held office.

Who can allege that our elected officials are not fulfilling their respective roles with craftsman-like precision? Can the majority of believers honestly make the claim that there is a material difference between how they are working to rectify our cultural problems and what their representatives are doing on a grand scale in Washington? According to a recent Forbes study, over half of Americans are living paycheck to paycheck and have less than $1,000 in cash on deposit at the bank.[30] Due to this financial pressure, we have developed a tendency to check our faith at the door, since speaking out at work could expose us to termination. When we are asked to engage a new business practice that places us in an ethical quandary, we have grown inclined to silence our dissent since we have mortgages to pay and mouths to feed at home. If this is how we handle ourselves privately, why should we expect a different public behavior from our politicians? We are only tasked with managing the affairs of one house, whereas they are expected to oversee the management of entire subdivisions, cities, counties, and states. If we lack the ability to face the pressure on a small scale, doesn't it stand to reason that the pressure would only mount for our representatives considering the magnitude of their responsibility?

When presented with an opportunity to take a stand for their faith, our politicians are predisposed to cave to financial pressures in the greater pursuit of job preservation because this is *precisely how we act* in our private lives. It is quite insincere to chide them when they mirror our behaviors by checking their faith at the door of the House or Senate.

Recent polls bring these tendencies to life. As recent as December of 2015, Gallup reported that Congress possessed a 13 percent approval rating.[31] Since the beginning of 2010, this rating has ranged as low as 9 percent to as high as 24 percent. In other words, for the last five years, greater than three in four Americans have consistently disapproved of how Congress handles its job. That piece of news is unsurprising. However, were you also aware that a January 2015 study by Pew Research found that Christians comprised roughly 92 percent of the then-current 114th session of Congress?[32] When polls reveal that only one-in-eight Americans finds favor with Congress, couldn't this poll double as a metric to measure how satisfied Christians are with the effectiveness of the church? If our representatives are a reflection of who we are, and 92 percent of them are Christian, isn't this the logical conclusion?

By now, the far-reaching implications of adamantly refusing to integrate our faith should be quite evident. Not only does it impair our personal spiritual growth, but it also constricts the growth of our nation due to our system of representative government. Remember that the pendulum of earthly authority never lies motionless in a culture. If we are not actively moving in the direction of God, and we most certainly are not, then we must then be gravitating toward the supremacy of the state. To understand how compartmentalizing our faith can have damaging consequences, we need only study the religious freedom restoration bills that surfaced in nearly half of our states in recent years. Reviewing the circumstances and results of a handful of these bills will help harden this point.

Arizona lawmakers passed Senate Bill 1062 in February of 2014, amidst a national climate featuring a growing number of lawsuits being filed against bakeries, photographers, caterers, and other businesses that typically provide wedding services.[33] Legal action was being brought upon a small number of these enterprises when they would decline the option to provide services for gay and lesbian weddings. Anticipating that the religious freedom of these types of businesses within the state of Arizona would soon come under attack, the state legislature passed a bill to ensure that people of faith would essentially not be sued for refusing to violate their religious beliefs.

Over the ensuing five days, the state came under intense political and financial pressure as a result of the bill.[34] A group of eighty businesses issued a letter to Governor Jan Brewer with the hyperbolic threat that the legislation would "haunt [the] business community for decades to come" if it were to pass. The businesses included major international corporations such as Marriott, PetSmart, American Airlines, and Intel. The board of the Hispanic National Bar Association unanimously voted to relocate its annual convention from Phoenix to Boston the week following the passage of the bill. The National Football League issued an ominous statement regarding the upcoming 2015 Super Bowl, which was already scheduled to take place in Glendale, Arizona. Major League Baseball even decided to weigh in with their opposition.

If we faced this type of financial pressure in our personal lives, how would we respond? For Ms. Brewer, she was threatened with the potential loss of millions of dollars of revenues for her state. In the face of this pressure, she elected to veto the bill within seven days of its passage by the state legislature.[35] In public remarks to the media, she explained that the bill provided "the potential to create more problems than it purports to solve. It could divide Arizona in ways we cannot even imagine and no one would ever want." The Arizona religious freedom bill failed to pass the governor's desk.

Soon after this defeat, religious freedom traveled to the crossroads of America, otherwise known as the state of Indiana. The circumstances and setting were almost identical to those of Arizona; however, in this instance then-Governor Mike Pence signed his legislature's Religious Freedom Restoration Act (RFRA) into law on March 26, 2015.[36] In signing the bill, Pence shared the following remarks, "Today I signed the Religious Freedom Restoration Act, because I support the freedom of religion for every Hoosier of every faith. The Constitution of the United States and the Indiana Constitution both provide strong recognition of the freedom of religion but today, many people of faith feel their religious liberty is under attack by government action."

Within seven days, Pence and his state came under a barrage of national media attention, the majority of which painted the state as unwelcoming, culturally backward, and divisive. Some outlets branded the action as an invitation to discriminate. As was the case with Arizona, the state faced the potential loss of substantial revenue from businesses warning that they planned to either boycott the state or relocate existing conferences.[37] The NCAA President Mark Emmert noted his board was "gonna (sic) have to evaluate" its future in context with the new law. The American Federation of State, County and Municipal Employees (AFSCME) announced they had pulled their 2015 Women's Conference out of the state. The spokesman for the official tourism site of Indianapolis said his agency received 800 emails from people saying they planned to cancel their future travel plans to Indiana. The dispute became so unbridled that the credit rating company Moody's noted it was a "negative credit development" for the finances of both Indiana and its capital city of Indianapolis. Even the Disciples of Christ denomination threatened to relocate its annual conference!

Facing this extreme backlash, Governor Pence and the state legislature completely reversed the direction in a remarkable capitulation to the homosexual lobby. Pence signed an amendment into law just one week later that prohibited businesses from using the new law as a legal defense for refusing to provide goods or services. It also forbade any discrimination based on sexual orientation or gender identity.[38] In other words, the amendment placed the new RFRA in direct contravention to the First Amendment right to freely exercise religion.

The third highly publicized pit stop for religious freedom reached Georgia in February of 2016. This state's house passed the bill in a unanimous vote of 161–0 before the senate made a minor adjustment to include what was termed the "Pastor Protection Act."[39] This latter initiative provided pastors with the legal ability to refuse to perform same-sex weddings if they conflicted with their religious beliefs. After the bill's passage in the state senate and before any action could be taken by Georgia Governor Nathan Deal, the state came under fierce pressure from multi-billion dollar companies such as The Home Depot, Coca-Cola, Delta, and the National Football League.[40]

In the face of this pressure, Governor Deal elected to veto the bill[41]. In public remarks shared with the media, he explained that the bill "doesn't reflect the character of our state or the character of our people." There is a profound truth in Mr. Deal's statement, since there is little evidence to support that the general public will stand for their faith regardless of consequence. Does his decision not make complete sense when considering his role is to represent the *will* of the people?

Arizona Governor Brewer, Indiana Governor Pence, and Georgia Governor Deal all vetoed these religious freedom bills. These three Republican governors attend Lutheran, Baptist, and evangelical churches, respectively. Despite our more-than-vocal allegations and disparagements, their vetoes do not render them cowardly or hypocritical . . . they make us cowards! Our governors are doing precisely what we elected them to do. If we fail to stand for our beliefs in the workplace to save a $50,000-per-year job, why would we expect our governors to stand for religious freedom when faced with millions of dollars of lost tax revenue? We have not given them the strength and protection necessary to enable them to take a bold stance for their faith in government.

Voting new people into office isn't going to solve the problem. Until we choose to live our faith, we should continue to expect attacks on our precious First Amendment rights. This is why our leaders take no action to hold any senior members of the Internal Revenue Service accountable for its disgraceful targeting of no less than 466 independent conservative groups during an election year.[42] Progressives have every intention of supplanting the authority of God with their chosen high priests of secularism, and Christians have only emboldened them by relaxing their calling to prioritize their faith through every facet of their lives.

Jesus explained that Christians are the salt of the earth, but he provided a frightening warning immediately following this assertion: a salt that loses its saltiness is no longer good for anything except to be thrown out and trampled underfoot.[43] Jesus never minced his words. The whole purpose of salt is to preserve, and if we lack the stamina to preserve our rights to speech, assembly, and religion, then they must similarly be thrown to the ground and trampled underfoot. The overwhelming evidence documented throughout this book confirms that progressives would like nothing more! When (not if) the First Amendment finally gets repealed, the party to hold culpable will be the Christian community of believers!

Whether the true reason is financial pressure or something else, progressives sense a general apathy from the faith community and they are seizing upon the opportunity. When the kingdom of man is determined to usurp God as the ultimate supplier of human rights, and the Christian community has rationalized away the central tenets of the faith, that which was once eternal now becomes perishable. The First Amendment must be annulled for the crime of interfering with human progress.

Let's conclude the chapter by examining a piece of ripened judicial fruit. Every action has purpose, and we should not overlook the meaning of the littlest of measures when attempting to truly understand the authenticity of modern judicial perspective. How has our system of justice "evolved" to preserve its relevance within the culture? Within mere hours of the Supreme Court's ruling in favor of gay marriage in June 2015, the Obama administration illuminated the White House in rainbow colors to rejoice over the most significant secular achievement of the decade.[44] The immediacy of the action proved that it was a premeditated effort to electrify the emotions of secular disciples across the land as well as inspire those beyond our shores. Contrast this unsolicited response from the White House to one that was specifically besought just over one year later. Following an ambush that left five police officers dead in Dallas, Texas, the Federal Law Enforcement Officers Association asked the Obama administration to illuminate the White House in blue.[45] This request was made to honor the lives of these members of law enforcement who dedicated their lives to preserving law and order in their local community. The request was rejected by the administration, with the official spokesman blithely explaining that it was simply *"not something we plan to do at this point."*[46]

While this juxtaposition should forewarn anyone desirous of a civil society, it is important to recognize that these are simply the defiled fruits of an entangled system of justice. When those 56 signers of our Constitution entered the labor and delivery unit of that stuffy Philadelphia State House in 1787, their exhaustive efforts produced the first blind judicial system in the history of the world. The miraculous conception of the Supreme Court and the White House was only made possible by the heavy Christian influence upon eighteenth-century colonial America. At birth, these two separate branches of government were deeply rooted in a system of biblical justice. Today, these entities wholly reject their natural birth identity. Instead, they express their new judicial proclivities in the form of an evolved social fairness doctrine that disproportionately administers justice in accordance with an arbitrarily tiered class system.

If the Supreme Court and the White House were born of biblical justice but now identify as social justice warriors, wouldn't we expect these transjudicial activists to redefine their own purpose for existence? Who can feign astonishment now that these entities have chosen to carry the torch for those individuals who also reject their God-given identities? Might this be precisely the same legal framework encountered by Jesus Christ during his ministry when he spurred the following admonition in the eleventh chapter of the Gospel of Luke?

> "Woe to you experts in the law, because you have taken away the key to knowledge. You yourselves have not entered, and you have hindered those who were entering" (Luke 11:52).

When the primary adviser of the high court becomes the weathervane of popular opinion, tranquility must be uprooted since the preservation of law and order becomes a matter of secondary importance. Once a society becomes indifferent to its own tranquility, it soon ceases to be a society.

EIGHT

The Cancer of Redemptive Utilitarianism

*I know your deeds, that you are neither cold nor hot.
I wish you were either one or the other! So, because
you are lukewarm – neither hot nor cold – I am
about to spit you out of my mouth.*

~ Revelation 3:15–16

There is little value to a farmer whose proficiency is limited to assessing the quality of fruit growing in the garden. Even a child is equipped with this rudimentary skill set. If the farmer indeed lacks any ability to appraise the health of the embedded root structures or the overall quality of the topsoil, he is of little use to the plantation. In a similar fashion, this book is meaningless without an assessment of the root cause of our rotting cultural institutions.

Thus far, the previous five chapters have merely identified that our societal produce contains a disproportionate amount of spoilage that has tainted our overall harvest. Sadly, we have painfully observed scientific progress stagnating, schools developing into sanctuaries of secular thought, illusions becoming reality, future generations relapsing, and the court system increasingly opting to legislate the tyranny of the mob.

This cultural spoilage is hardly the *cause* of our national decay; rather, it is the *effect* of a more significant concern buried deep within our root structure. I am quite certain that when presented with a tree that produces rotted fruit, the average American would consider it foolish to apportion blame upon the fruit. Academically, we can accept this as a given; however, when the time comes to apply this principle, why then does the average American reflexively do just that?

Everything that is wrong with our country comes straight out of Washington, DC! It's those awful Democrats! It's the spineless Republicans! Occasionally, we place blame upon entire generations, despite the fact that they have never held public office, led a business, or developed any form of public policy. It's those entitled Millennials! We even shamefully cast all of our condemnation upon the shoulders of a man. It's all Barack Obama's fault!

It is not the culture that drives the church; it is the church that drives the culture.

The silence of Christians and church leaders has directly led the general public to embrace a worldview that is progressively more secular and narcissistic in nature. Those who have not welcomed Jesus Christ into their hearts, whether acting as individuals or as part of a larger group, have little to do with the problem, as they simply represent the fruit of the relapsed application of our faith.

To dive into the actual root structure of our problem, we only need to dive into the Gospel of Jesus Christ. His words from John 15 provide the true wellspring of enlightenment, and they fully explain why our cultural institutions are in a critical state of collapse:

> "I am the vine; you are the branches. If you remain in me and I in you, you will bear much fruit; apart from me you can do nothing. If you do not remain in me, you are like a branch that is thrown away and withers; such branches are picked up, thrown into the fire and burned" (John 15:5–6).

Simply put, our culture has become a living example of why faith without works is dead. We have plunged into the abyss of darkness because we have voluntarily separated ourselves from the one true vine. When a culture withholds the teachings of Jesus Christ from its people, the eradication of civility soon becomes its sole accomplishment. Even worse, it submits that the church in fact holds no love for Jesus Christ:

> "Jesus replied, 'If anyone loves me, he will obey my teaching. My Father will love him, and we will come to him and make our home with him. He who does not love me will not obey my teaching. These words you hear are not my own; they belong to the Father who sent me'" (John 14:23–24).

To truly understand the collapse of our cultural institutions, we have no choice but to cast our gaze upon the church. As exhaustively outlined in our previous chapters, these institutions are in complete shambles because of our voluntary departure from countless Scriptural truths, oftentimes in deference to our own understanding. Though it brings about great discomfort and can often be downright unforgiving, honestly assessing our cultural root structure through the piercing lens of self-reflection can explain why we are flirting with such perilous times. Could our swelling culture war be the result of a passively reticent church configuration that has become so narrowly focused on extending the grace of God that it has all but abandoned the truth that suffering is indispensable to the faith?

Rather than explain to our fellow man why faith without works is dead ("doing what is right"), many churches and Christians are merely diluting the Gospel with the foolishness of human understanding ("doing what is easy"). In the supposed name of compassion, a countless number of these believers oversell the message that salvation is completely devoid of personal responsibility. This message of "cheap grace" is embraced as the best way of shepherding the lost into the gates of heaven. In actuality, there could be no more effective strategy with which we can trigger our impending downfall.

In a desperate attempt to reach the unchurched, far too many pastors prepare Sunday services by formatting a square piece of scripture, not to fit reality, but to fit the round hole of the latest entertainment offering from the secular world. Developing a series of sermons around a culturally relevant illustration proves that even the church is not immune to the gravitational pull of the secular culture. By employing this approach, pastors use a piece of fiction as a spiritual icebreaker for visitors before preaching a message that typically consists of a creative adaptation to dangle the carrot of free grace before a culturally hypnotized unbeliever.

While these efforts may yield a handful of new attendees, the *exclusive* pursuit of this approach keeps the church mired in the everlasting purgatory of irrelevance for two reasons. First, in an attempt to woo what will likely be less than two percent of its daily congregants, these churches sacrifice the spiritual development of the remaining 98 percent. Sacrificing the spiritual growth of those most committed to advancing the Kingdom of God for the benefit of a small few who have a high probability of not returning the following Sunday sets the church on an unsustainable course. The undertaking institutes a platform of surface-level Christianity, a concept that frustrates deep-rooted evangelicals. Since this process overhauls a once healthy spiritual diet in favor of one wholly comprised of spiritual milk from a bottle, longstanding congregants begin to stagnate.

Over time, they gradually lose their fire and leave the church. These once hot members of the church are then replaced by new recruits who never progress beyond a lukewarm state due to the perpetual newborn diet. It is truly a tragic case of the church dousing its own fire in an attempt to retain a modicum of cultural relevance. The third chapter of the book of Revelation provides a pretty clear warning to any individual or group of believers pursuing this approach:

> "I know your deeds, that you are neither cold nor hot. I wish you were either one or the other! So, because you are lukewarm – neither hot nor cold – I am about to spit you out of my mouth" (Rev. 3:15–16).

More importantly, however, this watered-down ministry promotes latency as opposed to action. Slowly but surely, this process of lukewarming the church leads churchgoers to evangelize by using the phrase *look at what my church is talking about* rather than *look at what my church is doing.* By promoting these types of "series," the church becomes increasingly secular in nature, giving way to the rise of comfortable Christianity. This is the environment capable of producing the paralytic apathy necessary to completely ignore the demise of the culture transpiring beyond the safety of the church walls. The Gospel of Jesus Christ is not a call to the passivity of indifference; it is a call to action of love. The collective action of the church should not mirror that of the priest in the Parable of the Good Samaritan while our nation lays half dead on the side of the road.

Please do not misinterpret these words. Churches should absolutely evangelize the Gospel to the unchurched. These evangelistic efforts, however, should not be exclusively limited to, or measured by, increases in Sunday attendance. The American people are desperate to see the church and its parishioners taking bold and courageous actions in defense of their faith. Much like a child learns from his father through his actions, not by his words, this latter approach would win far more hearts into the kingdom, as we will further explore in our final chapter.

For now, we must appreciate that preaching the Gospel through a narrow window of personal salvation produces a harvest of millions of apathetic followers. When authentic Christianity is perverted to promote the new age philosophy of redemptive utilitarianism, believers become conditioned to discredit the value of repentance. But without repentance, there can be no Christianity. As it is written:

". . . unless you repent, you too will all perish" (Luke 13:5).

"I tell you that in the same way there will be more rejoicing in heaven over one sinner who repents than over ninety-nine righteous persons who do not need to repent" (Luke 15:7).

Using Jesus for salvation is no different than using a woman for sex or a man for money. Love does not make its dwelling within such selfish acts.

To fully grasp the egocentrism nurtured by this redemptive utilitarianism, reflect upon the spiritually backward solution being entertained by an increasing number of believers. The *Chicago Tribune* published an article in August of 2016 about the "American Redoubt," a term used to describe the survivalist flight of Christians and political conservatives to the American northwest. The first two paragraphs of the piece explain how a couple in their 60s cashed out of the stock market, invested in gold and silver, stockpiled food and ammunition, and retreated to several wooded acres in northern Idaho in fear of a total economic collapse. The couple, as well as the various other members of the "prepper" movement, plan to provide for each other as they attempt to insulate themselves from our country's deepening political, racial, and economic polarization.

Although the author of the article notes that the survivalists are "mostly Christian," there is nothing in the piece to suggest that his time spent with the survivalists had much of a life-changing impact. In fact, his concluding editorial remarks imply that he observed a complete oneness between the actions of the redoubters and the values of the world:

"What they have looks like an idyllic retirement experience: his and hers recliners in front of a big-screen TV, a 'side-by-side' all-terrain vehicle in the barn, an art studio for (the retired wife), a carpentry and machine shop for (the retired husband), and a sweet-natured dog named Moose."[1]

Could there be a better demonstration of lighting a lamp and then hiding it in a clay jar? Preparing for the coming tribulation by waiting to deploy a strategy of self-preservation is the exact opposite of what we should be doing to express our love for our fellow man! Have we been called to only care for likeminded individuals?

How's this for irony? The Emperor Nero is widely remembered for fiddling while Rome was burning, a historical event leading to the deaths of scores of Christians. Two thousand years later, scores of Christians are stockpiling and preparing only so they may sleep comfortably while America burns.

The survivalist movement represents one tactic to address the breakdown of our culture, but its structural flaw is that it seeks to save the individual by abandoning and disregarding the culture at large. A second approach is much more prevalent, pursuing an "inside the box" strategy by using the prescribed boundaries of a presidential election to restore the health of our culture.

In 2008, American voters were fleeced by a narcissist who carefully wrapped Marxist redistribution theory inside of a package promising "hope and change," completely outside the framework of a biblical worldview. As a nation, we embraced the direction and leadership of this man with open arms, so much so that his re-election in 2012 was hardly in doubt. What cultural legacy do we have to bequeath our children from these last eight years? Forsaking the Lord for the empty promises of the kingdom of man has greatly accelerated the erosion of our religious liberty, mandating us to purchase defective healthcare and punishing businesses who promote traditional marriage. It has greatly accelerated the erosion of our economic liberty by turning the Federal Reserve into a printing press, inflating the money supply by $3.6 trillion. It has even greatly accelerated the erosion of our security by exposing our military impotence for all of the world to see during the rise of the Islamic State. Of course, these are just the first fruits, and it is *far* from a comprehensive list!

Not surprisingly, Christians were quite eager to see the near despotism of Barack Obama come to an end. What was surprising, however, is who they flocked to as his replacement. The week after coronating him to the highest office in the land, Fox News reported that 81 percent of white evangelicals voted for Donald Trump.[2] Earlier during the primaries, every single state in the deep south, a region commonly referred to as the "Bible Belt," voted to nominate Trump as the Republican Party candidate. Mr. Trump is a man who has openly defended the right of women to murder living babies during the birthing process, has boasted about his adulterous relationships with married women, has mocked the disabled, and has admitted in an interview that he is unsure whether he has ever asked for God's forgiveness. During a campaign rally in Iowa, he bragged that he could shoot somebody in the middle of 5th Avenue in New York City, and he likely wouldn't lose any of his voting base.[3,4,5,6,7]

Donald Trump is a mirror image of Barack Obama. He is a man who carefully wraps authoritarianism inside of a package promising hope and change, completely outside the framework of a biblical worldview. In short, evangelicals have chosen to solve the problems of our day by replacing one deceitful narcissist with another, placing their utmost hope and trust not in God, but in man. His influential Christian supporters are so desperate to return the authority of the White House not to God but to the Republican Party, that they willingly overlook Trump's rejection of the core tenets of the faith.

Ann Coulter, a conservative author who has stated that Christianity fuels everything she writes, wrote a book entitled *In Trump We Trust* during the 2016 campaign season.[8] This book followed an earlier tweet in which she insinuated that her support for Trump was so fierce that she wouldn't care if he wanted to perform abortions in the White House.[9] Dr. James Dobson, an evangelical Christian and founder of Focus on the Family, formally endorsed Trump in July of 2016, touting his commitment to "defend the sanctity of human life."[10] Liberty University president Jerry Falwell Jr. compared Trump to his late father, a former Southern Baptist televangelist. In an interview with CNN's Erin Burnett the month before the election, Falwell casually dismissed serious allegations of Trump's sexual misconduct by explaining that the ethical character of a presidential candidate represented a "rabbit trail" in the electoral process.[11] In an incredible display of mental gymnastics, Mr. Falwell declared that words speak louder than actions by explaining that the candidates' stated positions on the issues are what the voters need to emphasize. Liberty University is the largest evangelical Christian university in the country. How can a man of his high position be so embarrassingly unaware of the following Scriptures?

"Dear children, let us not love with words or speech but with actions and in truth" (1 John 3:18).

"Not many of you should become teachers, my fellow believers, because you know that we who teach will be judged more strictly" (James 3:1).

Falwell, Coulter, and Dobson have each been blessed with a megaphone of influence in the community of believers, yet in their individual actions, these cultural shepherds are abusing their God-given platforms to lead many believers astray.

The technical term to define the strategy being employed by a countless number of evangelicals to address the issues of our day can be summed up in one word: *idolatry*. By lining up in droves to offer blind support to a man, especially one who has not shown any evidence of repentance or spiritual conversion, these believers are showing that this oldest plight facing humanity is alive and well.

More importantly, however, this sizable group of believers is seeking cultural restoration within the incredibly small box of the man-made election construct. This framework suggests that the portal for political engagement appears once every four years. All periods falling outside of this window denote times in which the portal is replaced by a grievance box. Once a presidential election concludes, Christians must then return to a three-and-a-half-year hibernation in which they sleep away their accountability until the reappearance of the portal of opportunity.

Far too many conservative Christians ascribe to the political portal theory. The 2016 presidential election cycle featured a #NeverTrump movement on Twitter, a concerted effort by a minority of Republicans and other conservatives to refuse to support Donald Trump purely on principal. These people were relentlessly attacked by the majority of party supporters on nearly all conservative media outlets, often being compared to petulant children. Longtime Republican party supporter Wayne Allen Root even suggested that #NeverTrumpers were traitors who would ultimately be responsible for ending America, capitalism, freedom, and their children's future. He went on to state that any Christian not voting for Trump is "either ignorant, delusional, or incredibly selfish with an ego so big (they) don't care about anyone but (themselves)."[12]

By demanding unity with a complete disregard to conscience, Mr. Root is among those holding a resolute faith that the only means to restore the country is through the narrow framework of an election cycle. What he fails to see is that changing our elected officials cannot ultimately solve the problem because these representatives are merely reflections of who we are. The proposed solution of simply voting a new person into office attempts to avoid the difficulties of both individual and societal reformation, choosing to instead outsource these responsibilities onto the shoulders of a third party. By penning such fear-laced rhetoric, it is hard not to conclude that the underlying purpose of this op-ed is to point a giant finger at a diminutive group of people as being responsible for what he believes will be the end of civilization.

Ascribing to the political portal theory is one of the greatest gifts conservative Christians can give to the state authority. The action shows that we are eager participants in the advancement of the separation of church and state fallacy. To borrow from a popular university trend, our behaviorisms are beginning to turn all periods falling outside of the quadrennial election cycle into a state-sponsored safe space that forbids political engagement. Just as the solution to our societal ills does not involve abandoning and disregarding the culture at large, it also does not include the mass transfer of our personal responsibility. Simply instilling new leadership will not magically restore the brokenness of the culture in any way, shape, or form. Can a house resting upon a cracked foundation be wholly repaired by applying a fresh coat of paint?

The world is embracing hybrid technology because this is precisely how the church has chosen to power and operate its engine within the culture. The church has essentially replaced the Gospel of Jesus Christ with a hybrid battery that figuratively disengages the engine of God when the culture encounters a sinful delicacy, choosing in these instances to operate on the man-made electricity of human compassion. Because we have all been given over to our sinful desires in one way or another, however, the church practically functions as an enabler of sin despite its best intentions!

As mentioned earlier in this chapter, American churches have soothed themselves into the assurance that the only worthwhile element of Christianity is grace. Instead of reshaping our values to conform to the biblical way of life, we have reshaped the biblical way of life to conform to our values. Rather than striving to convict the hearts of Christians to take up their cross, too many of our preachers instead promote a prosperity gospel advocating that the primary will of the Lord is for all believers to acquire material wealth and comfort. Others choose to ignore the wrath of God and turn hell into an allegorical fantasy, displaying a vulnerability to the thought that only an unjust God would employ such primitive punishment. These influences contribute to the concoction of a synthetic, false gospel that the grace of God is completely devoid of truth, repentance, personal responsibility, or any concern for our fellow man.

The North Raleigh Community Church epitomizes this synthetic, false gospel. NRCC brands itself as an unambiguously Christian church, and it primarily serves the inner-city residents of North Carolina's state capital. Like most churches, the organization publicly posts its statement of faith on its website.[13] This statement practically functions as an owner's manual to the twenty-first-century spiritual hybrid battery.

The very first paragraph openly confesses that the "(church) community isn't really organized around a set of doctrines we all believe." Church leaders profess to believe in Jesus and the Holy Spirit; however, the Bible is curiously omitted from the over 600-word summary of core beliefs. As a substitute, the church applies a mixture of ancient sacred texts, history, psychology, and science, in addition to "wisdom from our own time." As of January 2017, there were no scriptural references to be found anywhere on the site; however, there is a prominent reference to an ancient Zen proverb to stimulate reflection among the church community.[14]

NRCC's fifth core belief scandalously professes that "compared to the vastness of God's grace and forgiveness, sin is just not that big a deal." Naturally, there are no references to repentance, the fallen nature of man, his resultant need for a Savior, or the need to participate in the Great Commission. Even though the wages of sin is death,[15] the church simply cannot help but fall into the trap of acting as a modern-day Greek Siren to lure those in search of what certainly appears to be lifestyle validation and/or cheap grace.

Curiously, while the Bible was unable to attain the publicly esteemed status as a "sacred text" worthy of guidance and instruction, church leaders seem to have rolled out the red carpet for the values of the secular world. When documenting the history of the Christian church, its founders outline a litany of offenses to explain why "the Church had lost its moral authority." NRCC takes "Christian culture" to task by exposing its intolerance, hypocrisy, hatred, ignorance, sexual exploitation of children, financial exploitation of adults, antagonism toward science, and hostility to the LGBT and female communities.[16] As if this were not enough, they then add the catch-all bucket of "and a whole lot more" before pivoting to highlight their desire to reduce their environmental footprint.

Have you ever wondered why the tolerance and inclusion of the world tends to be intolerant and excluding of Christianity? When the church cannot tolerate the Gospel of Jesus Christ, neither will the culture. Remember, the church drives the culture. Think critically: is it possible for the national court system to turn into the weathervane of popular opinion without the church first paving the way through these types of downright rudderless value statements?

When the church preaches grace with no consideration to repentance, it is consciously electing to mirror the same strategy used by T-ball organizations to promote character development. Dispensing participation trophies, whether on the baseball diamond or in the church, artificially inflates the self-worth of the faith's youngest participants. When these little ones are brought to Christ not as a result of the impact the church is making in the community, but by the selfish promise of a free ticket into heaven, they tend to give no value to the thought of making subsequently uncomfortable adjustments to their sinful lifestyles. This is how the distribution of a heavenly participation trophy stunts the spiritual growth of a Christian in the same degree that a traditional participation trophy stunts the growth of an aspiring athlete. Both misrepresent the need for their participants to constantly refine their discipline through practice and hard work. In the majority of cases, the tragic result of this approach leads believers to fail to reach their full potential by encouraging them to breakdown at the first encounter of spiritual difficulty.

Hillsong Church has become one such printing press for spiritual participation trophies in America, and this cultural leviathan has a presence in three of our six largest cities. Since its founding, the strategic plan of Hillsong has been to target some of the world's largest cities by flagrantly catering to celebrities; conducting its services in a nightclub; having its pastors swagger to the stage in trendy outfits; integrating viral videos and photographs into their services; promoting a hip, concert-like ambiance in their church; and adopting a strategy of ethical neutrality to live in peace alongside those who have given over to their sinful desires.

Hillsong trumpets its statement of beliefs on its website, with the very first core belief stated as follows:

"We believe that the Bible is God's Word. It is accurate, authoritative and applicable to our everyday lives."[17]

Hillsong NYC Pastor Carl Lentz was given a remarkable opportunity to preach the Gospel of Jesus Christ before a national audience during an interview with Katie Couric in December of 2013.[18] During this interview, he quoted a grand total of zero scriptures, explained that his church is not about behavioral modification, and confessed that his church is not trying to change anybody. He further explained that "our church meets in a club because most people recognize the club."

When pressed lightly on the subject of homosexuality, Lentz put forth that "very rarely did Jesus ever talk about morality or social issues." These remarks were echoed by Hillsong Australia Pastor Joel Houston less than one year later, who stated that the subject of homosexuality is "too important for us just to reduce it down to a yes or no answer."[19]

In September of 2016, Lentz again offered a curious interpretation of Hillsong's foremost core belief. Taking to the Facebook wall of the church, he prominently explained that the church will not say "all lives matter" because "all lives are not at risk right now." Instead, the church would be touting that "BLACK LIVES MATTER" because "right now, black lives apparently are worth LESS on our streets."[20] (Capitalization copied from original posting). Lentz reveals his persuasion to relative truth through his use of the word *apparently*. If he would only consult the absolute truth of the Bible, he would understand why submitting to the cultural trade winds only leads to division. As it is written in Galatians 3:

> "There is neither Jew nor Gentile, neither slave nor free, nor is there male and female, for you are all one in Christ Jesus" (Gal. 3:28).

Judging by these two accounts, Lentz has no problem departing from the teachings of the Bible. And since he remains gainfully employed by the church, Hillsong apparently has no problem abandoning its core values. How can any pastor possibly suggest that all lives are not at risk of eternal damnation? Hebrews 4 explains that the actual word of God is sharper than any double-edged sword, penetrating to divide soul and spirit, joints and marrow. Shrewdly sensing that this sword could slice right through the vitality of the Hillsong business model, Lentz astutely elects to leave it in its sheath. Perhaps his decision is mindful of the billion-dollar record label held by parent company Hillsong Music Australia.[21] Regardless of the true reason, instances such as these explain how the church forsakes the wisdom of its elders to chase the aforementioned mirage of cultural relevance. There is little difference between this and a man leaving his wife of twenty years to pursue a relationship with a young woman. Regrettably, America has far too many examples of both such circumstances.

One of the shortest books in the Bible is the one-chapter book of Jude, and it is the final letter to the church before the book of Revelation. Proving that those ignorant of history are only doomed to repeat it, the fourth verse of this book could very well have been written about Christianity in twenty-first-century America:

"For certain men whose condemnation was written about long ago have secretly slipped in among you. They are godless men, who change the grace of our God into a license for immorality and deny Jesus Christ our only Sovereign and Lord" (Jude 4).

Might there be symbolism in Jude's placement in the Bible and where our culture finds itself today, teetering on the brink of complete collapse? The shape-shifting Christianity of cultural conformity promises personal salvation at the expense of total societal upheaval. Have we truly become this narcissistic?

While the influential purpose of the church has stagnated in the United States, the desired church growth resulting from our diluted message has completely vanished. In May of 2015, the Pew Research Center released a report entitled, "America's Changing Religious Landscape."[22] The publication indicts the church by simply partaking of its fruit. The findings show that believers are rapidly declining across every single demographic in our culture. For every new convert brought to Christianity, there are more than four that are choosing to leave the faith.[23] As a testament to our failure to pursue the biblical approach to parenting, Millennials (born 1981–1996) are three times more likely than the Silent Generation (born 1928–1945) to respond that they are unaffiliated with the Christian faith.

The Gospel of Jesus Christ changes individual hearts and minds to produce a greater degree of righteousness in the culture. With our spiritual results suggesting the contrary, the inescapable conclusion is that, broadly speaking, our churches have not been preaching the full Gospel of Jesus Christ. For this reason, it is the community of Christians who retains the exclusive culpability for the rampant turmoil and division we see permeating throughout our nation.

We must never forget that the best barometer of the effectiveness of the church is the overall health of the culture. The church does not make its dwelling within the constructed confines of a building (it lives within YOU), and church services are not limited to one hour per week (they are limited to 168). The church has not been called to preside over the death of the civil society as we rejoice over our individual salvation.

This has been a remarkably difficult and heartbreaking chapter to write, but I have penned these words with a steadfast love for the church, its pastors, and the American people. To stand behind this claim, let me now reveal how we can definitively break the chains that threaten American exceptionalism.

NINE

Uproot and Unite!

*"Comrades, don't take down our cross. I can give you
my head instead. Even if they take my head, I can
still find happiness with God!"*

~ Yang Zhumei

assive problems require massive solutions, and massive
solutions can only be achieved through massive
collaboration from a group of individuals who have
mutually pledged to restore a greater purpose in their lives by
enacting massively difficult personal lifestyle changes. To
understand the odds that lay before us, we need to consult and
develop an appreciation for the historical lifecycle of
civilization.[1] First deduced by the Scottish historian Alexander
Fraser Tytler, this sequence begins in the chains of bondage and

progresses through the following nine stages as listed in the following diagram:

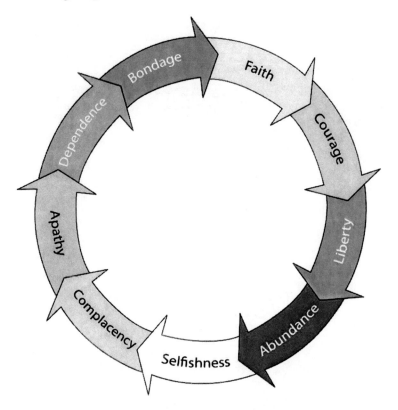

Tytler Lifecycle of Human Civilization

America is midway through the eighth step of this progression. Our apathy is best expressed by our ongoing tolerance of the Great American Holocaust, an active genocidal movement that has been *ten times as powerful* as the Jewish Holocaust during World War II. Not only is there no end in sight to this infanticide, but we have been idle bystanders while an open market has emerged to facilitate the buying and selling of these infant body parts. And what is one of the arguments used to attempt to justify these heinous crimes? *We can use the organs to broaden our understanding of science!*

Without any sense of shame, progressives attempt to hide their wicked exploits behind the same banner of science that they so steadfastly reject when it embarrassingly supports the divine hand of providence. In the name of this academically duplicitous research, the dean of the University of New Mexico School of Medicine recently admitted to allowing *high school students* to dissect the brains of aborted babies during a summer camp at the university.[2] The University of Minnesota has also openly admitted to using aborted babies to conduct "medical research."[3] Indiana University paid a price of $200 per infant brain to help develop medical treatments.[4] When this was discovered, the university countersued, claiming that the state's abortion restrictions threaten their "academic freedom" and risks stifling efforts to uncover treatment for neurological disorders.[5] Is there truly nothing that we will not tolerate as Christians?

Wake up, slumbering believer! Must you have no fear for the Lord? Do you not know that you will be held to account for the blood of the unborn? Unlike our worldly system of justice, the biblical standard of justice is resolute. The words of the prophet Ezekiel should resound an echo through every church, convicting the heart of every Christian:

> "When I say to a wicked person, "You will surely die,"
> and you do not warn them or speak out to dissuade
> them from their evil ways in order to save their life, that

wicked person will die for their sin, and I will hold you accountable for their blood" (Ezek. 3:18).

Having dismissed what can hardly be deemed fleeting remedies in our prior chapter, the time has come to define the literal calling of our generation and propose the actions necessary to heed this calling. Put simply, we are charged with determining the next stage in our lifecycle of human civilization. Of course, our current momentum and broader historical susceptibilities suggest that we will heedlessly transfer our people from apathy into the final stage of bondage. While this is undoubtedly the likely outcome, it is far from a certainty thanks to the grace and patience of God. The only absolute certainty at this point is that we will not remain in a state of apathy for long due to the fertility of our individual and cultural topsoil. Continuing to produce bad fruit will guarantee our slavery, but working to uproot the poisonous tree will begin to reverse the course. We cannot remain in the eighth stage because we are incapable of producing no fruit. This is how, even in our advanced state of depravity, God has so graciously given us the wherewithal to circumvent slavery.

Before we can even begin to formulate an action plan to sidestep the impending captivity, it is essential to comprehend the gravity of the task at hand. To emerge successful in our mission, not only will we have to prove ourselves to be an outlier in the annals of history, but we will also have to break a mold of human nature first demonstrated (and consistently revisited) by the Israelites throughout the Old Testament.

The biblical account that best illustrates what we are up against falls in the sixteenth chapter of the book of Exodus. At this point in their flight from slavery, the Israelites had just crossed the Red Sea, leaving the pursuing Egyptians drowned in the floodwaters behind them as they were on their way to the promised land. Naturally, the assembly immediately raised their voices in a song of celebration and thanksgiving to the Lord to commemorate the event. Not long thereafter, though, the gratitude quickly subsided as the community received their first test while wandering through the desert. At this juncture, the grumblings of the Israelites tell us everything we need to know about the basic human condition:

> "In the desert the whole community grumbled against Moses and Aaron. The Israelites said to them, 'If only we had died by the LORD's hand in Egypt! There we sat around pots of meat and ate all the food we wanted, but you have brought us out into this desert to starve this entire assembly to death'" (Exod. 16:2).

Barely six weeks had transpired since witnessing a miracle with their very eyes and receiving the blessing of freedom for the first time in 400 years, and the Israelites were already begging to be returned to the hands of their captors. And all because there was a temporary shortage of food and water. This account is a lesson on the default human condition, and the moral of the story is that human nature prefers slavery to faith.

I do not include this excerpt to discourage the reader, but rather to establish a baseline for understanding why the proposed solution must be revolutionary. If we were to be judged according to our instinctive tendencies and the greater human experience, slavery would be inevitable. For this reason, pursuing mainstream, conventional solutions, or making minor adjustments to our day-to-day routines will only assure our slavery. Similarly, submitting to the notion that we can each "right the ship" individually in our own lives, without giving consideration to our neighbors and fellow countrymen, will also only assure slavery. How, then, can we defy these massive headwinds and leapfrog the stage of bondage to safely return to the starting point of spiritual faith?

Devising a biblical solution for the problems of the modern era requires an understanding of the two enigmatic characteristics of a biblical solution: simplicity and difficulty. To address every multifaceted aspect of the human experience, the Old Covenant presented only ten affirmative commandments the Israelites were to obey. When the New Covenant expanded the eternal tent to include citizens of every nation, Jesus reduced this list to only two: love the Lord your God with all your heart and with all your soul and with all your mind, and love your neighbor as yourself.[6]

It is staggering to think only these two commandments separate us from prosperity and a civil society. Despite this simplicity, however, the executional degree of difficulty is so extreme that it prompted the late G. K. Chesterton to lament:

> "The Christian ideal has not been tried and found wanting; it has been found difficult and left untried."[7]

If the Bible is indeed absolute truth, and biblical solutions are grounded in simplicity and difficulty, then reason would dictate that the solution to our perils must be demanding despite a general lack of complexity.

To realize the fundamental restoration of America, Christians must satisfy two, and only two, affirmative directives:

1. Uniting the entire church community of believers to incorporate their faith into every aspect of their lives, no matter the cost; and,
2. Uprooting the suffocating weeds of secular influence in the culture.

If just the Christians of this land would commit to these two obligations, the ensuing conservation of the United States of America will go down in history as an even greater achievement than its initial founding. The odds are far steeper, since no civilization in the history of the world has demonstrated such an enlightenment as to skip the phase of slavery once progressing into the stage of cultural apathy. Lest there be any doubt of the truth of this declaration, we need only consult 2 Chronicles 7,

> "[I]f my people, who are called by my name, will humble themselves and pray and seek my face and turn from their wicked ways, then I will hear from heaven, and I will forgive their sin and will heal their land . . . "But if you turn away and forsake the decrees and commands I have given you and go off to serve other gods and worship them, then I will uproot Israel from my land, which I have given them, and will reject this temple I have consecrated for my Name" (2 Chron. 7:14, 19–20).

We are living in historic times, and though none of us has the opportunity to be a *founding* father or mother, the power to be a *resuscitating* father or mother rests within each of us. We must answer this call, for if we choose not to revitalize our culture, the conferral of slavery will be the legacy for which we will all have to give account on Judgment Day! Again, this slavery will be inescapable in the event we continue to enlist a divorced network of reticent churches to counter the unified secular front. Does a military general enter the battlefield using less than two percent of his resources? Why would we then think the coupling of a 90-minute Sunday service with a 90-minute midweek Bible study is sufficient to repel these forces of darkness? There are 168 hours in a week. How can we in any fashion preserve what we have so providentially inherited from the toil and faith of our progenitors by limiting our faith time commitment to merely three hours per week?

So what does this first component look like? How do we unite the church to stand on its convictions? The answer to these questions can be found in the part of the church in which the fire burns with the greatest intensity. In 2010, United States churches dispatched an estimated 127,000 missionaries, many to parts of the world whose central governments are openly hostile to the Gospel of Jesus Christ. One of these nations happens to be the largest atheistic country in the world, so it should come as no surprise that we would have to dig a metaphorical hole to China to comprehend the magnitude of our responsibility.[8]

Wenzhou is a city in southeastern China that has become known as the "Jerusalem of the East." The city is home to seven million residents, one million of which are Christians.[9] In 2007, Communist Party (CP) officials in this city approved the construction of the Sanjiang Church, an architectural project that was later lauded by officials as a "model engineering project." Since the date of this approval, however, the ongoing spread of Christianity throughout China has become so vibrant that CP officials have begun to subsequently pursue creative efforts to crackdown upon this troublesome spiritual influence.

Just as we have seen here in the United States, CP officials have concluded that the solution to their predicament lies within the governing framework of the legal system. I know . . . who could have seen that coming? The reason secular leaders have and will always continue to pursue this route is because, just like a dog hiding a bone, it permits them to submerge their accountability underneath the ever-mutating wisdom of the world. In this case, these leaders have attempted to clandestinely bury their actual national policy of church persecution behind a system of ambiguous stipulations buried within urban development and beautification laws. Sound familiar?

With Wenzhou standing as the Christian stronghold of mainland China, the CP has aggressively enforced its modified legal approach in this second largest city of the Zhejiang province. After receiving its initial approval, the Sanjiang church took six years and upwards of $5 million to complete, officially opening the doors in December of 2013. [10] Four short months following the grand opening, CP leaders mobilized under the orders of the central authority to demolish this now suddenly outmoded engineering project. How these Wenzhou Christians reacted to the persecution at the hands of their government is a lesson that American Christians must study and apply if we have any desire to save the future of our country.

In the days leading up to its scheduled demolition date, Bible-carrying believers encircled the church to protect it from oncoming bulldozers. The group of Christians included men and women, as well as the elderly and disabled. As the authorities descended on the church, Yang Zhumei, a 74-year-old Chinese woman, pleaded with these officials to leave the church alone. Holding their hands, she begged, "Comrades, don't take down our cross. I can give you my head instead. Even if they take my head, I can still find happiness with God!"

A second woman, Li Jingliu, echoed Yang's sentiments, "I will guard the church until the very end, without fearing hardship or death. God will punish those who try to take down the cross."[11]

Despite the impassioned actions of these and many other Wenzhou believers, the church was demolished on April 28, 2014.

The display represented a remarkable unification of the Christian community in defense of their faith. By joining in an effort to risk their precious lives to save the church, these believers sent a striking message to their central government that their faith is an immovable element of their moral fabric. But didn't they ultimately fail? By no means! Though the demolition was undeniably tragic, the fact that the church was demolished will do nothing to stifle the faith in the long run. As the apostle Paul wrote, the church is not merely a building in which likeminded believers congregate:

> "Don't you know that you yourselves are God's temple and that God's Spirit lives within you? If anyone destroys God's temple, God will destroy him; for God's temple is sacred, and you are that temple" (1 Cor. 3:16).

The message we must learn from our Wenzhou brethren is that the Christianity of conviction fuels rampant church growth. James Miller, a Professor of Chinese Religions at Queen's University in Canada, estimated that there were a total of 4 million Christians living in China at the time the CP rose to power in 1949.[12] Less than 70 years later, following courageous missionary efforts that have produced a community of fearless believers in the mainland, a recent article in *The Economist* estimated that the number of Christians living in China total upwards of 100 million as of November 2014.[13] In many instances, these believers convene in secret, underground churches, many of which are located in private homes just as in the days of the Acts of the Apostles. This dedication has resulted in numerous sources now projecting that China will be the largest Christian country in the world within ten to fifteen years.

This growth comes in the face of an undeclared governmental war on the faith. According to the International Christian Concern, a non-denominational organization committed to assisting persecuted Christians worldwide, CP officials and their supporters have already torn down 64 churches in the Zhejiang province as of May 2014.[14] The international non-profit Christian human rights organization, ChinaAid, reported that authorities dismantled 50 crosses in one day alone in Wenzhou, and another eighty-five house churches were warned to stop gathering or else face closure by the end of that same month.[15] This is just one province! Yet the Christian ranks continue to swell. Only when the people place their unwavering trust in the Lord can a peaceful group of non-combative Christians emerge victorious over a regime committed to the destruction of many of their houses of worship.

This achievement requires a deeper look inside the numbers to highlight the power of the Gospel of Jesus Christ. When the United States sent 127,000 missionaries into the world in 2010, this figure represented only 0.07 percent of its total number of Christian believers (using the Gallup estimate that 77 percent of American adults are Christian). This percentage reflects one out of every 1,422 believers. Keep in mind that not every one of these believers were directly sent into China, so the actual number is far smaller than this already miniscule percentage.

To echo the words of the Apostle Paul, do you not know that a little yeast leavens the whole batch of dough?[16] If the Lord can gradually convert the most secular, atheistic, and communist country in the world with less than seven hundredths of a percent of American Christians over the span of a couple of generations, could there be any limit to what he could do here if we would only awaken from our deep slumber? Of course, the United States is not the only country dispatching its Christian missionaries, but it is worth noting that the number sent in 2010 was nearly four times as high as the next highest country.

In China, the Christianity of conviction has led to exponential church growth, laying the groundwork for increased liberty for the people. As the nation has gradually begun to embed capitalistic principles into its economic policy, millions of Chinese people have been lifted out of extreme poverty. China has been the world's fastest-growing economy for several years in the past two decades. With respect to basic human rights, the central government formally ended its disastrous "one child policy"[17] in October of 2015. Can any free thinker reject the possibility that Christianity might just be the driving force behind these societal improvements?

Christian believers here in the United States must learn from their Chinese brethren. We must implore the church to reject its unintended role as an enabler to sin, and this undertaking requires the enlistment of all Bible-believing churches across the land. Evangelism is a struggle that is best accomplished by deploying a crowd of believers, not just one individual. As it is written in the fourth chapter of the book of Ecclesiastes:

"Two are better than one, because they have a good return for their labor" (Eccl. 4:9).

Mega churches that have been blessed with substantial financial resources must abandon the failed church model of empire building, branching, and evangelizing within established cultural norms. Instead, these larger churches should be targeting the nation's largest cities, leading massive efforts to end the abortion industry in America.

Abortion, in essence, is modern-day child sacrifice. As any student of history is well aware, child sacrifice represents the line of demarcation between cultures that are civilized or barbaric in nature. Its practice is generally limited to those cultures that either do not know or have wholly abandoned the ways of the Lord. Christians must understand that secular humanists view man (and woman) as the author, creator, and giver of life. This is the essential reason why child sacrifice has become the highest sacrament of a humanistic worldview. Preserving child sacrifice has nothing to do with anything other than the notion that man is god. Alas, child sacrifice (infanticide) is the most effective mechanism with which to promote narcissism and foster selfishness within a culture.

Ending abortion drives a stake right through the heart of secular humanism. Rather than sacrificing our children to a heathen world view, ending this barbaric custom would begin to sacrifice a heathen world view before our magnificent Creator. Putting an end to the abortion industry would represent a magnificent cultural pronouncement that we are indeed "one nation under God" and that we are turning from our sinful ways. It is the church and its followers that must take ownership of ending this wicked ritual. Only one thing is certain: abortion will never go away so long as we continue to outsource our responsibility to our politicians. As reflections of who we are, once we elect to outsource, so will they.

Again, the churches that have been blessed with the most abundant resources must spearhead the efforts to end barbarism in America. Is it any wonder that a culture that rejects the sanctity of life soon becomes a culture that dies a slow and painful death? This is the most important civil rights issue in the history of the United States of America. Slavery was a heinous evil, but at least slaves were granted the right to life.

Secondly, the church must reclaim its rightful ownership as the entity responsible for caring for the underprivileged. Expanding the healing influence of the church requires the active efforts of *all* believers. The current church model of a passive, culturally-relevant lecture series is meaningless if we refuse to first commit to these two greater missions.

The majority of church services should feature the active engagement of believers, in detached groupings, working tirelessly to construct living quarters and hospitals to provide transitional care for the sick, poor, and destitute. Other groups would be tasked with the construction of safe houses for unwed teenage girls who have fallen pregnant. With respect to the sermon, praise, and worship, these aspects would transpire on site. Through love and financial provision, these centers can counter the deplorable aims of the abortion lobby which suggest that unwed mothers should turn their wombs into private concentration camps for the unborn. This is how the church can reject the government's botched attempt to care for the underprivileged. The "exception" church service would be that which we are currently accustomed to, with the primary purpose of the engagement to provide a periodic progress report and realign participant groups to strengthen camaraderie.

Smaller churches would pursue similar goals, only channeling their efforts to suburban and rural parts of the country. These entities should unite with their neighboring churches to accomplish the same goals, with the understanding that infanticide is the most substantial civil rights issue since the enslavement of the Negro. These smaller churches most certainly should not be seeking to increase attendance without regard to these neighbors. Pastors everywhere must realize that the kingdom cannot not advance until we commit actions of such significance.

In the same fashion, Christian business leaders must take to heart that to those whom much has been given, much will be required. These leaders should actively seek to unite with others who share their faith. Think of how much stronger the influence of Christianity would be if 100,000 business leaders joined in a national faith co-operative, making the pledge that any assault on the religious freedom of one business would be an assault on them all. Would the federal government mobilize to close a catering business refusing to serve a gay wedding if it would result in the closure of 100,000 businesses and the loss of millions of American jobs? Does any believer lack the faith that we could #Unite100K on Twitter and land a critical blow to the Washington elites in an instant? Use the cultural platforms to advance the Kingdom of God, and incentivize businesses that stand on the courage of their convictions!

Lastly, we must once and for all end the practice of depleting our quiver by unloading a round of arrows on those who are not against us. Jesus spoke of this human tendency in the ninth chapter of the Gospel of Luke:

An argument started among the disciples as to which of them would be the greatest. Jesus, knowing their thoughts, took a little child and had him stand beside him. Then he said to them, "Whoever welcomes this little child in my name welcomes me; and whoever welcomes me welcomes the one who sent me. For it is the one who is least among you all who is the greatest." "Master," said John, "we saw someone driving out demons in your name and we tried to stop him, because he is not one of us." "Do not stop him," Jesus said, "for whoever is not against you is for you" (Luke 9:46–50).

Though there are several lessons in this teaching, one of the most seldom taught is that the Great Commission should not feature a relentless attack on Jews and Mormons. Despite the obvious differences within each of these separate religious convictions, we should be embracing these individuals should they wish to link arms with us in our efforts to reject the secular culture and restore God's supremacy. Similarly, we should not be searching for reasons to take umbrage with Christian denominations over mere technicalities. For example, while we must hold those churches that reject sin and repentance to account, the mere concept of predestination should not prevent believers from locking arms. If these believers are welcoming little children in the name of Jesus Christ, we should not divert our attention from what needs to be done by seeking to stop them at any cost. Fundamentally restoring the church, and by extension the nation, can only be achieved by first achieving the greater unity of purpose.

It is beyond debate that the reestablishment of church unity can certainly carry its own weight as it pertains to circumventing slavery. If this is the case, what is the point of suggesting that two affirmative directives are necessary to fundamentally restore the culture?

By pursuing the second action, uprooting the suffocating weeds of secular influence, Christians can take advantage of the vacuum-abhorrence theory held by Aristotle that dates back to the fourth century BC. This theory posits that nature abhors a vacuum. Christians and unbelievers share the penchant for our godless contemporary culture, which provides a suffocating influence over virtually every facet of their lives. I will not spend any additional time belaboring this point, as it has been addressed exhaustively in the middle chapters of this book. What you must understand is that uprooting the primary secular influence from your personal life would create an ideological vacuum that must ultimately be filled by a competing worldview. Just like everyone else, you have been created with a heart of limitless fertility, and the subsequent void of your suddenly rejected cultural ideology cannot be replaced with nothing. In this fashion, pursuing efforts to uproot the suffocating weeds of secularism from your life helps to upgrade the engine we will all use to speed out of this cultural cesspool of depravity. With time being of the essence, this step is critically important. In addition, it features the added benefit of depleting resources from the very institutions being used to siphon morality out of the culture.

What we must undertake is the exact same strategy employed by progressives roughly one century ago. The founding of the progressive movement was hinged upon uprooting the two most significant cultural influences of their time: the will of the parents and the resolve of the church. At the outset, these goals must have seemed downright impossible considering the norms of that era. I have already outlined the initial objective of Woodrow Wilson to make children as unlike their father as possible, and the rallying cry of progressives everywhere became a unified effort to dethrone the influence of the church. Though it took a century, this cultural mission has been nothing short of a wild success. Thus, we know this blueprint has the ability to produce results should we choose to make the arduous commitment.

One hundred years later, the norms of our era present a similar challenge to those of us nostalgic for the return of family values and a God-fearing culture. In keeping with biblical wisdom, the actions necessary to drain the influence of the secularism are exceptionally difficult, particularly because their root structures have been so deeply engrained into our personal constitution. Exhibiting the fortitude and moral strength to surgically remove these roots at the risk of complete social vilification is the literal definition of courage. In the midst of this challenge, however, simplicity rears its head through the surprisingly few number of excisions that are necessary as part of this surgical procedure. What must we do to fumigate the infestation of secular thought?

Just two actions have the power of separating the oxygen from this toxic ideology. While these two steps would not completely cut the circulation of secular humanism, they have the potential to put it on life support by sterilizing its ability to poison future generations. Curiously, one of these steps is simple, while the other is quite difficult! Nevertheless, *both* are essential steps to take for the believer adamant about reprioritizing his life in hopes of restoring the future of his children.

The simple action we can all pursue to take the legs out from under secularism is to turn off the television. We have already seen television's devastating ability to charter a new reality by misrepresenting basic human relationships in chapter five. Without this device, there is no chance our nation could have embraced gay marriage or transgenderism. Without its constant media attention, the domestic terrorist group known as Black Lives Matter could not function, improving the stability of overall race relations. The police force and respect for the rule of law would not be under assault. We would not be electing reality television stars to the office of the presidency, and professional impostors (actors and actresses) would no longer be asked to give academic commencement addresses to graduating seniors or domestic policy advice to elected representatives. We would be far less likely to glorify adultery, and we most definitely would not be desensitized to violence. We would discontinue sacrificing every Sabbath between September and February upon the altar of the National Football League. Without its shrine to the false god of fame, our deepest aspirations for our children would no longer feature placing them in settings most conducive to the destructive influence of the secular world.

By functioning as little more than a weapon of mass distraction, television has become today's opiate of the masses. When it comes to cultural enrichment, it is a completely worthless asset. Yet according to the NPD Group market research company, the average American cable bill was $123 per month in 2015.[18] Thus, a Christian who subscribes to cable television allocates weeks and weeks of time (over 1,800 hours a year assuming he consumes the five hour daily allotment referenced in chapter five) and close to $1,500 per year for this "amenity." After considering its overall impact on the culture, for all intents and purposes, how exactly should this not be viewed as a tithe to the church of secularism? There are a grand total of zero redemptive qualities in this device!

The television is the carotid artery of the culture, principally responsible for circulating depravity from the heart of the power-hungry elites to the furthest capillaries of our nation. Why must we so willingly preserve the blood flow when we have the power to cause massive damage to our central corruption system by simply deactivating these nerve endings? While it certainly may feel difficult to cut the cord on this beacon of the kingdom of man, it does not require any degree of considerable effort whatsoever. For the sake of the Kingdom of God, Christians have no choice but to take this abrupt action.

The truly difficult excision requires a paradigm shift in the lives of Christian parents. Believers have spent the last five decades trusting that it is in the best interests of their children to obediently usher them off to government instructional facilities that openly reject the Gospel of Jesus Christ, refuse to provide a basic understanding of financial literacy, and fail to instruct the merits of civic responsibility. These facilities do not ascribe to an absolute standard of morality and they generally avoid disciplining students out of fear of legal reprisal. An increasing number are beginning to subvert classical academic curricula in order to exaggerate the importance of sexual preference, a matter that is well outside the scope of any academic curriculum. Plain and simple, these institutions are not preparing our children for the trials and tribulations of adulthood.

Presumably for these reasons, many parents have already removed their children from these institutions in favor of private or charter schools. While this is an improvement in most instances, many fail to realize that these remain federally regulated entities, explaining why so many of these latter establishments have also adopted the Common Core State Standards Initiative.

There is only one form of education in the United States today that is not funded or regulated by the federal government. It is the oldest and most tradition-rich form of instruction known to humanity. This method of education is known as homeschooling, and it is spreading like wildfire. In fact, the US Department of Education recently released data showing that children enrolled at home schools throughout the country surged 62 percent to nearly 1.8 million in the ten-year period ending in 2012.[19] Can anybody refer to this as a fringe element if the percentage of homeschooled children (3.4 percent) far exceeds the percentage of Americans identifying as lesbian, gay, or bisexual (2.3 percent)? After recollecting the chronic overrepresentation of LGBT characters on television, this statistic suggests that these programs should begin portraying nearly every child as a homeschool student.

To promote the best chance of spiritual revival, Christian parents must pioneer a nationwide exodus out of the American public school system and restore their primary responsibility for directly educating their children out of their own personal home school. This is a remarkably difficult venture that will unquestionably overhaul any element of established equilibrium in the life of a parent. Yet we are called to raise our children in the ways of the Lord, and by rejecting the teachings of the Bible, the schools to which we are sending our children are attempting to pursue an enlightened education at the expense of truth. Even amidst the presence of a countless number of teachers who possess an active faith and noble character, the previously described factors prove that the system is currently resting upon a foundation of sand. Who among us finds this foundation preferable to the one we have formed in our own home?

As Christians, our generation must rally around the ambition of making the words home, church, and school completely interchangeable within our culture. It was this societal framework, not one operating under a bloated federal department of education, that the Lord used to produce the American experiment and unleash freedom, liberty, and prosperity upon the masses. To those who possess the means, home school your children as well as the child of your underprivileged neighbor. To the church, mobilize and organize to rescue the children of unattached parents from secular contamination during their most impressionable years. These are the exceptionally difficult cultural pursuits we have been called to confront. That which we refuse to uproot will only continue to ensnare.

Judging by the concerns commonly expressed by those most faithful to the pursuit of academic excellence, the homeschooling movement should be widely embraced by the culture. One of the premier measurements of quality education is the student-to-teacher ratio, since a lower ratio allows the child to receive more individualized attention from the teacher. The Center for Public Education suggests[20] that a class size of no more than 15 to 18 students appears to provide students with the most advantageous learning environment. Homeschooling lowers that ratio to as low as 1:1, granting a student exclusive access to his teacher upon demand. When compared to this benchmark, there is simply no better approach to education.

A second prerequisite for academic excellence is the presence of a fully qualified and competent teacher. Assuming that the primary educator of the home school was a high school graduate from an institution within the public school system, we can rest assured this condition would be fully satisfied. When a high school distributes a diploma, this ceremonial proceeding verifies that a student has developed a mastery of the essential skills and subject matter necessary to enter the workforce. Surely this mastery would include the aptitude to impart these same skills and instruction upon a child or adolescent. For if a public school cannot prepare an individual to share these concepts, that would sure seem to suggest an incompetence that would threaten its societal value, wouldn't it?

Third, diversity is an indispensable priority of the public school system. Since no two home schools are alike, this academic approach represents the ultimate form of avoiding a monopoly of educational thought. That is, unless the scope of diversity does not expand beyond something as disgracefully shallow as skin tone.

Lastly, progressives seem to be convinced that the best measurement of how much we care about our children is how much we spend on them. By reducing the enrollment at public institutions, homeschooling would increase the amount of federal funding per student for those individuals who remain at the traditional public school. If a school district had 1,000 students and a $10,000,000 budget, the school could allocate $10,000 per student towards its mission to educate these children. If 200 of these students left the school the following year to be homeschooled, this amount would increase to $12,500 for each of the remaining students.

It would appear quite duplicitous for an esteemed academic to oppose the idea of homeschooling after verifying that this instructional method satisfies every independent metric on their own measuring scale. Yet this duplicity will rear its ugly head when the state elects to prohibit any effort to home school. This is an absolute certainty. In February of 1995, the United States ambassador to the United Nations, Madeline Albright, signed the United Nations Convention on the Rights of the Child (UNCRC), a treaty that subjects every parental decision to a governmental review panel.[21] Although this treaty was not ratified by the United States Senate at the time, does any freethinker truly believe these seeds will lay dormant in an ideological garden that has developed a voracious lust for power? Have we learned nothing from the overthrow of the Bible from our public schools?

This is one of the vehicles through which our impending slavery will be delivered. Shall we wait like listless dupes while we yet have the power of God to advance His kingdom? Will we leave a biblical solution untried if the literal consequences will be the enslavement of our children? Will our grandchildren remember us as the generation who so providentially inherited affluence from the toil and faith of our progenitors, only to willingly bestow a legacy of slavery upon our posterity? There is only one way to combat this unprecedented dishonor:

BELIEVERS OF THE WORLD . . . UNITE!

End Notes

PREFACE

1. http://www.gallup.com/poll/159548/identify-christian.aspx.
2. http://www.americanrhetoric.com/speeches/mlkihaveadream.htm.

CHAPTER ONE

1. http://www.nytimes.com/2016/02/09/opinion/i-miss-barack-obama.html?_r=0.
2. http://www.newsmax.com/Newsfront/david-brooks-new-york-times-convert-christianity/2015/04/17/id/639149/.
3. http://founders.archives.gov/documents/Jefferson/03-09-02-0209.
4. http://data.worldbank.org/indicator/EG.ELC.ACCS.ZS.
5. Lewis, C. S. *Mere Christianity*. New York: Macmillan Publishing Company, 1952.
6. http://www.forbes.com/sites/billflax/2011/05/12/do-marxism-and-christianity-have-anything-in-common/#5e7c4b5b6676.
7. https://jonathanturley.org/2012/06/19/looking-for-socialism-try-buying-a-drink-in-one-of-americas-state-controlled-liquor-stores/.
8. http://pamelageller.com/2014/08/islamic-state-using-dolls-train-children-behead-infidels.html/.
9. www.fusion.net/story/275184/supreme-court-abortion-joyful-experience.
10. http://kristenvbrown.com/.

CHAPTER TWO

1. http://lostepisodes.us/robert-c-winthrop-speaker-of-the-u-s-house-the-massachusetts-bible-society/.
2. http://www.cnn.com/2014/11/14/politics/obamacare-voters-stupid-explainer/index.html.
3. https://www.washingtonpost.com/news/wonk/wp/2016/10/05/washingtons-governing-elite-actually-think-americans-are-morons/.
4. John 12:8.
5. http://www.mrctv.org/blog/leaked-emails-show-clinton-camp-mocking-catholics.
6. http://www.truthrevolt.org/news/emails-reveal-clinton-camp-plotting-revolution-against-catholic-church.

7. http://hotair.com/archives/2016/10/12/podesta-hey-whos-catholic-spring-reject-churchs-middle-ages-dictatorship/.
8. http://www.theblaze.com/contributions/hillary-clintons-plan-to-change-your-deep-seated-cultural-codes-religious-beliefs/.
9. http://www.huffingtonpost.com/2014/06/16/hillary-clinton-bible_n_5500041.html.
10. http://www.americanthinker.com/blog/2016/10/viewers_guide_to_the_latest_james_okeefe_project_veritas_action_video.html.
11. http://michellemalkin.com/2008/03/30/sunday-meditation-obama-and-the-punishment-of-unborn-life/.
12. http://townhall.com/columnists/johnhawkins/2016/01/12/everything-you-need-to-know-about-socialism-in-20-quotes-n2103130.
13. http://www.thefreedictionary.com/communism.
14. http://www.wnd.com/2005/11/33619/#IWHcX0uVKVpBX7Re.99.
15. Ibid.
16. http://www.hillaryhq.com/2015/01/i-consider-myself-proud-modern-american.html.
17. http://www.foxnews.com/us/2015/03/18/presbyterian-church-formally-approves-gay-marriage-in-church-constitution.html.
18. Proverbs 3:5.

CHAPTER THREE

1. http://www.scientificamerican.com/article/its-time-to-end-the-war-on-salt/.
2. http://www.cbsnews.com/news/cutting-back-salt-may-be-worse-for-heart-health-study/.
3. http://news.heart.org/reduced-salt-intake-critical-american-heart-association-says/.
4. http://dailycaller.com/2015/03/05/new-york-city-global-warming/.
5. http://nypost.com/2015/01/26/snowmageddon-2015-whats-closing-in-nyc/.
6. http://www.redstate.com/diary/jimjamitis/2016/09/19/heretic-scientists-forced-use-pseudonyms-get-work-published/.
7. http://www.npr.org/2013/06/25/195497342/obamas-climate-strategy-doesnt-require-congressional-approval.
8. http://www.forbes.com/sites/larrybell/2012/07/17/that-scientific-global-warming-consensus-not/#37b794f71690.
9. http://www.washingtontimes.com/news/2015/jul/7/nobel-physicist-obama-dead-wrong-global-warming/.
10. http://www.ecowatch.com/al-gore-at-sxsw-we-need-to-punish-climate-change-deniers-and-put-a-pri-1882022405.html.
11. http://dailycaller.com/2014/03/17/u-s-college-professor-demands-imprisonment-for-climate-change-deniers/#ixzz47f2xha8t.
12. http://www.theatlantic.com/politics/archive/2014/07/elizabeth-warrens-11-commandments-of-progressivism/455955/.
13. http://www.pbs.org/faithandreason/transcript/dawk-frame.html.
14. http://www.telegraph.co.uk/technology/facebook/10930654/Facebooks-71-gender-options-come-to-UK-users.html.

15. http://time.com/3630012/google-infinite-gender-options/.

16. http://www.cnn.com/2014/11/18/living/okcupid-expands-gender-orientation-options/index. html.

17. http://www.sfgate.com/business/technology/article/Tinder-update-allows-gender-options-beyond-man-10615649.php.

18. http://www.latimes.com/local/lanow/la-me-ln-uc-gender-20150806-story.html.

19. http://www.huffingtonpost.com/entry/bathrooms-across-brown-universitys-campus-are-now-stocked-with-free-tampons-pads_us_57d03400e4b0a48094a6df9e.

20. http://dailyfreepress.com/2016/09/11/editorial-tampons-all-bathrooms-intersectionality/.

21. http://www.mediaite.com/online/brown-university-to-put-tampons-in-all-bathrooms-to-set-a-tone-of-trans-inclusivity/.

22. https://www.brown.edu/about/administration/controller/sites/brown.edu.about. administration.controller/files/uploads/FINAL_JUNE%2030%202015%20FS.pdf.

23. http://www.academia.org/tampons-could-be-available-in-mens-restrooms-at-cornell/.

24. http://www.campusreform.org/?ID=8205.

25. http://nypost.com/2016/08/27/forcing-doctors-to-operate-team-obamas-new-low-in-the-name-of-trans-rights/.

26. http://www.thenewatlantis.com/docLib/20160819_TNA50SexualityandGender.pdf.

27. http://www.biology-online.org/dictionary/Life.

28. http://www.webmd.com/baby/ss/slideshow-conception.

29. https://publications.nigms.nih.gov/insidelifescience/genetics-numbers.html.

30. http://clinicquotes.com/scientists-speak-before-the-senate-human-life-begins-at-conception/.

31. Ibid.

32. Ibid.

33. http://www.telegraph.co.uk/science/2016/04/26/bright-flash-of-light-marks-incredible-moment-life-begins-when-s/.

34. http://mynorthwest.com/358693/jason-rantz-taken-aback-by-this-answer-on-abortion/.

35. https://www.scientificamerican.com/article/hillary-clinton-declares-i-believe-in-science/.

36. http://rzim.org/just-thinking/just-thinking-magazine-21-1/.

37. https://duckduckgo. com/?q=%22lochner+v.+new+york%22+minimum+wage+unconstitutional&t=ffsb&ia=web.

38. http://legal-dictionary.thefreedictionary.com/Schechter+Poultry+Corp.+v.+United+States.

39. http://www.laborrights.org/living-wage-solutions.

40. http://takingnote.blogs.nytimes.com/2014/03/07/f-d-r-makes-the-case-for-the-minimum-wage/?_r=0.

41. http://object.cato.org/sites/cato.org/files/pubs/pdf/PA701.pdf.

42. http://fightfor15.org/about-us/.

43. http://www.huffingtonpost.com/2014/11/15/most-dangerous-cities_n_6164864. html?slideshow=true.

44. http://fightfor15homecare.org/why-we-strike/.

45. http://www.hoovers.com/company-information/cs/competition.Yum_Brands_Inc. c235d3abd45851ff.html.

46. http://beta.fortune.com/fortune500/yum-brands-218/.

47. John 12:8.
48. http://www.forbes.com/sites/timworstall/2015/08/11/wendys-explains-what-really-happens-with-a-minimum-wage-rise-job-losses/#4235e6478dc3.
49. http://www.investors.com/politics/policy/wendys-serves-up-kiosks-as-wages-rise-hits-fast-food-group/.

CHAPTER FOUR

1. http://www.evolutionnews.org/2008/07/the_dehumanizing_impact_of_mod009211.html.
2. http://progressingamerica.blogspot.com/2012/05/progressivism-purpose-of-colleges-it-to.html.
3. http://www.huffingtonpost.com/2012/02/08/debbie-squires-education-official-says-teachers-know-better-than-parents_n_1264025.html.
4. https://www.acf.hhs.gov/sites/default/files/ecd/draft_hhs_ed_family_engagement.pdf.
5. http://www.law.harvard.edu/students/orgs/jlpp/Vol29_No3_Davis.pdf.
6. http://caselaw.findlaw.com/us-9th-circuit/1051665.html.
7. http://www.christianitytoday.com/ct/2002/juneweb-only/6-24-41.0.html.
8. Romans 1:22.
9. http://www.cnsnews.com/news/article/msnbc-we-have-break-through-idea-kids-belong-their-parents.
10. William Shirer, *The Rise and Fall of the Third Reich* New York: Simon and Schuster, 1960), 249.
11. Ibid.
12. Karl Marx to Friedrich Engels (June 21, 1854); *Marx-Engels Werke* (Berlin, 1959), XXVIII, p. 371.
13. Ibid.
14. http://www.oecd.org/edu/eag2013%20(eng)--FINAL%2020%20June%202013.pdf.
15. http://www.cbsnews.com/news/us-education-spending-tops-global-list-study-shows/.
16. http://www.breitbart.com/texas/2015/01/03/expert-most-us-college-freshmen-read-at-7th-grade-level/.
17. http://www.cnn.com/2016/05/12/politics/transgender-bathrooms-obama-administration/index.html.
18. https://www.washingtonpost.com/local/education/ill-group-sues-obama-administration-over-transgender-students-bathroom-access/2016/05/04/5c57ad12-1206-11e6-93ae-50921721165d_story.html.
19. http://www.wnd.com/2016/09/school-allows-partially-clothed-boy-to-twerk-in-girls-locker-room/.
20. http://www.foxnews.com/story/2009/12/16/rewriting-our-history-changing-our-traditions.html.
21. http://www.cnn.com/2011/US/07/14/california.lgbt.education/index.html.
22. http://www.lgbthistorymonth.com/broward-school-board-1st-recognize-lgbt-history-month.
23. http://dailycaller.com/2016/06/01/washington-state-to-teach-transgenderism-to-kindergartners/.

24. http://www.prideschoolatlanta.org/about-us/.
25. http://www.uuca.org/about-us/our-mission-history/.
26. Ibid.
27. Sabsovich, Leonid M. *Sotsialisticheskie goroda* (Moscow: Gosizdat RSFSR Moskovskii rabochii, 1930).
28. http://www1.nyc.gov/office-of-the-mayor/news/108-14/transcript-mayor-de-blasio-unprecedented-recruitment-training-high-quality-pre-k#/0.
29. http://www.peoplesworld.org/article/de-blasio-takes-over-in-new-york/.
30. http://www.corestandards.org/about-the-standards/.
31. 1 Corinthians 3:19.
32. http://muse.jhu.edu/article/40863.
33. http://oneradionetwork.com/geo-politics/lily-tang-williams-marching-toward-communism-bleak-future-america-american-education-following-path-march-3-2015/.
34. http://www.nsta.org/docs/ngss/201302_NGSS-Bybee.pdf.
35. http://www.nextgenscience.org/pe/ms-ess3-5-earth-and-human-activity.
36. www.educationnews.org/education-policy-and-politics/new-sex-ed-standards-for-suggested-for-elementary-schools/.
37. http://www.activistpost.com/2013/12/4th-grade-common-core-math-problem.html.
38. http://www.thenewamerican.com/culture/education/item/16192-common-core-a-scheme-to-rewrite-education.
39. http://www2.ed.gov/pubs/NatAtRisk/risk.html.
40. http://nypost.com/2016/03/18/upstate-town-board-votes-against-reciting-pledge-of-allegiance/.
41. http://neatoday.org/2013/12/03/what-do-the-2012-pisa-scores-tell-us-about-u-s-schools-2/.
42. http://forms.act.org/research/policymakers/cccr15/findings.html.
43. https://www.washingtonpost.com/blogs/college-inc/post/study-two-fifths-of-high-school-graduates-are-unprepared/2011/12/12/gIQArZKnpO_blog.html.
44. http://www.evolutionnews.org/2008/07/the_dehumanizing_impact_of_mod009211.html.

CHAPTER FIVE

1. http://www.rasmussenreports.com/public_content/politics/mood_of_america/right_direction_or_wrong_track/.
2. http://www.nydailynews.com/life-style/average-american-watches-5-hours-tv-day-article-1.1711954.
3. http://filmworld24.com/breaking-bad-torrent-hd-movie-download/.
4. http://w2.parentstv.org/MediaFiles/PDF/Studies/2014_Family_Study_Report.pdf.
5. http://www.hollywoodreporter.com/review/mick-review-959625.
6. http://www.indiewire.com/2017/01/the-mick-review-kaitlin-olson-fox-comedy-spoilers-1201763679.
7. http://www.lifesitenews.comnews/new-fox-comedy-breaks-moral-compass-includes-children-in-sexual-gender-conf.

8. https://www.washingtonpost.com/national/health-science/health-survey-gives-government-its-first-large-scale-data-on-gay-bisexual-population/2014/07/14/2db9f4b0-092f-11e4-bbf1-cc51275e7f8f_story.html.

9. www.glaad.org/files/2013WWATV.pdf.

10. http://articles.latimes.com/2009/feb/01/business/fi-abcfamily.1.

11. http://www.gallup.com/poll/183383/americans-greatly-overestimate-percent-gay-lesbian.aspx.

12. http://medscape.com/viewarticle/448017.

13. http://reason.com/poll/2014/08/19/august-2014-reason-rupe-national-survey.

14. http://www.cbsnews.com/news/south-carolina-moms-arrest-over-daughter-alone-in-park-sparks-debate/.

15. http://www.cdc.gov/nchs/pressroom/95facts/fs_439s.htm.

16. http://www.divorcesource.com/blog/why-women-file-80-percent-of-divorces/.

17. Popenoe, David. *Life Without Father: Compelling New Evidence That Fatherhood and Marriage Are Indispensable for the Good of Children and Society* (1996).

18. http://www.fathers.com/statistics-and-research/the-consequences-of-fatherlessness/.

19. http://onlinelibrary.wiley.com/wol1/doi/10.1111/j.1532-7795.2004.00079.x/full.

20. http://www.nytimes.com/roomfordebate/2013/06/03/what-are-fathers-for/children-are-better-off-with-a-father-than-without-one.

21. http://www.wnd.com/2007/06/42105/.

22. Nielsen. 2010 U.S. television universe estimates. New York, NY: Nielsen; 2009.

23. http://www.americanbible.org/uploads/content/State%20of%20the%20Bible%20Report%20 2013.pdf.

24. http://www.vanityfair.com/hollywood/2016/12/apprentice-producer-donald-trump-president?mbid=social_twitter.

25. https://www.youtube.com/watch?v=DjbZEYrRpPE.

26. http://www.nasdaq.com/aspx/call-transcript.aspx?StoryId=3968783&Title=facebook-fb-mark-elliot-zuckerberg-on-q1-2016-results-earnings-call-transcript.

27. http://www.pewinternet.org/2015/08/19/the-demographics-of-social-media-users/.

28. http://zephoria.com/top-15-valuable-facebook-statistics.

29. http://www.pewinternet.org/2015/08/19/the-demographics-of-social-media-users/.

30. http://zephoria.com/top-15-valuable-facebook-statistics mith, Michael B. and Bravo, Veronica, "Date Distraction," *USA Today* 8 Feb. 2017: A1+.

31. http://www.menshealth.com/sex-women/sex-robots.

32. http://www.pewinternet.org/files/2014/08/Future-of-AI-Robotics-and-Jobs.pdf.

CHAPTER SIX

1. http://www.rasmussenreports.com/public_content/business/general_business/january_2013/just_15_think_today_s_children_will_be_better_off_than_their_parents.

2. http://www.rasmussenreports.com/public_content/politics/mood_of_america/right_direction_wrong_track_nov21.

3. http://www.simplypsychology.org/piaget.html.

4. https://www.commonsensemedia.org/research/zero-to-eight-childrens-media-use-in-america-2013.
5. http://blog.sfgate.com/sfmoms/2012/08/31/toddlers-tiaras-scandal-4-year-old-destiny-smokes-cigarette-on-stage/.
6. https://www.commonsensemedia.org/research/zero-to-eight-childrens-media-use in america-2013.
7. http://www.huffingtonpost.com/2015/06/29/smartphone-behavior-2015_n_7690448.html.
8. Ibid.
9. http://www.huffingtonpost.com/2015/04/01/pew-study-cell-phones_n_6985004.html.
10. https://ca.news.yahoo.com/blogs/daily-buzz/study-thanks-to-portable-devices-our-attention-165215074.html.
11. http://www.fba2z.com/political3.php#axzz4RBAWjUUp.
12. http://www.cnn.com/2015/10/23/politics/grumpy-cat-obama-republicans/index.html.
13. http://www.kltv.com/story/29279529/e-texas-police-shut-down-girls-lemonade-stand-demand-permit.
14. http://www.huffingtonpost.com/2011/06/17/us-open-lemonade-fine-neighbors-parking_n_878949.html.
15. http://www.foxnews.com/us/2011/08/02/iowa-police-shut-down-4-year-olds-lemonade-stand.html.
16. Ibid.
17. http://www.thegatewaypundit.com/2015/02/new-jersey-police-crack-down-on-teens-for-illegal-snow-shoveling/.
18. http://www.nytimes.com/2015/02/20/nyregion/new-jersey-teenagers-eager-to-shovel-snow-and-an-encounter-with-the-police.html?_r=0.
19. http://abcnews.go.com/US/classroom-beating-florida-student-pummeled-teacher-sits-back/story?id=12279310.
20. http://www.dallasnews.com/opinion/editorials/2011/05/12/editorial-classroom-fight-videos-underscore-need-for-teacher-to-exercise-authority.
21. http://q13fox.com/2013/03/29/teacher-watches-as-students-fight/.
22. http://www.fox23.com/news/muldrow-teacher-arrested-for-allowing-students-to-fight/454954200.
23. http://www.theblaze.com/stories/2011/05/11/shock-classroom-video-teacher-watches-as-student-beats-classmate-in-head/.
24. http://articles.sun-sentinel.com/2010-12-19/news/fl-jeaga-middle-students-20101219_1_jeaga-middle-school-fights-palm-beach-schools/2.
25. http://www.huffingtonpost.com/2011/06/20/rosalina-gonzales-sentenced-for-spanking-_n_880432.html.
26. http://www.usatoday.com/story/news/nation-now/2015/01/05/florida-spanking-police-supervision/21290053/.
27. http://www.kob.com/albuquerque-news/belen-parents-punish-son-by-making-him-live-in-tent/4180172/.
28. https://sustainabledevelopment.un.org/post2015/transformingourworld.
29. http://www.end-violence.org/.

30. https://www.washingtonpost.com/local/education/boy-suspended-for-chewing-breakfast-pastry-into-a-gun-shape-will-get-hearing/2013/09/13/8326c878-1bf6-11e3-8685-5021e0c41964_story.html.

31. http://www.huffingtonpost.com/david-a-grimes/united-nations-committee-affirms-abortion-as-a-human-right_b_9020806.html.

32. https://www.hrw.org/legacy/english/docs/2007/06/20/iran16211.htm.

33. http://www.cnsnews.com/news/article/penny-starr/400-million-lives-prevented-through-one-child-policy-chinese-official-says.

34. http://www.prb.org/pdf08/fgm-wallchart.pdf.

35. http://www.npr.org/2016/08/18/479349760/should-we-be-having-kids-in-the-age-of-climate-change.

36. http://money.cnn.com/2015/11/04/pf/college/college-tuition/index.html.

37. http://www.realtor.org/topics/metropolitan-median-area-prices-and-affordability.

38. http://www.pewsocialtrends.org/2014/02/11/chapter-1-education-and-economic-outcomes-among-the-young/.

39. Ibid.

40. http://www.businessinsider.com/18-34-years-olds-living-with-parents-2014-6.

41. http://www.pewresearch.org/2012/05/17/college-graduation-weighing-the-cost-and-the-payoff/.

42. http://www.heritage.org/research/reports/2016/07/big-debt-little-study-what-taxpayers-should-know-about-college-students-time-use.

43. http://cnsnews.com/news/article/penny-starr/university-new-mexico-fights-sexual-assault-sex-week.

44. http://www.michigancapitolconfidential.com/22537.

45. http://leadership.oregonstate.edu/sites/leadership.oregonstate.edu/files/documents/student_social_justice_learning_modules_summary.pdf.

46. http://religion.ssrc.org/reforum/Gross_Simmons.pdf.

CHAPTER SEVEN

1. http://williamsinstitute.law.ucla.edu/wp-content/uploads/Gates-How-Many-People-LGBT-Apr-2011.pdf.

2. http://admissions.yale.edu/what-yale-looks-for.

3. http://yaledailynews.com/blog/2014/03/27/6-26-percent-of-applicants-admitted-to-class-of-2018/.

4. http://www.usnews.com/education/best-colleges/the-short-list-college/articles/2015/11/03/10-colleges-and-universities-with-the-most-competitive-admissions-rates.

5. http://www.foxnews.com/us/2015/12/16/yale-fail-ivy-leaguers-caught-on-video-clamoring-to-kill-first-amendment.html.

6. http://dailycaller.com/2015/06/10/california-trains-professors-to-avoid-microaggressions/.

7. http://www.merriam-webster.com/words-at-play/microaggression-words-were-watching.

8. http://www.capoliticalreview.com/blog/uc-president-napolitano-to-receive-570k-base-salary/.

9. http://www.thecollegefix.com/wp-content/uploads/2015/06/UCMicro.jpg.

10. http://www.thecollegefix.com/post/23555/

11. Ibid.

12. Ibid.

13. http://calendar.missouri.edu/event/workplace_diversity_series_rmicroaggressions_at_mizzou#.WD-eGlQ8_Gs.

14. Ibid.

15. http://www.uc.edu/news/NR.aspx?id=23526.

16. http://www.freerepublic.com/focus/f-news/3446137/posts.

17. http://www.washingtontimes.com/news/2016/jun/27/richard-posner-no-value-in-studying-us-constitutio/.

18. http://caselaw.findlaw.com/us-9th-circuit/1051665.html.

19. http://dailysignal.com/2012/02/08/justice-ginsburg-i-would-not-look-to-the-u-s-constitution/.

20. http://sacea.org/education/doma1.pdf.

21. http://www.npr.org/sections/thetwo-way/2013/06/26/195857796/supreme-court-strikes-down-defense-of-marriage-act.

22. http://usatoday30.usatoday.com/news/washington/2010-07-06-arizona-immigration_N.htm.

23. http://www.nytimes.com/2016/07/06/us/politics/hillary-clinton-fbi-email-comey.html.

24. http://www.chron.com/news/politics/houston/article/Council-passes-equal-rights-ordinance-5510672.php.

25. http://www.msnbc.com/craig-melvin/houston-passes-equal-rights-ordinance.

26. https://www.washingtonpost.com/national/religion/houston-subpoenas-pastors-sermons-in-gay-rights-ordinance-case/2014/10/15/9b848ff0-549d-11e4-b86d-184ac281388d_story.html?utm_term=.204ac2e6f875.

27. http://www.texasmonthly.com/the-daily-post/houston-city-attorneys-subpoenaed-sermons-from-pastors-they-suspect-fought-the-ordinance-from-the-pulpit/.

28. http://www.washingtontimes.com/news/2014/oct/15/houston-backs-off-church-sermon-subpoenas-in-trans/.

29. http://www.mystatesman.com/news/news/opinion/mackowiak-hero-provisions-ignored-safety-and-commo/npRCj/.

30. http://www.esquire.com/news-politics/news/a41147/half-of-americans-less-than-1000/.

31. http://www.gallup.com/poll/1600/Congress-Public.aspx.

32. http://www.newsmax.com/Newsfront/congress-christians-protestants-religion/2015/01/06/id/616640/.

33. http://www.azleg.gov/legtext/51leg/2r/bills/sb1062s.pdf.

34. http://money.cnn.com/2014/02/25/news/economy/arizona-anti-gay-bill/index.html.

35. http://www.politico.com/story/2014/02/jan-brewer-vetoes-arizona-sb-1062-104018.

36. http://www.indystar.com/story/news/politics/2015/03/25/gov-mike-pence-sign-religious-freedom-bill-thursday/70448858/.

37. http://www.lgbtqnation.com/2015/04/indiana-faces-long-road-to-restore-battered-image-after-religious-freedom-law/.

38. http://www.indystar.com/story/news/politics/2015/04/01/indiana-rfra-deal-sets-limited-protections-for-lgbt/70766920/.

39. http://www.cnn.com/2016/02/19/politics/georgia-religious-freedom-bill/index.html.

40. http://cnsnews.com/news/article/rudy-takala/religious-freedom-bill-faces-stiff-opposition-gop-led-ga-legislature.

41. https://www.washingtonpost.com/news/post-nation/wp/2016/03/28/georgia-governor-to-veto-religious-freedom-bill-criticized-as-anti-gay/.

42. http://www.redstate.com/streiff/2016/06/06/irs-reveals-targeted-400-conservative-groups-scrutiny/.

43. Matthew 5:13.

44. http://www.cnn.com/2015/06/26/politics/white-house-rainbow-marriage/index.html.

45. http://lawofficer.com/special-topics/white-house-ignored-request-to-illuminate-white-house-in-blue/.

46. http://www.westernjournalism.com/white-house-addresses-decision-not-to-support-cops-with-blue-light-display/.

CHAPTER EIGHT

1. http://www.chicagotribune.com/news/nationworld/ct-american-redoubt-20160827-photogallery.html.

2. http://fox17online.com/2016/11/16/fox-news-trump-won-81-percent-of-white-evangelical-vote.

3. http://libertynews.com/2015/07/flashback-donald-trump-supported-partial-birth-abortion-and-universal-healthcare-video/.

4. http://www.cnn.com/2016/01/27/politics/ben-sasse-donald-trump-affairs-salesman-iowa/.

5. http://www.nbcnews.com/politics/2016-election/hes-not-war-hero-donald-trump-mocks-john-mccains-service-n394391.

6. http://www.politico.com/story/2016/06/trump-forgiveness-god-224068.

7. http://www.cnn.com/2016/01/23/politics/donald-trump-shoot-somebody-support/index.html.

8. http://humanevents.com/2006/06/06/emexclusive-interview-emcoulter-says-book-examines-mental-disorder-of-liberalism/.

9. http://www.mediaite.com/online/coulter-i-dont-care-if-donald-trump-performs-abortions-in-the-white-house/.

10. http://www.lifenews.com/2016/07/21/james-dobson-endorses-donald-trump-he-will-defend-the-sanctity-of-human-life/.

11. http://www.redstate.com/aglanon/2016/10/13/jerry-falwell-jr.-disgrace-liberty-university-resign/.

12. Root, Wayne Allen. "Never-Trump Fools: Wake Up!" *Whistleblower*. September 2016.

13. http://www.northraleighcommunitychurch.org/what-we-believe/.

14. http://www.northraleighcommunitychurch.org/the-four-practices/.

15. Romans 6:23.

16. http://www.northraleighcommunitychurch.org/our-story/.

17. http://hillsong.com/what-we-believe.

18. https://www.youtube.com/watch?v=_3wLm6pPvRY.
19. http://www.nytimes.com/2014/10/18/us/megachurch-pastor-signals-shift-in-tone-on-gay-marriage.html.
20. http://www.theblaze.com/news/2016/09/28/hillsong-nyc-pastor-carl-lentz-at-this-church-we-are-not-saying-all-lives-matter-right-now/.
21. http://www.nylon.com/articles/hillsong-the-worlds-sexiest-church/#page-1.
    http://www.pewforum.com/2015/05/12/americas-changing-religious-landscape.
22. http://www.hoovers.com/company-information/cs/competition.Yum_Brands_Inc.c235d3abd45851ff.html.
23. http://www.usatoday.com/story/news/nation/2015/05/12/christians-drop-nones-soar-in-new-religion-portrait/27159533/.

CHAPTER NINE

1. http://townhall.com/columnists/terrypaulson/2008/11/02/democracies_die_when_liberty_gives_way_to_dependence
2. http://www.thecollegefix.com/post/28617.
3. Ibid.
4. http://www.lifenews.com/2016/11/15/indiana-university-caught-paying-200-for-brains-of-aborted-babies-for-research/.
5. http://www.indystar.com/story/news/politics/2016/05/24/judge-says-iu-cant-join-suit-against-abortion-law/84868934/.
6. Matthew 22:34–40.
7. https://www.chesterton.org/who-is-this-guy/.
8. http://www.reuters.com/article/us-missionary-massachusetts-idUSTRE81J0ZD20120220.
9. http://www.christianitytoday.com/gleanings/2014/may/walls-came-tumbling-down-china-jerusalem-wenzhou-sanjiang.html.
10. http://www.latimes.com/world/worldnow/la-fg-wn-china-massive-church-demolished-20140429-story.html.
11. http://www.telegraph.co.uk/news/worldnews/asia/china/10745248/Christians-form-human-shield-around-church-in-Chinas-Jerusalem-after-demolition-threat.html.
12. http://research.omicsgroup.org/index.php/Christianity_in_China.
13. http://www.economist.com/news/briefing/21629218-rapid-spread-christianith-forcing-official-rethink-religion-cracks.
14. https://world.wng.org/2014/05/chinese_christians_prepare_for_more_church_demolitions.
15. http://www.chinaaid.org/2014/05/house-church-persecution-continues-in.html.
16. 1 Corinthians 5:6.
17. http://www.nytimes.com/2015/10/30/world/asia/china-end-one-child-policy.html.
18. http://www.fool.com/investing/general/2015/02/01/the-average-american-pays-this-amount-for-cable-ho.aspx.
19. http://www.christianheadlines.com/blog/homeschoolers-in-u-s-number-nearly-2-million.html.

20. http://www.centerforpubliceducation.org/Main-Menu/Organizing-a-school/Class-size-and-student-achievement-At-a-glance/Class-size-and-student-achievement-Research-review.html?css=print.
21. http://fas.org/sgp/crs/misc/R40484.pdf.

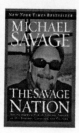